Messa

Yo

People

Messages to Young People

"Remember now thy Creator in the days of thy youth."

Ellen G. White

The Stanborough Press Ltd

This edition published 2023,
The Stanborough Press Ltd,
Alma Park, Grantham, Lincolnshire.

British Library Cataloguing in Publication Data.
A catalogue record for this book is available from the British Library.

ISBN 978-1-78665-163-1

Cover design by Abigail Murphy.

Printed in China.

Preface

We live in an age of spiritual and cultural confusion. To arrive at truth and to know God's will for our lives, we need help. We need guidance in our efforts to build characters that will fit us for eternal life in heaven.

Ellen White was only 17 years old when she was called by the Lord to begin her work for Him, a work that would provide the kind of help we need. She knew the struggles that children and youth have with the powers of darkness, and she also knew the life of victory in Christ. During the years of her nearly 70-year ministry, she wrote messages of instruction, sympathy, reproof, and encouragement, many of them addressed specifically to young people. These messages directed the minds of the youth to Christ and to His Word as the only source of strength in building noble Christian characters.

While much that Ellen White wrote for youth has been published in her books, many articles that appeared in the *Youth's Instructor* and in other places have not been preserved in permanent form. These instructions are a precious heritage, and should be in the hands of all our young people today. Therefore, the General Conference Youth Department has gone over all that she has written in our periodicals from the beginning of her work, and has made selections of particular relevance to young people. The work of gathering and arranging the articles comprising this volume was entered into unitedly by the trustees of the Ellen G. White Estate and the directors of the Youth Department.

In chapter 2 of this book Mrs. White tells us that God is calling for young people with uncorrupted hearts, strong and brave, and determined to fight successfully the struggle before them, that they may glorify God and bless humanity. God has standards to be upheld, and He calls the youth to a life of service for Him. "Salvation" and "service" should be the watchwords on our lips and in our hearts every day. God wants the youth to be His helping hand in carrying the message of Christ's soon return to the world (*Testimonies for the Church*, vol. 7, p. 64). And in her book *Education* she says, "With such an army of workers as our youth, rightly trained, might furnish, how soon the message of a crucified, risen, and soon-coming Saviour might be carried to the whole world!" (p. 271).

The messages in the present compilation are timeless. They were valid when written, and they are even more urgent now as we approach Christ's soon return. It is our earnest prayer that these messages may be a great strength to Adventist young people all around the world as they seek to perfect Christian character and complete the great task given to the remnant church—to take "the Advent message to all the world in this generation."

General Conference Youth Department

Contents

Section III. Gaining Victories

Section IV. Walking in the Light

Section V. Preparation for the Life Work

INTRODUCTION

Building Character for Eternity

I have a deep interest in the youth, and I greatly desire to see them striving to perfect Christian characters, seeking by diligent study and earnest prayer to gain the training essential for acceptable service in the cause of God. I long to see them helping one another to reach a higher plane of Christian experience.

Christ came to teach the human family the way of salvation, and He made this way so plain that a little child can walk in it. He bids His disciples follow on to know the Lord; and as they daily follow His guidance, they learn that His going forth is prepared as the morning.

You have watched the rising sun, and the gradual break of day over earth and sky. Little by little the dawn increases, till the sun appears; then the light grows constantly stronger and clearer until the full glory of noontide is reached. This is a beautiful illustration of what God desires to do for His children in perfecting their Christian experience. As we walk day by day in the light He sends us, in willing obedience to all His requirements, our experience grows and broadens until we reach the full stature of men and women in Christ Jesus.

The youth need to keep ever before them the course that Christ followed. At every step it was a course of overcoming. Christ did not come to the earth as a king, to rule the nations. He came as a humble man, to be tempted, and to overcome temptation, to follow on, as we must, to know the Lord. In the study of His life we shall learn how much God through Him will do for His children. And we shall learn that, however great our trials may be, they cannot exceed what Christ endured that we might know the way, the truth, and the life. By a life of conformity to His example, we are to show our appreciation of His sacrifice in our behalf.

The youth have been bought with an infinite price, even the blood of the Son of God. Consider the sacrifice of the Father in permitting His Son to make this sacrifice. Consider what Christ gave up when He left the courts of heaven and the royal throne, to give His life a daily sacrifice for men. He suffered reproach and abuse. He bore all the insult and mockery that wicked men could heap upon Him. And when His earthly ministry was accomplished, He suffered the death of the cross. Consider His sufferings on the cross—the nails driven into His hands and feet, the derision and abuse from those He came to save, the hiding of His Father's face. But it was by all this that Christ made it possible for all who will to have the life that measures with the life of God.

A Faithful Friend

When Christ ascended to the Father, He did not leave His followers without help. The Holy Spirit, as His representative, and the heavenly angels, as ministering spirits, are sent forth to aid those who against great odds are fighting the good fight of faith. Ever remember that Jesus is your helper. No one understands as well as He your peculiarities of character. He is watching over you, and if you are willing to be guided by Him, He will throw around you influences for good that will enable you to accomplish all His will for you.

In this life we are preparing for the future life. Soon there is to be a grand review, in which every soul who is seeking to perfect a Christian character must bear the test of God's searching questions: Have you set an example that others were safe in following? Have you watched for souls as those that must give an account? The heavenly host are interested in the youth; and they are intensely desirous that you will bear the test, and that to you will be spoken the words of approval, "Well done, good and faithful servant; . . . enter thou into the joy of thy Lord."

Let the youth remember that here they are to build characters for eternity, and that God requires them to do their best. Let those older in experience watch over the younger ones; and when they see them tempted, take them aside, and pray with them and for them. The Lord would have us recognize the great sacrifice of Christ for us by showing an interest in the salvation of those He came to save. If the youth will seek Christ, He will make their efforts effectual. Mrs. E. G. White, *Youth's Instructor*, November 21, 1911.

SECTION 1
God's Purpose for the Youth

In order that the work my go forward in all its branches, God calls for youthful vigor, zeal, and courage. He has chosen the youth to aid in the advancement of His cause. To plan with clear mind and execute with courageous hand demands fresh, uncrippled energies. Young men and women are invited to give God the strength of their youth, that through the exercise of their powers, through keen thought and vigorous action, they may bring glory to Him and salvation to their fellow men. Gospel Workers, *p. 67.*

CHAPTER 2

A Call to the Youth

God wants the youth to become men of earnest mind, to be prepared for action in His noble work, and fitted to bear responsibilities. God calls for young men with hearts uncorrupted, strong and brave, and determined to fight manfully in the struggle before them, that they may glorify God, and bless humanity. If the youth would but make the Bible their study, would but calm their impetuous desires, and listen to the voice of their Creator and Redeemer, they would not only be at peace with God, but would find themselves ennobled and elevated. It will be for your eternal interest, my young friend, to give heed to the instructions in the Word of God, for they are of inestimable importance to you.

I entreat you to be wise, and consider what will be the result of leading a wild life, uncontrolled by the Spirit of God. "Be not deceived; God is not mocked: for whatsoever a man soweth, that shall he also reap. For he that soweth to his flesh shall of the flesh reap corruption." For your soul's sake, for Christ's sake, who gave Himself to save you from ruin, pause on the threshold of your life, and weigh well your responsibilities, your opportunities, your possibilities. God has given you an opportunity to fill a high destiny. Your influence may tell for the truth of God; you may be a co-laborer with God in the great work of human redemption. . . .

Called to a High Destiny

O that young men might appreciate the high destiny to which they are called! Ponder well the paths of your feet. Begin your work with high and holy purpose, and be determined that through the power of the grace of God, you will not diverge from the path of rectitude. If you begin to go in a wrong direction, every step will be fraught with peril and disaster, and you will go on straying from the path of truth, safety, and success. You need your intellect strengthened, your moral energies quickened, by divine power.

The cause of God demands the highest powers of the being, and there is urgent need in many fields for young men of literary qualifications. There is need of men who can be trusted to labor in extensive fields that are now white to the harvest. Young men of ordinary ability, who give themselves wholly to God, who are uncorrupted by vice and impurity, will be successful, and will be enabled to do a great work for God. Let young men heed the admonition, and be sober-minded.

How many youth have wasted their God-given strength in folly and dissipation! How many painful histories rise before me of youth who have become mere wrecks of humanity, mentally, morally, physically, because of indulgence in vicious habits! Their constitutions are ruined, their life usefulness greatly impaired, because of indulgence in unlawful pleasures.

I entreat of you, careless, reckless youth of today, be converted, and become laborers together with God. Let it be the study of your life to bless and save others. If you seek help from God, His power working in you will bring to naught all opposing powers, and you will become sanctified through the truth. Sin is alarmingly prevalent among the youth of today, but let it be your purpose to do what you can to rescue souls from the power of Satan.

Be Light Bearers

Carry light wherever you go; show that you have strength of purpose, that you are not a person of indecision, easily swayed by the persuasions of evil associates. Do not yield a ready assent to the suggestions of those who dishonor God, but rather seek to reform, reclaim, and rescue souls from evil.

Resort to prayer, persuade in meekness and lowliness of spirit those who oppose themselves. One soul saved from error, and brought under the banner of Christ, will cause joy in heaven, and place a star in your crown of rejoicing. A soul saved will, through his godly influence, bring other souls to a knowledge of salvation, and thus the work will multiply, and only the revealings of the day of judgment will make manifest the extent of the work.

Do not hesitate to work for the Lord because you think you can do but little. Do your little with fidelity; for God will work with your efforts. He will write your name in the book of life as one worthy to enter into the joy of the Lord. Let us earnestly entreat the Lord that laborers may be raised up, for the fields are white to the harvest; the harvest is great, and the laborers are few. . . .

Cherish Broad Ideas

Young men should have broad ideas, wise plans, that they may make the most of their opportunities, catch the inspiration and courage that animated the apostles. John says, "I have written unto you, young men, because ye are strong, and the word of God abideth in you, and ye have overcome the wicked one." An elevated standard is presented before the youth, and God is inviting them to come into real service for Him. True-hearted young men who delight to be learners in the school of Christ, can do a great work for the Master, if they will only give heed to the command of the Captain as it sounds down along the lines to our time, "Quit you like men, be strong."

You are to be men who will walk humbly with God, who will stand before Him in your God-given manhood, free from impurity, free from all contamination from the sensuality that is corrupting this age. You must be men who will despise all falsity and wickedness, who will dare to be true and brave, holding aloft the blood-stained banner of Prince Emmanuel. Your talents will increase as you use them for the Master, and they will be esteemed precious by Him who has bought them with an infinite price. Do not sit down and neglect to do anything, simply because you cannot do some great thing, but do whatever your hands find to do, with thoroughness and energy. . . .

The Call to Enlist

Christ is calling for volunteers to enlist under His standard, and bear the banner of the cross before the world. The church is languishing for the help of young men who will bear a courageous testimony, who will with their ardent zeal stir up the sluggish energies of God's people, and so increase the power of the church in the world. Young men are wanted who will resist the tide of worldliness, and lift a voice of warning against taking the first steps in immorality and vice.

But first the young men who would serve God, and give themselves to His work, must cleanse the soul temple of all impurity, and enthrone Christ in the heart; then they will be enabled to put energy into their Christian effort, and will manifest enthusiastic zeal in persuading men to be reconciled to Christ. Will not our young men respond to the invitation of Christ, and answer, "Here am I; send me"? Young men, press to the front, and identify yourselves as laborers together with Christ, taking up the work where He left it, to carry it on to its completion. *Review and Herald*, June 16, 1891.

Essential Elements of Character

God does not bid the youth to be less aspiring. The elements of character that make a man successful and honored among men—the irrepressible desire for some greater good, the indomitable will, the strenuous exertion, the untiring perseverance—are not to be crushed out. *Patriarchs and Prophets*, p. 602.

CHAPTER 3

Seeking to Please Him

The Lord has a special work to do for us individually. As we see the wickedness of the world brought to light in the courts of justice and published in the daily papers, let us draw near to God, and by living faith lay hold of His promises, that the grace of Christ may be manifest in us. We may have an influence, a powerful influence, in the world. If the convicting power of God is with us, we shall be enabled to lead souls that are in sin to conversion.

Our simplicity will accomplish much in this work. We are not to try to climb up to high positions or to gain the praise of men. Our aim should not be to be the greatest. We are to have an eye single to the glory of God. We are to work with all the intelligence that God has given us, placing ourselves in the channel of light, that the grace of God can come upon us to mold and fashion us to the divine similitude. Heaven is waiting to bestow its richest blessings upon those who will consecrate themselves to do the work of God in these last days of the world's history. We shall be tested and tried; we may be called to spend wakeful nights; but let such times be spent in earnest prayer to God, that He may give understanding, and quicken the mind to discern the privileges that are ours. *Review and Herald*, April 1, 1909.

CHAPTER 4

Standards of Success

"The fear of the Lord is the beginning of wisdom." Many of our youth do not feel the necessity of bringing their powers into vigorous exercise to do their best at all times and under all circumstances. They do not have the fear of God before their eyes, and their thoughts are not pure and elevated.

All heaven is cognizant of every thought and every action. Your actions may be unseen by your associates, but they are all open to the inspection of angels. The angels are commissioned to minister unto those who are striving to overcome every wrong habit, and stand clear from the devices of Satan.

Faithful Integrity

The power of little acts of evil, of small inconsistencies to mold character, are not estimated as they should be. The grandest and most elevated principles are revealed to us in the Word of God. They are given to us to strengthen every effort for good, to control and balance the mind, to lead us to aspire to reach a high standard.

In the history of Joseph, Daniel, and his fellows, we see how the golden chain of truth may bind the youth to the throne of God. They could not be tempted to turn aside from their course of integrity. They valued the favor of God above the favor and praise of princes, and God loved them and spread His shield over them. Because of their faithful integrity, because of their determination to honor God above every human power, the Lord signally honored them before men. They were honored by the Lord God of hosts, whose power is over all the works of His hand in heaven above and the earth beneath. These youth were not ashamed to display their true colors. Even in the court of the king, in their words, their habits, their practices, they confessed their faith in the Lord God of heaven. They refused to bow to any earthly mandate that detracted from the honor of God. They had strength from heaven to confess their allegiance to God.

You should be prepared to follow the example of these noble youth. Never be ashamed of your colors; put them on, unfurl them to the gaze of men and angels. Do not be controlled by false modesty, by false prudence which suggests to you a course of action contrary to this advice. By your choice words and a consistent course of action, by your propriety, your earnest piety, make a telling confession of your faith, determined that Christ shall occupy the throne in the soul temple; and lay your talents without reserve at His feet to be employed in His service.

Complete Consecration

For your present and eternal good it is best to commit yourself wholly to the right, that the world may know where you are standing. Many are not wholly committed to the cause of God, and their position of wavering is a source of weakness in itself, and a stone of stumbling to others. With principles unsettled, unconsecrated as they are, the waves of temptation sweep them away from what they know to be right, and they do not make holy endeavor to overcome every wrong, and through the imputed righteousness of Christ, perfect a righteous character.

The world has a right to know just what may be expected from every intelligent human being. He who is a living embodiment of firm, decided, righteous principles, will be a living power upon his associates; and he will influence others by his Christianity. Many do not discern and appreciate how great is the influence of each one for good or evil. Every student should understand that the principles which he adopts become a living, molding influence upon character. He who accepts Christ as his personal Saviour, will love Jesus, and all for whom Christ has died; for Christ will be in him a well of water springing up unto everlasting life. He will surrender himself without reservation to the rule of Christ.

Assert Your Liberty

Make it the law of your life from which no temptation or side interest shall cause you to turn, to honor God, because He "so loved the world, that He gave his only-begotten Son, that whosoever believeth in Him should not perish, but have everlasting life." As a redeemed, free moral agent, ransomed by an infinite price, God calls upon you to assert your liberty, and employ your God-given powers as a free subject of the kingdom of heaven. Be no longer under the thralldom of sin, but as a loyal subject to the King of kings, prove your loyalty to God.

Through Jesus Christ show that you are worthy of the sacred trust with which the Lord has honored you in bestowing upon you life and grace. You are to refuse to be in subjection to the power of evil. As soldiers of Christ we must deliberately and intelligently accept His terms of salvation under every circumstance, cherish right principles, and act upon them. Divine wisdom is to be a lamp to your feet. Be true to yourselves, be true to your God. Everything that can be shaken will be shaken; but rooted and grounded in the truth, you will abide with those things that cannot be shaken. The law of God is steadfast, unalterable; for it is the expression of the character of Jehovah. Make up your mind that you will not by word or influence cast the least dishonor upon its authority.

Complete Surrender

To have the religion of Christ means that you have absolutely surrendered your all to God, and consented to the guidance of the Holy Spirit. Through the gift of the Holy Spirit moral power will be given you, and not only will you have your former intrusted talents for the service of God, but their efficiency will be greatly multiplied. The surrender of all our powers to God greatly simplifies the problem of life. It weakens and cuts short a thousand struggles with the passions of the natural heart. Religion is as a golden cord that binds the souls of both youth and aged to Christ. Through it the willing and obedient are brought safely through dark and intricate paths to the city of God.

There are youth who have only common faculties, and yet by education and discipline under teachers who are actuated by high and pure principles, they may come forth from the training process qualified for some position of trust to which God has called them. But there are young men who will make a failure because they have not determined to overcome natural inclinations, and they will not listen to the voice of God in His Word. They have not barricaded their souls against temptation, and determined to do their duty at all hazards. They are like one who in a perilous journey refuses any guide or instruction whereby he may escape accident and ruin, and goes on in a certain course of destruction.

Choosing Your Destiny

O that every one might realize that he is the arbiter of his own destiny! Your happiness for this life, and for the future, immortal life lies with yourself. If you choose, you may have associates who, by their influence, will cheapen your thoughts, your words, and your morals. You can give loose rein to appetite and passion, despise authority, use coarse language, and degrade yourself to the lowest level. Your influence may be such as to contaminate others, and you may be the cause of ruining those whom you might have brought to Christ. You may lead from Christ, from right, from holiness, and from heaven. In the judgment the lost may point to you and say, "If it had not been for his influence, I would not have stumbled and made a mock of religion. He had light, he knew the way to heaven. I was ignorant, and went blindfolded on my way to destruction." O, what answer can we give to such a charge? How important it is that every one shall consider where he is leading souls. We are in view of the eternal world, and how diligently we should count the cost of our influence. We should not drop eternity out of our reckoning, but accustom ourselves to ask continually, Will this course be pleasing to God? What will be the influence of my action upon the minds of those who have had much less light and evidence as to what is right?

Heart-searching Questions

O, that the youth would search the Scriptures, and do as they think Christ would have done under similar circumstances! Our opportunities to gain knowledge from heaven have placed upon us large responsibilities, and with intense solicitude, we should inquire, Am I walking in the light? Am I, according to the great light given me, leading in the right way, or making such crooked paths that the lame shall be turned out of the way? . . .

We should be pervaded with a deep, abiding sense of the value, sanctity, and authority of the truth. The bright beams of heaven's light are shining upon your pathway, dear youth, and I pray that you may make the most of your opportunities. Receive and cherish every heaven-sent ray, and your path will grow brighter and brighter unto the perfect day. *Youth's Instructor*, February 2, 1893.

CHAPTER 5

Our Day of Opportunity

There are lessons for us to learn at this time from the experience of those who labored for God in past generations. How little we know of the conflicts and trials and labors of these men, as they fitted themselves to meet the armies of Satan. Putting on the whole armor of God, they were able to stand against the wiles of Satan. . . .

These men who in the past gave themselves to God and to the uplifting of His cause were as true as steel to principle. They were men who would not fail nor be discouraged; men who, like Daniel, were full of reverence and zeal for God, full of noble purposes and aspirations. They were as weak and helpless as any of those who are now engaged in the work, but they put their whole trust in God. They had wealth, but it consisted of mind and soul culture. This every one may have who will make God first and last and best in everything. Although destitute of wisdom, knowledge, virtue, and power, we may receive all these if we will learn from Christ the lessons that it is our privilege to learn.

The Kind of Workers Needed

In this time we have opportunities and advantages that it was not easy to obtain in generations past. We have increased light, and this has come through the work of those faithful sentinels who made God their dependence, and received power from

Him to let light shine in clear, bright rays to the world. In our day we have increased light to improve, as in times past men and women of noble worth improved the light that God gave them. They toiled long to learn the lessons given them in the school of Christ, and they did not toil in vain. Their persevering efforts were rewarded. They bound themselves up with the mightiest of all powers, and yet they were ever longing for a deeper, higher, and broader comprehension of eternal realities, that they might successfully present the treasures of truth to a needy world.

Workers of this character are needed now. Those who are men in the sight of God, and who are thus recorded on the books of heaven, are those who, like Daniel, cultivate every faculty in such a way as best to represent the kingdom of God in a world lying in wickedness. Progress in knowledge is essential; for when employed in the cause of God, knowledge is a power for good. The world needs men of thought, men of principle, men who are constantly growing in understanding and discernment. The press is in need of men to use it to the best advantage, that the truth may be given wings to speed it to every nation, and tongue, and people.

Our Source of Efficiency

We need to make use of the youth who will cultivate honest industry, who are not afraid to put their powers to task. Such youth will find a position anywhere, because they falter not by the way; in mind and soul they bear the divine similitude. Their eye is single, and constantly they press onward, and upward, crying, Victory. But there is no call for the indolent, the fearful and unbelieving, who by their lack of faith and their unwillingness to deny self for Christ's sake, keep the work from advancing. . . . .

God calls for those who will be workers together with Him. Connected with Christ, human nature becomes pure and true. Christ supplies the efficiency, and man becomes a power for good. Truthfulness and integrity are attributes of God, and he who possesses these attributes possesses a power that is invincible. *Review and Herald*, March 10, 1903.

Righteousness Within

Righteousness within is testified to by righteousness without. He who is righteous within is not hard-hearted and unsympathetic, but day by day he grows into the image of Christ, going on from strength to strength. He who is being sanctified by the truth will be self-controlled, and will follow in the footsteps of Christ until grace is lost in glory. The righteousness by which we are justified is imputed; the righteousness by which we are sanctified is imparted. The first is our title to heaven, the second is our fitness for heaven. *Review and Herald*, June 4, 1895.

CHAPTER 6

Heights that May Be Attained

Dear youth, what is the aim and purpose of your life? Are you ambitious for education that you may have a name and position in the world? Have you thoughts that you dare not express, that you may one day stand upon the summit of intellectual greatness; that you may sit in deliberative and legislative councils, and help to enact laws for the nation? There is nothing wrong in these aspirations. You may every one of you make your mark. You should be content with no mean attainments. Aim high, and spare no pains to reach the standard.

Religion the Basis of Life

The fear of the Lord lies at the foundation of all true greatness. Integrity, unswerving integrity, is the principle that you need to carry with you into all the relations of life. Take your religion into your school life, into your boarding house, into all your pursuits. The important question with you now is, how to so choose and perfect your studies that you will maintain the solidity and purity of an untarnished Christian character, holding all temporal claims and interests in subjection to the higher claims of the gospel of Christ.

You want now to build as you will be able to furnish, to so relate yourself to society and to life that you may answer the purpose of God in your creation. As disciples of Christ, you are not debarred from engaging in temporal pursuits; but you should carry your religion with you. Whatever the business you may qualify yourself to engage in, never entertain the idea that you cannot make a success of it without sacrificing principle.

High Responsibilities

Balanced by religious principle, you may climb to any height you please. We would be glad to see you rising to the noble elevation God designs that you shall reach. Jesus loves the precious youth; and He is not pleased to see them grow up with uncultivated, undeveloped talents. They may become strong men of firm principle, fitted to be intrusted with high responsibilities, and to this end they may lawfully strain every nerve.

But never commit so great a crime as to pervert your God-given powers to do evil and destroy others. There are gifted men who use their ability to spread moral ruin and corruption; but all such are sowing seed that will produce a harvest which they will not be proud to reap. It is a fearful thing to use God-given abilities in such a way as to scatter blight and woe instead of blessing in society. It is also a fearful thing to fold the talent intrusted to us in a napkin, and hide it away in the world; for this is casting away the crown of life. God claims our service. There are responsibilities for every one to bear; and we can fulfill life's grand mission only when these responsibilities are fully accepted, and faithfully and conscientiously discharged.

Influence of Religion

Says the wise man, "Remember now thy Creator in the days of thy youth." But do not for a moment suppose that religion will make you sad and gloomy and will block up the way to success. The religion of Christ does not obliterate or even weaken a single faculty. It in no way incapacitates you for the enjoyment of any real happiness; it is not designed to lessen your interest in life, or to make you indifferent to the claims of friends and society. It does not mantle the life in sackcloth; it is not expressed in deep-drawn sighs and groans. No, no; those who in everything make God first and last and best, are the happiest people in the world. Smiles and sunshine are not banished from their countenance. Religion does not make the receiver coarse and rough, untidy, and uncourteous; on the contrary, it elevates and ennobles him, refines his taste, sanctifies his judgment, and fits him for the society of heavenly angels and for the home that Jesus has gone to prepare.

Let us never lose sight of the fact that Jesus is a wellspring of joy. He does not delight in the misery of human beings, but loves to see them happy. Christians have many sources of happiness at their command, and they may tell with unerring accuracy what pleasures are lawful and right. They may enjoy such recreations as will not dissipate the mind or debase the soul, such as will not disappoint, and leave a sad after-influence to destroy self-respect or bar the way to usefulness. If they can take Jesus with them, and maintain a prayerful spirit, they are perfectly safe. . . .

Our Stewardship of Talents

Young friends, the fear of the Lord lies at the very foundation of all progress; it is the beginning of wisdom. Your heavenly Father has claims upon you; for without solicitation or merit on your part He gives you the bounties of His providence; and more than this, He has given you all heaven in one gift, that of His beloved Son. In return for this infinite gift, He claims of you willing obedience. As you are bought with a price, even the precious blood of the Son of God, He requires that you make a right use of the privileges you enjoy. Your intellectual and moral faculties are God's gifts, talents intrusted to you for wise improvement, and you are not at liberty to let them lie dormant for want of proper cultivation, or be crippled and dwarfed by inaction. It is for you to determine whether or not the weighty responsibilities that rest upon you shall be faithfully met, whether or not your efforts shall be well directed and your best.

We are living in the perils of the last days. All heaven is interested in the characters you are forming. Every provision has been made for you, that you should be a partaker of the divine nature, having escaped the corruption that is in the world through lust. Man is not left alone to conquer the powers of evil by his own feeble efforts. Help is at hand, and will be given every soul who really desires it. Angels of God, that ascend and descend the ladder that Jacob saw in vision, will help every soul who will to climb even to the highest heaven. They are guarding the people of God, and watching how every step is taken. Those who climb the shining way will be rewarded; they will enter into the joy of their Lord. *Fundamentals of Christian Education*, pp. 82-86.

A High Ideal to Reach

Higher than the highest human thought can reach is God's ideal for His children. Godliness—godlikeness—is the goal to be reached. Before the student there is opened a path of continual progress. He has an object to achieve, a standard to attain, that includes everything good, and pure, and noble. He will advance as fast and as far as possible in every branch of true knowledge. But his efforts will be directed to objects as much higher than mere selfish and temporal interests as the heavens are higher than the earth. *Education*, pp. 18, 19.

Channels of God's Grace

It is the privilege of every soul to be a living channel through which God can communicate to the world the treasures of His grace, the unsearchable riches of Christ. There is nothing that Christ desires so much as agents who will represent to the world His Spirit and character. There is nothing that the world needs so much as the manifestation through humanity of the Saviour's love. All heaven is waiting for channels through which can be poured the holy oil to be a joy and blessing to human hearts. *Christ's Object Lessons*, p. 419.

CHAPTER 7

Standards of Efficiency

Grave responsibilities rest upon the youth. God expects much from the young men who live in this generation of increased light and knowledge. He expects them to impart this light and knowledge. He desires to use them in dispelling the error and superstition that cloud the minds of many. They are to discipline themselves by gathering up every jot and tittle of knowledge and experience. God holds them responsible for the opportunities and privileges given them. The work before them is waiting for their earnest effort, that it may be carried forward from point to point, as the time demands.

If the youth will consecrate their minds and hearts to God's service, they will reach a high standard of efficiency and usefulness. This is the standard that the Lord expects the youth to attain. To do less than this is to refuse to make the most of God-given opportunities. This will be looked upon as treason against God, a failure to work for the good of humanity.

Qualifying for Service

Those who strive to become laborers for God, who seek earnestly to acquire in order to impart, will constantly receive light from God that they may be channels of communication. If, like Daniel, young men and young women will bring all their habits, appetites, and passions into conformity to the requirements of God, they will qualify themselves for higher work. They should put from their minds all that is cheap and frivolous. Nonsense and amusement-loving propensities should be discarded, as out of place in the life and experience of those who are living by faith in the Son of God, eating His flesh and drinking His blood.

They should realize that though all the advantages of learning may be within their reach, they may yet fail of obtaining that education which will fit them for work in some part of the Lord's vineyard. They cannot engage in God's service without the requisite qualifications of intelligent piety. If they give to pleasure and amusement the precious mind that should be strengthened by high and noble purposes, they degrade the powers that God has given them, and are guilty before Him, because they fail to improve their talents by wise use.

Their dwarfed spirituality is an offense to God. They taint and corrupt the minds of those with whom they associate. By their words and actions they encourage a careless inattention to sacred things. Not only do they imperil their own souls, but their example is detrimental to all with whom they come in contact. They are utterly incompetent to represent Christ. Servants of sin, careless, reckless, and foolish, they scatter away from Him.

Those who are satisfied with low attainments fail of being workers together with God. To those who let the mind drift where it will drift if not guarded, Satan makes suggestions which so fill the mind that they are trained in his army to decoy other souls. They may make a profession of religion, they may have a form of godliness; but they are lovers of pleasure more than lovers of God.

Cleverness not Piety

There are youth who have a certain kind of cleverness, which is acknowledged and admired by their associates, but their ability is not sanctified. It is not strengthened and solidified by the graces and trials of experience, and God cannot use it to benefit humanity and glorify His name. Under the guise of godliness, their powers are being used to erect false standards, and the unconverted look to them as an excuse for their wrong course of action. Satan leads them to amuse their associates by their nonsense and so-called wit. Everything that they undertake is cheapening; for they are under the control of the tempter, who directs and fashions their characters, that they may do his work.

They have ability, but it is untrained; they have capacity, but it is unimproved. Talents have been given them; but they misuse and degrade them by folly, and drag others down to their own low level. Christ paid the ransom for their souls by self-denial, self-sacrifice, humiliation, by the shame and reproach He endured. This He did that He might rescue them from the bondage of sin, from the slavery of a master who cares for them only as he can use them to ruin souls. But they make the love of the Redeemer in their behalf of no avail to them, and He looks with sadness on their work.

Such youth meet with eternal loss. How will their fun and frolic appear to them in the day when every man shall receive from the Judge of all the earth according to the deeds done in the body? They have brought to the foundation wood, hay, and stubble, and all their life work will perish. What a loss!

O, how much better is the condition of those who act their part in God's service, looking to Jesus for His approval, writing daily in their account-book their mistakes, their errors, their sorrow, the victories they have gained over temptation, their joy and peace in Christ! Such youth will not have to meet their life record with shame and dismay. *Youth's Instructor*, June 22, 1899.

The Chosen Agency

Our confession of His faithfulness is Heaven's chosen agency for revealing Christ to the world. We are to acknowledge His grace as made known through the holy men of old; but that which will be most effectual is the testimony of our own experience. We are witnesses for God as we reveal in ourselves the working of a power that is divine. Every individual has a life distinct from all others, and an experience differing essentially from theirs. God desires that our praise shall ascend to Him, marked with our own individuality. *The Ministry of Healing*, p. 100.

CHAPTER 8

Climbing the Heights

In perfecting a Christian character, it is essential to persevere in right doing. I would impress upon our youth the importance of perseverance and energy in the work of character-building. From the earliest years it is necessary to weave into the character principles of stern integrity, that the youth may reach the highest standard of manhood and womanhood. They should ever keep the fact before their eyes that they have been bought with a price, and should glorify God in their bodies and spirits, which are His. . . .

Daily Advancement

It is the work of the youth to make advancement day by day. Peter says, "Add to your faith virtue; and to virtue knowledge; and to knowledge temperance; and to temperance patience; and to patience godliness; and to godliness brotherly kindness; and to brotherly kindness charity. For if these things be in you, and abound, they make you that ye shall neither be barren nor unfruitful in the knowledge of our Lord Jesus Christ."

All these successive steps are not to be kept before the mind's eye, and counted as you start; but fixing the eye upon Jesus, with an eye single to the glory of God, you will make advancement. You cannot reach the full measure of the stature of Christ in a day, and you would sink in despair could you behold all the difficulties that must be met and overcome. You have Satan to contend with, and he will seek by every possible device to attract your mind from Christ.

Meeting Obstacles

But we must meet all obstacles placed in our way, and overcome them one at a time. If we overcome the first difficulty, we shall be stronger to meet the next, and at every effort will become better able to make advancement. By looking to Jesus, we may be overcomers. It is by fastening our eyes on the difficulties and shrinking from earnest battle for the right, that we become weak and faithless.

By taking one step after another, the highest ascent may be climbed, and the summit of the mount may be reached at last. Do not become overwhelmed with the great amount of work you must do in your lifetime, for you are not required to do it all at once. Let every power of your being go to each day's work, improve each precious opportunity, appreciate the helps that God gives you, and make advancement up the ladder of progress step by step. Remember that you are to live but one day at a time, that God has given you one day, and heavenly records will show how you have valued its privileges and opportunities. May you so improve every day given you of God, that at last you may hear the Master say, "Well done, thou good and faithful servant." *Youth's Instructor*, January 5, 1893.

CHAPTER 9

Partnership With God

You have within your reach more than finite possibilities. A man, as God applies the term, is a son of God. "Now are we the sons of God, and it doth not yet appear what we shall be: but we know that, when He shall appear, we shall be like Him; for we shall see Him as He is. And every man that hath this hope in him purifieth himself, even as He is pure." It is your privilege to turn away from that which is cheap and inferior, and rise to a high standard—to be respected by men and beloved by God.

The religious work which the Lord gives to young men, and to men of all ages, shows His respect for them as His children. He gives them the work of self-government. He calls them to be sharers with Him in the great work of redemption and uplifting. As a father takes his son into partnership in his business, so the Lord takes His children into partnership with Himself. We are made laborers together with God. Jesus says, "As Thou hast sent Me into the world, even so have I also sent them into the world." Would you not rather choose to be a child of God than a servant of Satan and sin, having your name registered as an enemy of Christ?

Young men and women need more of the grace of Christ, that they may bring the principles of Christianity into the daily life. The preparation for Christ's coming is a preparation made through Christ for the exercise of our highest qualities. It is the privilege of every youth to make of his character a beautiful structure. But there is a positive need of keeping close to Jesus. He is our strength and efficiency and power. We cannot depend on self for one moment. . . .

Reaching Higher and Higher

However large, however small, your talents, remember that what you have is yours only in trust. Thus God is testing you, giving you opportunity to prove yourself true. To Him you are indebted for all your capabilities. To Him belong your powers of body, mind, and soul, and for Him these powers are to be used. Your time, your influence, your capabilities, your skill—all must be accounted for to Him who gives all. He uses his gifts best who seeks by earnest endeavor to carry out the Lord's great plan for the uplifting of humanity.

Persevere in the work that you have begun, until you gain victory after victory. Educate yourselves for a purpose. Keep in view the highest standard, that you may accomplish greater and still greater good, thus reflecting the glory of God. *Youth's Instructor*, January 25, 1910.

SECTION II
The Conflict With Sin

The example of Christ shows us that our only hope of victory is in continual resistance of Satan's attacks. He who triumphed over the adversary of souls in the conflict of temptations understands Satan's power over the race, and has conquered him in our behalf. As an overcomer, He has given us the advantage of His victory, that in our efforts to resist the temptations of Satan we may unite our weakness to His strength, our worthlessness to His merits. And sustained by His enduring might under the strength of temptation, we may resist in His all-powerful name, and overcome as He overcame. Signs of the Times, *March 4, 1880.*

CHAPTER 10

Satan, a Mighty Foe

Fallen man is Satan's lawful captive. The mission of Jesus Christ was to rescue him from his power. Man is naturally inclined to follow Satan's suggestions, and he cannot of himself successfully resist so terrible a foe, unless Christ, the mighty conqueror, dwells in him, guiding his desires, and giving him strength. God alone can limit the power of Satan. He is going to and fro in the earth, and walking up and down in it. He is not off his watch for a single moment, through fear of losing an opportunity to destroy souls. It is important that God's people understand this, that they may escape his snares.

Satan in Disguise

Satan is preparing his deceptions that in his last campaign against the people of God, they may not understand that it is he. 2 Corinthians 11:14: "And no marvel; for Satan himself is transformed into an angel of light." While some deceived souls are advocating that he does not exist, he is taking them captive, and is working through them to a great extent. Satan knows better than God's people the power that they can have over him, when their strength is in Christ.

When they humbly entreat the mighty Conqueror for help, the weakest believers in the truth, relying firmly upon Christ, can successfully repulse Satan and all his host. He is too cunning to come openly, boldly, with his temptations, for then the drowsy energies of the Christian would arouse, and he would rely upon the strong and mighty Deliverer. But Satan comes in unperceived, and in disguise he works through the children of disobedience, who profess godliness. Satan will go to the extent of his power to harass, tempt, and mislead God's people.

He who dared to face, and tempt, and taunt our Lord, and who had power to take Him in his arms and carry Him to a pinnacle of the temple, and up into an exceeding high mountain, will exercise his power to a wonderful degree upon the present generation, who are far inferior in wisdom to their Lord, and who are almost wholly ignorant of Satan's subtlety and strength.

In a marvelous manner will he affect the bodies of those who are naturally inclined to do his bidding. Satan exults for his own sake that he is regarded as a fiction. When he is made light of, and is represented by some childish illustration, or as some animal, it suits him well. He is thought so inferior that minds are wholly unprepared for his wisely laid plans, and he almost always succeeds well. If his power and subtlety were understood, minds would be prepared to successfully resist him. . . .

The Battle for Each Soul

I saw evil angels contending for souls, and angels of God resisting them. The conflict was severe. Evil angels were crowding about them, corrupting the atmosphere with their poisonous influence, and stupefying their sensibilities. Holy angels were anxiously watching these souls, and were waiting to drive back Satan's host. But it is not the work of good angels to control minds against the will of the individuals. If they yield to the enemy, and make no effort to resist him, then the angels of God can do but little more than hold in check the host of Satan, that they should not destroy, until further light be given to those in peril, to move them to arouse and look to heaven for help. Jesus will not commission holy angels to extricate those who make no effort to help themselves.

If Satan sees he is in danger of losing one soul, he will exert himself to the utmost to keep that one. And when the individual is aroused to his danger, and, with distress and fervor, looks to Jesus for strength, Satan fears he shall lose a captive, and he calls a re-enforcement of his angels to hedge in the poor soul, and form a wall of darkness around him, that heaven's light may not reach him. But if the one in danger perseveres, and in helplessness and weakness casts himself upon the merits of the blood of Christ, Jesus listens to the earnest prayer of faith, and sends a re-enforcement of those angels which excel in strength to deliver him.

Satan cannot endure to have his powerful rival appealed to, for he fears and trembles before His [Christ's] strength and majesty. At the sound of fervent prayer, Satan's whole host trembles. . . . And when angels, all-powerful, clothed with the armory of heaven, come to the help of the fainting, pursued soul, Satan and his host fall back, well knowing that their battle is lost. *Review and Herald*, May 13, 1862.

CHAPTER 11

The Character of the Conflict

The will of man is aggressive, and is constantly striving to bend all things to its purposes. If it is enlisted on the side of God and right, the fruits of the Spirit will appear in the life; and God has appointed, "glory, honor, and peace, to every man that worketh good."

When Satan is permitted to mold the will, he uses it to accomplish his ends. He instigates theories of unbelief, and stirs up the human heart to war against the Word of God. With persistent, persevering effort, he seeks to inspire men with his own energies of hate and antagonism to God, and to array them in opposition to the institutions and requirements of heaven and the operations of the Holy Spirit. He enlists under his standard all evil agencies, and brings them into the battlefield under his generalship to oppose evil against good.

Call to Oppose Powers of Evil

It is Satan's work to dethrone God from the heart, and to mold human nature into his own image of deformity. He stirs up all evil propensities, awakening unholy passions and ambitions. He declares, All this power, these honors, and riches and sinful pleasures will I give thee; but his conditions are that integrity shall be yielded, conscience blunted. Thus he degrades the human faculties, and brings them into captivity to sin.

God calls upon men to oppose the powers of evil. He says, "Let not sin therefore reign in your mortal body, that ye should obey it in the lusts thereof. Neither yield ye your members as instruments of unrighteousness unto sin: but yield yourselves unto God, as those that are alive from the dead, and your members as instruments of righteousness unto God."

The Christian life is a warfare. But "we wrestle not against flesh and blood, but against principalities, against powers, against the rulers of the darkness of this world, against spiritual wickedness in high places." In this conflict of righteousness against unrighteousness we can be successful only by divine aid. Our finite will must be brought into submission to the will of the Infinite; the human will must be blended with the divine. This will bring the Holy Spirit to our aid; and every conquest will tend to the recovery of God's purchased possession, to the restoration of His image in the soul.

Aid of the Holy Spirit

The Lord Jesus acts through the Holy Spirit; for it is His representative. Through it He infuses spiritual life into the soul, quickening its energies for good, cleansing it from moral defilement, and giving it a fitness for His kingdom. Jesus has large blessings to bestow, rich gifts to distribute among men. He is the wonderful Counselor, infinite in wisdom and strength; and if we will acknowledge the power of His Spirit, and submit to be molded by it, we shall stand complete in Him. What a thought is this! In Christ "dwelleth all the fullness of the Godhead bodily. And ye are complete in Him." Never will the human heart know happiness until it is submitted to be molded by the Spirit of God. The Spirit conforms the renewed soul to the model, Jesus Christ. Through the influence of the Spirit, enmity against God is changed into faith and love, and pride into humility. The soul perceives the beauty of truth, and Christ is honored in excellence and perfection of character. As these changes are effected, angels break out in rapturous song, and God and Christ rejoice over souls fashioned after the divine similitude. . . .

The Price of Victory

The warfare between good and evil has not grown less fierce than it was in the days of the Saviour. The path to heaven is no smoother now than it was then. All our sins must be put away. Every darling indulgence that hinders our spiritual progress must be cut off. The right eye or the right hand must be sacrificed, if it causes us to offend. Are we willing to renounce our own wisdom, and to receive the kingdom of heaven as a little child? Are we willing to part with our self-righteousness? Are we willing to sacrifice the approbation of men? The prize of eternal life is of infinite value. Are we willing to welcome the Holy Spirit's aid, and co-operate with it, putting forth efforts and making sacrifices proportionate to the value of the object to be obtained? *Review and Herald*, Feb. 10, 1903.

CHAPTER 12

Satan's Special Effort

I have been shown that we must be guarded on every side, and perseveringly resist the insinuations and devices of Satan. He has transformed himself into an angel of light, and is deceiving and leading thousands captive. The advantages he takes of the science of the human mind is tremendous. Here, serpentlike, he imperceptibly creeps in to corrupt the work of God. The miracles and works of Christ, he makes all human.

If Satan should make an open, bold attack upon Christianity, it would bring the Christian in distress and agony at the feet of his Redeemer, and the strong and mighty Deliverer would affright the bold adversary away. But Satan, transformed into an angel of light, works upon the mind to allure from the only safe and right path. The sciences of phrenology, psychology, and mesmerism have been the channel through which Satan has come more directly to this generation, and wrought with that power which was to characterize his work near the close of probation. . . .

As we near the close of time, the human mind is more readily affected by Satan's devices. He leads deceived mortals to account for the works and miracles of Christ upon general principles. Satan has ever been ambitious to counterfeit the work of Christ, and establish his own power and claims. He does not generally do this openly and boldly. He is artful, and knows that the most effectual way for him to accomplish his work is to come to poor fallen man in the form of an angel of light.

Satan came to Christ in the wilderness in the form of a beautiful young man—more like a monarch than a fallen angel. He came with Scripture in his mouth. Said he, "It is written, etc." Our suffering Saviour meets him with Scripture, saying, "It is written." Satan takes the advantage of the weak, suffering condition of Christ. He took upon Him our human nature. . . .

Confidence in Self Fatal

If Satan can so befog and deceive the human mind, and lead mortals to think there is an inherent power in themselves to accomplish great and good works, they cease to rely upon God to do that for them which they think exists in themselves to do. They acknowledge not a superior power. They give not God the glory He claims, and which is due to His great and excellent Majesty. Satan's object is thus accomplished. He exults that fallen man presumptuously exalts himself, as he exalted himself in heaven, and was thrust out. He knows that the ruin of man is just as sure if he exalts himself as his was certain.

Destroying Confidence

He has failed in his temptations to Christ in the wilderness. The plan of salvation has been carried out. The dear price has been paid for man's redemption. And now Satan seeks to tear away the foundation of the Christian's hope, and turn the minds of men in a channel that they may not be benefited or saved by the great sacrifice offered. He leads fallen man, through his "all deceivableness of unrighteousness," to believe that he can do very well without an atonement; that he need not depend upon a crucified and risen Saviour; that man's own merits will entitle him to God's favor, and then he destroys man's confidence in the Bible, well knowing if he succeeds here, and the detector which places a mark upon himself is destroyed, he is safe.

He fastens the delusion upon minds that there is no personal devil, and those who believe this make no effort to resist and war against that which does not exist, and poor blind mortals finally adopt the maxim, "Whatever is, is right." They acknowledge no rule to measure their course. Satan leads many to believe that prayer to God is useless, and but a form. He well knows how needful is meditation and prayer, to keep Christ's followers aroused to resist his cunning and deceptions. Satan's devices will divert the mind from these important exercises, that the soul may not lean for help upon the mighty One, and obtain strength from Him to resist his attacks. . . .

It will serve his purpose well if we neglect the exercise of prayer, for then his lying wonders are more readily received. Satan accomplishes his object in setting his deceitful temptations before man, that which he failed to accomplish in tempting Christ. He sometimes comes in the form of a lovely young person, or in a beautiful shadow. He works cures, and is worshiped by deceived mortals as a benefactor of our race. . . .

Control of the Mind

I was shown that Satan cannot control minds unless they are yielded to his control. Those who depart from the right are in serious danger now. They separate themselves from God and from the watch-care of the angels of God, and Satan, ever upon the watch to destroy souls, begins to present to such his deceptions, and they are in the utmost peril. And if they see and try to resist the powers of darkness and to free themselves from Satan's snare, it is not an easy matter. They have ventured on Satan's ground, and he claims them. He will not hesitate to engage all his energies, and call to his aid all his evil host to wrest a single human being from the hand of Christ.

Those who have tempted the devil to tempt them will have to make desperate efforts to free themselves from his power. When they begin to work for themselves, then angels of God whom they have grieved will come to their rescue. Satan and his angels are unwilling to lose their prey. They contend and battle with the holy angels, and the conflict is severe. And if those who have erred continue to plead, and in deep humility confess their wrongs, angels who excel in strength will prevail and wrench them from the power of the evil angels.

The Curtain Lifted

As the curtain was lifted and I was shown the corruption of this age, my heart sickened, my spirit nearly fainted within me. I saw that the inhabitants of the earth were filling up the measure of the cup of their iniquity. God's anger is kindled, and will be no more appeased until the sinners are destroyed out of the earth.

Satan is Christ's personal enemy. He is the originator and leader of every species of rebellion in heaven and earth. His rage increases, and we do not realize his power. If our eyes could be opened to discern the fallen angels at their work with those who feel at ease and consider themselves safe, we should not feel so secure. Evil angels are upon our track every moment. We expect a readiness on the part of bad men to act as Satan suggests; but while our minds are unguarded against Satan's invisible agents, they will assume new ground, and will work marvels and miracles in our sight. Are we prepared to resist them by the Word of God, the only weapon we can use successfully.

Some will be tempted to receive these wonders as from God. The sick will be healed before us. Miracles will be performed in our sight. Are we prepared for the trial when the lying wonders of Satan shall be more fully exhibited? Will not many souls be ensnared and taken? Forms of error, and departure from the plain precepts and commandments of God and giving heed to fables are fitting minds for these lying wonders of Satan. We must all now seek to arm ourselves for the contest in which we must soon engage. Faith in God's Word, prayerfully studied and practically applied will be our shield from Satan's power, and will bring us off conquerors through the blood of Christ. *Review and Herald*, February 18, 1862.

CHAPTER 13

Temptation No Excuse for Sin

There is not an impulse of our nature, not a faculty of the mind or an inclination of the heart, but needs to be, moment by moment, under the control of the Spirit of God. There is not a blessing which God bestows upon man, nor a trial which he permits to befall him, but Satan both can and will seize upon it to tempt, to harass, and destroy the soul, if we give him the least advantage. Therefore however great one's spiritual light, however much he may enjoy of the divine favor and blessing, he should ever walk humbly before the Lord, pleading in faith that God will direct every thought and control every impulse.

All who profess godliness are under the most sacred obligation to guard the spirit, and to exercise self-control under the greatest provocation. The burdens placed upon Moses were very great; few men will ever be so severely tried as he was; yet this was not allowed to excuse his sin. God has made ample provision for His people; and if they rely upon His strength, they will never become the sport of circumstances. The strongest temptation cannot excuse sin. However great the pressure brought to bear upon the soul, transgression is our own act. It is not in the power of earth or hell to compel any one to do evil. Satan attacks us at our weak points, but we need not be overcome. However severe or unexpected the assault, God has provided help for us, and in His strength we may conquer. *Patriarchs and Prophets*, p. 421.

CHAPTER 14

Fortitude

Those who are finally victorious will have seasons of terrible perplexity and trial in their religious life; but they must not cast away their confidence, for this is a part of their discipline in the school of Christ, and it is essential in order that all dross may be purged away. The servant of God must endure with fortitude the attacks of the enemy, his grievous taunts, and must overcome the obstacles which Satan will place in his way.

Satan will seek to discourage the followers of Christ, so that they may not pray or study the Scriptures, and he will throw his hateful shadow athwart the path to hide Jesus from the view, to shut away the vision of His love, and the glories of the heavenly inheritance. It is his delight to cause the children of God to go shrinkingly, tremblingly, and painfully along, under continual doubt. He seeks to make the pathway as sorrowful as possible; but if you keep looking up, not down at your difficulties, you will not faint in the way, you will soon see Jesus reaching His hand to help you, and you will only have to give Him your hand in simple confidence, and let Him lead you. As you become trustful, you will become hopeful.

In the Strength of the Lord

Jesus is the light of the world, and you are to fashion your life after His. You will find help in Christ to form a strong, symmetrical, beautiful character. Satan cannot make of none effect the light shining forth from such a character. The Lord has a work for each of us to do. He does not provide that we shall be sustained by the influence of human praise and petting; He means that every soul shall stand in the strength of the Lord. God has given us His best gift, even His only-begotten Son, to uplift, ennoble, and fit us, by putting on us His own perfection of character, for a home in His kingdom. Jesus came to our world and lived as He expects His followers to live. If we are self-indulgent, and too lazy to put forth earnest effort to cooperate with the wonderful work of God, we shall meet with loss in this life, and loss in the future, immortal life.

God designs that we shall work, not in a despairing manner, but with strong faith and hope. As we search the Scriptures, and are enlightened to behold the wonderful condescension of the Father in giving Jesus to the world, that all who believe on Him should not perish but have everlasting life, we should rejoice with joy unspeakable and full of glory. Everything that can be gained by education, God means that we shall use for the advancement of the truth. True, vital godliness must be reflected from the life and character, that the cross of Christ may be lifted up before the world, and the value of the soul be revealed in the light of the cross. Our minds must be opened to understand the Scriptures, that we may gain spiritual power by feeding upon the bread of heaven. *Review and Herald*, April 8, 1890.

CHAPTER 15

The Soul Temple

A faithful obedience to God's requirements will have a surprising influence to elevate, develop, and strengthen all man's faculties. Those who have in youth devoted themselves to the service of God, are found to be the men of sound judgment and keen discrimination. And why should it not be so? Communion with the greatest Teacher the world has ever known, strengthens the understanding, illuminates the mind, and purifies the heart—elevates, refines, and ennobles the whole man. "The entrance of Thy words giveth light; it giveth understanding unto the simple."

God's Ideal

Among the youth who profess godliness, there is a large class who may seem to contradict this statement. They make no advancement in knowledge or in spirituality. Their powers are dwarfing, rather than developing. But the psalmist's words are true of the genuine Christian. It is not, indeed, the bare letter of God's Word that gives light and understanding; it is the word opened and applied to the heart by the Holy Spirit. When a man is truly converted, he becomes a son of God, a partaker of the divine nature. Not only is the heart renewed, but the intellect is strengthened and invigorated. There have been many instances of persons who before conversion were thought to possess ordinary and even inferior ability, but who after conversion seemed to be entirely transformed. They then manifested remarkable power to comprehend the truths of God's Word, and to present these truths to others. Men of high intellectual standing have considered it a privilege to hold intercourse with these men. The Sun of Righteousness, shedding its bright beams into their minds, quickened every power into more vigorous action.

God will do a great work for the youth, if they will by the aid of the Holy Spirit receive His Word into the heart and obey it in the life. He is constantly seeking to attract them to Himself, the Source of all wisdom, the Fountain of goodness, purity, and truth. The mind which is occupied with exalted themes becomes itself ennobled.

Desecrated Shrines

Those who profess to serve God, and yet make no advancement in knowledge and piety, are Christians only in name. The soul-temple is filled with desecrated shrines. Frivolous reading, trifling conversation, and worldly pleasure, occupy the mind so completely that there is no room left for the entrance of God's Word. Worldliness, frivolity, and pride take the place which Christ should occupy in the soul. . . .

Degradation Through Sensual Indulgence

Those who seek as their chief good the indulgence of appetite and passion, are never good or truly great men. However high they may stand in the opinion of the world, they are low, vile, and corrupt in God's estimation. Heaven has ordered that the mark of their depravity shall be written upon their very countenance. Their thoughts are of the earth, earthly. Their words reveal the low level of the mind. They have filled the heart with vileness, and well-nigh effaced therefrom the image of God. The voice of reason is drowned, and judgment is perverted. Oh, how is man's entire nature debased by sensual indulgence! When the will is surrendered to Satan, to what depths of vice and folly will not men descend! In vain does truth appeal to the intellect; for the heart is opposed to its pure principles. *Signs of the Times*, December 1, 1881.

Help in Temptation

By faith and prayer all may meet the requirements of the gospel. No man can be forced to transgress. His own consent must be first gained; the soul must purpose the sinful act, before passion can dominate over reason, or iniquity triumph over conscience. Temptation, however strong, is never an excuse for sin. "The eyes of the Lord are over the righteous, and His ears are open unto their prayers." Cry unto the Lord, tempted soul. Cast yourself, helpless, unworthy, upon Jesus, and claim His very promise. The Lord will hear. He knows how strong are the inclinations of the natural heart, and He will help in every time of temptation.

Have you fallen into sin? Then without delay seek God for mercy and pardon. . . . Mercy is still extended to the sinner. The Lord is calling to us in all our wanderings, "Return, ye backsliding children, and I will heal your backslidings." *Testimonies for the Church*, Vol. 5, page 177.

CHAPTER 16

Ye Are Not Your Own

We sometimes hear the questions: Am I never to do as I please? Am I never to have my own way? Am I always to be restrained? Can I never act in accordance with my inclinations?

The less you follow natural inclinations, the better it will be for yourself and for others. The natural inclinations have been perverted, the natural powers misapplied. Satan has brought man into collision with God. He works continually to destroy the divine image in man. Therefore we must place a restraint on our words and actions.

Results of Complete Consecration

When the grace of God takes possession of the heart, it is seen that the inherited and cultivated tendencies to wrong must be crucified. A new life, under new control, must begin in the soul. All that is done must be done to the glory of God. This work includes the outward as well as the inward man. The entire being, body, soul, and spirit, must be brought into subjection to God, to be used by Him as an instrument of righteousness.

The natural man is not subject to the law of God; neither, indeed, of himself, can he be. But by faith he who has been renewed lives day by day the life of Christ. Day by day he shows that he realizes that he is God's property.

Body and soul belong to God. He gave His Son for the redemption of the world, and because of this we have been granted a new lease of life, a probation in which to develop characters of perfect loyalty. God has redeemed us from the slavery of sin, and has made it possible for us to live regenerated, transformed lives of service.

All Our Powers Belong to Him

God's stamp is upon us. He has bought us, and He desires us to remember that our physical, mental, and moral powers belong to Him. Time and influence reason, affection, and conscience, all are God's, and are to be used only in harmony with His will. They are not to be used in accordance with the direction of the world; for the world is under a leader who is at enmity with God.

The flesh, in which the soul tabernacles, belongs to God. Every sinew, every muscle, is His. In no case are we by neglect or abuse to weaken a single organ. We are to cooperate with God by keeping the body in the very best possible condition of health, that it may be a temple where the Holy Ghost may abide, molding, according to the will of God, every physical and spiritual power.

The mind must be stored with pure principles. Truth must be graven on the tablets of the soul. The memory must be filled with the precious truths of the Word. Then, like beautiful gems, these truths will flash out in the life.

The Price of a Soul

The value that God places on the work of His hands, the love He has for His children, is revealed by the gift He made to redeem men. Adam fell under the dominion of Satan. He brought sin into the world, and death by sin. God gave His only-begotten Son to save man. This He did that He might be just, and yet the justifier of all who accept Christ. Man sold himself to Satan, but Jesus bought back the race. . . .

You are not your own. Jesus has purchased you with His blood. Do not bury your talents in the earth. Use them for Him. In whatever business you may be engaged, bring Jesus into it. If you find that you are losing your love for your Saviour, give up your business, and say, "Here I am, Saviour; what wilt Thou have me to do?" He will receive you graciously, and love you freely. He will abundantly pardon; for He is merciful and long-suffering, not willing that any should perish. . . .

We, and all that we have, belong to God. We should not regard it as a sacrifice to give Him the affection of our hearts. The heart itself should be given to Him as a willing offering. *Youth's Instructor*, November 8, 1900.

Decision Called For

It is not safe for us to linger to contemplate the advantages to be reaped through yielding to Satan's suggestions. Sin means dishonor and disaster to every soul that indulges in it; but it is blinding and deceiving in its nature, and it will entice us with flattering presentations. If we venture on Satan's ground, we have no assurance of protection from his power. So far as in us lies, we should close every avenue by which the tempter may find access to us. *Thoughts from the Mount of Blessing*, p. 118.

CHAPTER 17

True Conversion

"Then will I sprinkle clean water upon you, and ye shall be clean: from all your filthiness, and from all your idols, will I cleanse you. A new heart also will I give you, and a new spirit will I put within you: and I will take away the stony heart out of your flesh, and I will give you an heart of flesh."

Many who speak to others of the need of a new heart do not themselves know what is meant by these words. The youth especially stumble over this phrase, "a new heart." They do not know what it means. They look for a special change to take place in their feelings. This they term conversion. Over this error thousands have stumbled to ruin, not understanding the expression, "Ye must be born again."

Not Feeling but a Changed Life

Satan leads people to think that because they have felt a rapture of feeling they are converted. But their experience does not change. Their actions are the same as before. Their lives show no good fruit. They pray often and long, and are constantly referring to the feelings they had at such and such a time. But they do not live the new life. They are deceived. Their experience goes no deeper than feeling. They build upon the sand, and when adverse winds come their house is swept away.

Many poor souls are groping in darkness, looking for the

feelings which others say they have had in their experience. They overlook the fact that the believer in Christ must work out his own salvation with fear and trembling. The convicted sinner has something to do. He must repent and show true faith.

When Jesus speaks of the new heart, He means the mind, the life, the whole being. To have a change of heart is to withdraw the affections from the world, and fasten them upon Christ. To have a new heart is to have a new mind, new purposes, new motives. What is the sign of a new heart? A changed life. There is a daily, hourly dying to selfishness and pride.

Practicality of Genuine Religion

Some make a great mistake by supposing that a high profession will compensate for real service. But a religion which is not practical is not genuine. True conversion makes us strictly honest in our dealings with our fellow men. It makes us faithful in our everyday work. Every sincere follower of Christ will show that the religion of the Bible qualifies him to use his talents in the Master's service.

"Not slothful in business." These words will be fulfilled in the life of every Christian. Even though your work may seem to be a drudgery, you may ennoble it by the way in which you do it. Do it as unto the Lord. Do it cheerfully, and with heaven-born dignity. It is the noble principles which are brought into the work that make it wholly acceptable in the Lord's sight. True service links the lowliest of God's servants on earth with the highest of His servants in the courts above. . . .

As sons and daughters of God, Christians should strive to reach the high ideal set before them in the gospel. They should be content with nothing less than perfection; for Christ says, "Be ye therefore perfect, even as your Father which is in heaven is perfect."

The Sanctified Life

Let us make God's holy Word our study, bringing its holy principles into our lives. Let us walk before God in meekness and humility, daily correcting our faults. Let us not by selfish pride separate the soul from God. Cherish not a feeling of lofty supremacy, thinking yourself better than others. "Let him that thinketh he standeth take heed lest he fall." Peace and rest will come to you as you bring your will into subjection to the will of Christ. Then the love of Christ will rule in the heart, bringing into captivity to the Saviour the secret springs of action. The hasty, easily roused temper will be soothed and subdued by the oil of Christ's grace. The sense of sins forgiven will bring that peace that passeth all understanding. There will be an earnest striving to overcome all that is opposed to Christian perfection. Variance will disappear. He who once found fault with those around him will see that far greater faults exist in his own character.

There are those who listen to the truth, and are convinced that they have been living in opposition to Christ. They are condemned, and they repent of their transgressions. Relying upon the merits of Christ, exercising true faith in Him, they receive pardon for sin. As they cease to do evil and learn to do well, they grow in grace and in the knowledge of God. They see that they must sacrifice in order to separate from the world; and, after counting the cost, they look upon all as loss if they may but win Christ. They have enlisted in Christ's army. The warfare is before them, and they enter it bravely and cheerfully, fighting against their natural inclinations and selfish desires, bringing the will into subjection to the will of Christ. Daily they seek the Lord for grace to obey Him, and they are strengthened and helped. This is true conversion. In humble, grateful dependence he who has been given a new heart relies upon the help of Christ. He reveals in his life the fruit of righteousness. He once loved himself. Worldly pleasure was his delight. Now his idol is dethroned, and God reigns supreme. The sins he once loved he now hates. Firmly and resolutely he follows in the path of holiness. *Youth's Instructor*, September 26, 1901.

The Cords of Satan

The pains of duty and the pleasures of sin are the cords with which Satan binds men in his snares. Those who would rather die than perform a wrong act are the only ones who will be found faithful. *Testimonies for the Church*. Vol. 5, p. 53.

CHAPTER 18

Counsel to an Indulged Daughter

You have a fearful record of the past year, which is laid open to the view of the Majesty of heaven and the myriads of pure, sinless angels. Your thoughts and acts, your desperate and unsanctified feelings, may have been concealed from mortals; but remember, the most trivial acts of your life are open to the view of God. You have a spotted record in Heaven. The sins you have committed are all registered there.

God's frown is upon you, and yet you appear destitute of feeling; you do not realize your lost and undone condition. At times you do have feelings of remorse; but your proud, independent spirit soon rises above this, and you stifle the voice of conscience.

You are not happy; yet you imagine that if you could have your own way unrestrained, you would be happy. Poor child! you occupy a position similar to that of Eve in Eden. She imagined that she would be highly exalted if she could only eat of the fruit of the tree which God had forbidden her even to touch, lest she die. She ate, and lost all the glories of Eden.

Controlling the Imagination

You should control your thoughts. This will not be an easy task; you cannot accomplish it without a close and even severe effort. Yet God requires this of you; it is a duty resting upon every accountable being. You are responsible to God for your thoughts.

If you indulge in vain imaginations, permitting your mind to dwell upon impure subjects, you are, in a degree, as guilty before God as if your thoughts were carried into action. All that prevents the action is the lack of opportunity.

Day and night dreaming and castle-building are bad and exceedingly dangerous habits. When once established, it is next to impossible to break up such habits, and direct the thoughts to pure, holy, elevated themes. You will have to become a faithful sentinel over your eyes, ears, and all your senses, if you would control your mind, and prevent vain and corrupt thoughts from staining your soul. The power of grace alone can accomplish this most desirable work. You are weak in this direction.

Subduing Passions and Affections

You have become wayward, bold, and daring. The grace of God has no place in your heart. In the strength of God alone can you bring yourself where you can be a recipient of His grace, an instrument of righteousness. Not only does God require you to control your thoughts, but also your passions and affections. Your salvation depends upon your governing yourself in these things. Passion and affection are powerful agents. If misapplied, if set in operation through wrong motives, if misplaced, they are powerful to accomplish your ruin, and leave you a miserable wreck, without God and without hope.

The imagination must be positively and persistently controlled, if the passions and affections are made subject to reason, conscience, and character. You are in danger, for you are just upon the point of sacrificing your eternal interests at the altar of passion. Passion is obtaining positive control of your entire being—passion of what quality? of a base, destructive nature. By yielding to it, you will embitter the lives of your parents, bring sadness and shame to your sisters, sacrifice your own character, and forfeit heaven and a glorious immortal life. Are you ready to do this? I appeal to you to stop where you are. Advance not another step in your headstrong, wanton course; for before you are misery and death. Unless you exercise self-control in regard to your passions and affections, you will surely bring yourself into disrepute with all around you, and will bring upon your character disgrace which will last while you live.

You are disobedient to your parents, pert, unthankful, and unholy. These miserable traits are the fruits of a corrupt tree. You are forward. You love the boys, and love to make them the theme of your conversation. "Out of the abundance of the heart the mouth speaketh." Habits have become powerful to control you; and you have learned to deceive in order to carry out your purposes and accomplish your desires. *Testimonies for the Church*, Vol. 2, pp. 560-562.

CHAPTER 19

Strength of Character Through Conflict

The first thirty years of the life of Christ were passed in the obscure village of Nazareth. The inhabitants of this village were proverbial for their wickedness, hence the inquiry of Nathaniel: "Can there any good thing come out of Nazareth?" The evangelists say but very little in regard to the early life of Christ. With the exception of a brief account of His accompanying His parents to Jerusalem, we have the simple statement only, "And the child grew, and waxed strong in spirit, filled with wisdom: and the grace of God was upon Him."

Christ is our example in all things. In the providence of God, His early life was passed in Nazareth, where the inhabitants were of that character that He was continually exposed to temptations, and it was necessary for Him to be guarded in order to remain pure and spotless amid so much sin and wickedness. Christ did not select this place Himself. His Heavenly Father chose this place for Him, where His character would be tested and tried in a variety of ways. The early life of Christ was subjected to severe trials, hardships, and conflicts, that He might develop the perfect character which makes Him a perfect example for children, youth, and manhood.

Children and youth are frequently situated where their surroundings are not favorable to a Christian life, and they quite readily yield to temptations, and plead as an excuse for pursuing a course of sin that their surroundings are unfavorable. Christ chose retirement, and through a life of industry, keeping His hands employed, He did not invite temptation, but kept aloof from the society of those whose influence was corrupting. Christ placed His feet in the most uneven path that children and youth will ever be called to travel. He did not have allotted to Him a life of affluence and indolence. His parents were poor, and dependent upon their daily toil for sustenance; therefore the life of Christ was one of poverty, self-denial, and privation. He shared with His parents their life of diligent industry.

Purity Not Dependent on Circumstances

None will ever be called to perfect Christian character under more unfavorable circumstances than that of our Saviour. The fact that Christ lived thirty years in Nazareth, from which many thought it a wonder if any good thing could come, is a rebuke to the youth who consider that their religious character must conform to circumstances. If the surroundings of youth are unpleasant and positively bad, many make this an excuse for not perfecting Christian character. The example of Christ would rebuke the idea that His followers are dependent upon place, fortune, or prosperity, in order to live blameless lives. Christ would teach them that their faithfulness would make any place or position, where the providence of God called them, honorable, however humble.

The life of Christ was designed to show that purity, stability, and firmness of principle are not dependent upon a life freed from hardships, poverty, and adversity. The trials and privations of which so many youth complain, Christ endured without murmuring. And this discipline is the very experience the youth need, which will give firmness to their characters, and make them like Christ, strong in spirit to resist temptation. They will not, if they separate from the influence of those who would lead them astray and corrupt their morals, be overcome by the devices of Satan. Through daily prayer to God, they will have wisdom and grace from Him to bear the conflict and stern realities of life, and come off victorious. Fidelity and serenity of mind can only be retained by watchfulness and prayer. Christ's life was an example of persevering energy, which was not allowed to become weakened by reproach, ridicule, privation or hardships.

Thus should it be with the youth. If trials increase upon them, they may know that God is testing and proving their fidelity. And in just that degree that they maintain their integrity of character under discouragements, will their fortitude, stability, and power of endurance increase, and they wax strong in spirit. *Youth's Instructor*, March, 1872.

Death Before Dishonor

Choose poverty, reproach, separation from friends, or any suffering, rather than to defile the soul with sin. Death before dishonor or the transgression of God's law, should be the motto of every Christian. *Testimonies for the Church*, Vol. 5, p. 147.

CHAPTER 20

Resisting Temptation

Those who are partakers of the divine nature will not give way to temptation. The enemy is working with all his might to overcome those who are striving to live the Christian life. He comes to them with temptations, in the hope that they will yield. Thus he hopes to discourage them. But those who have planted their feet firmly on the Rock of Ages will not yield to his devices. They will remember that God is their Father and Christ their Helper. The Saviour came to our world to bring to every tried, tempted soul strength to overcome even as He overcame. I know the power of temptation; I know the dangers that are in the way; but I know, too, that strength sufficient for every time of need is provided for those who are struggling against temptation.

Needless Temptations to Be Shunned

"God is faithful, who will not suffer you to be tempted above that ye are able; but will with the temptation also make a way to escape, that ye may be able to bear it." And we also have a part to act. We are not to place ourselves needlessly in the way of temptation. God says, "Come out from among them, and be ye separate, . . . and touch not the unclean thing; and I will receive you, and will be a Father unto you, and ye shall be My sons and daughters." If by associating with worldlings for pleasure, by conforming to worldly practices, by uniting our interests with unbelievers, we place our feet in the path of temptation and sin, how can we expect God to keep us from falling?

Keep yourselves away from the corrupting influences of the world. Do not go unbidden to places where the forces of the enemy are strongly entrenched.

Do not go where you will be tempted and led astray. But if you have a message for unbelievers, and if you live so near to God that you can speak to them a word in season, you can do a work that will help them and will honor God. "I pray not," Christ said, "that Thou shouldest take them out of the world, but that Thou shouldest keep them from the evil." *Review and Herald*, April 14, 1904.

Duty Above Inclination

When the youth attempt to break away from Satan's control, he will redouble his temptations. Taking advantage of their ignorance and inexperience, he attempts to obscure the distinction between right and wrong. He transforms himself into an angel of light, and beguiles by promises of pleasure in a forbidden path. If the youth have formed the habit of following inclination rather than duty, they will find it hard to resist temptation. They do not see the danger in indulging even once in forbidden pleasures. The suggestions of Satan will stir every lingering element of depravity in the heart. *Signs of the Times*, January 19, 1882.

CHAPTER 21

The Deceitfulness of Sin

Nothing is more treacherous than the deceitfulness of sin. It is the god of this world that deludes, and blinds, and leads to destruction. Satan does not enter with his array of temptations at once. He disguises these temptations with a semblance of good. He mingles with amusements and folly some little improvements, and deceived souls make it an excuse that great good is to be derived by engaging in them. This is only the deceptive part. It is Satan's hellish arts masked. Beguiled souls take one step, then are prepared for the next. It is so much more pleasant to follow the inclinations of their own hearts than to stand on the defensive, and resist the first insinuation of the wily foe, and thus shut out his in-comings.

Oh, how Satan watches to see his bait taken so readily, and to see souls walking in the very path he has prepared! He does not want them to give up praying and maintaining a form of religious duties; for he can thus make them more useful in his service. He unites his sophistry and deceptive snares with their experiences and professions, and thus wonderfully advances his cause.

Self-examination

There is a necessity for close self-examination, and to closely investigate in the light of God's Word, Am I sound, or am I rotten, at heart? Am I renewed in Christ, or am I still carnal at heart, with an outside, new dress put on? Rein yourself up to the tribunal of God, and see as in the light of God if there is any secret sin, any iniquity, any idol you have not sacrificed. Pray, yes, pray as you have never prayed before, that you may not be deluded by Satan's devices; that you may not be given up to a heedless, careless, and vain spirit, and attend religious duties to quiet your own conscience. . . .

One of the sins that constitute one of the signs of the last days, is that professed Christians are lovers of pleasure more than lovers of God. Deal truly with your own souls. Search carefully. How few, after a faithful examination, can look up to Heaven and say, "I am not one of those thus described. I am not a lover of pleasure more than a lover of God." How few can say, "I am dead to the world; the life I now live is by faith of the Son of God. My life is hid with Christ in God, and when He who is my life shall appear, then shall I also appear with Him in glory."

The love and grace of God! Oh precious grace! more valuable than fine gold. It elevates and ennobles the spirit beyond all other principles. It sets the heart and affections upon Heaven. While those around us may be engaged in worldly vanity, pleasure-seeking, and folly, the conversation is in heaven, whence we look for the Saviour; the soul is reaching out after God for pardon and peace, for righteousness and true holiness. Converse with God and contemplation of things above transform the soul into the likeness of Christ. *Review and Herald*, May 11, 1886.

CHAPTER 22

A Warning Against Skepticism

I feel the most intense anguish for our youth. I warn you, as one who knows the danger, not to be entrapped by Satan through the little knowledge of science which you may have acquired. It is better to have a pure and humble heart than all the knowledge you can possibly gain without the fear of the Lord.

The youth of today will be likely to meet skeptics and infidels wherever they may go, and how necessary that they be equipped, so that they may be able to give a reason of their hope with meekness and fear. Thomas Paine has passed into his grave, but his works live to curse the world, and those who doubt the truth of God's Word will place these infidel productions in the hands of the young and inexperienced, to fill their hearts with the poisonous atmosphere of doubt. The spirit of Satan works through wicked men to carry on his schemes for the ruin of souls.

Danger of Association with Skeptics

We are living in an age of licentiousness, and men and youth are bold in sin. Unless our youth are sacredly guarded, unless they are fortified with firm principles, unless greater care is manifested in choosing their associates and the literature which feeds the mind, they will be exposed to a society whose morals are as corrupt as were the morals of the inhabitants of Sodom. The appearance of the people of the world may be very attractive, but if they are continually throwing out suggestions against the Bible, they are dangerous companions, for they will ever seek to undermine the foundations of your faith, to corrupt the conscientiousness of old-fashioned, gospel religion.

The youth often come in contact with those of skeptical tendencies, and their parents are in ignorance of the fact until the terrible work of evil is consummated and the youth are ruined. The young should be instructed diligently, that they may not be deceived in regard to the true character of these persons, and not form friendships with this class, or listen to their words of sarcasm and sophistry. Unless our young people have moral courage to sever their connection with these persons when they discover their unbelief, they will be ensnared, and will think and talk as do their associates, speaking lightly of religion and the faith of the Bible.

Self-confidence and Blindness

Could the eyes of deluded youth be opened, they would see the exultant leer of Satan at his success in ruining souls. In every conceivable way he seeks to adapt his temptations to the various dispositions and circumstances of those whom he wishes to entangle. He will try every device, and if the subjects of these temptations do not seek God, they will be blinded to his deceptions, and will be self-confident, self-sufficient, and in ignorance of their condition and danger. They will soon come to despise the faith once delivered to the saints.

I speak to the youth as one who knows, as one to whom the Lord has opened the perils that attend their pathway. Self-confidence will lead you into the snare of the enemy. The youth do not ask counsel of God, and make Him their refuge and strength. They enter society with all assurance, confident that they are fully able to choose the right and to comprehend divine mysteries, because of their powers of reason, as though they could discover truth for themselves.

We fear more for those who are self-confident than for any others, for they will surely be entangled in the net that has been set by the great adversary of God and man. Some associate who has been chosen as a familiar friend, who has been tainted with the corruption of doubt, will instill his leaven of unbelief into the minds of this class. By fulsome flattery of their talent, their intellectual superiority, by inciting in them an ambition for high position, their attention will be gained, and moral blight will fall upon them. Those who are exalted in their own opinions will despise the blood of the Atoning Sacrifice, and will do despite to the Spirit of grace.

The children of Sabbath-keeping parents, who have had great light, who have been the objects of the tenderest solicitude, may be the ones who will leave a heritage of shame, who will sow to the wind and reap the whirlwind. In the judgment the names of those who have sinned against great light will be written with those who are condemned to be separated from the presence of the Lord and from the glory of His power. They will be lost, lost, and will be numbered with the scorners of the grace of Christ.

I would rather see my children laid in the grave than see them taking the path that leads to death. The terrible fact that I had nurtured children to fight against the God of heaven, to swell the ranks of apostates in the last days, to march under the black banner of Satan, would indeed be a thought of horror to me.

Moral Courage Needed

Our youth will meet temptations on every hand, and they must be so educated that they will depend upon higher power, higher teaching, than can be given by mortals. There are despisers of our Lord everywhere, who habitually throw contempt upon Christianity. They call it the plaything of children, invented to impose on the credulity of the ignorant.

Those who have not moral power cannot stand in defense of the truth; they have not courage to say: "Unless such conversation ceases, I cannot remain in your presence. Jesus, the world's Redeemer, is my Saviour; in Him is centered my hope of eternal life." But this is the very way in which to silence them. If you argue with them, they will have arguments with which to meet you, and nothing you may say will touch them; but if you live for Christ, if you are firm in your allegiance to the God of heaven, you may do for them that which argument will fail to do, and convince them of the fallacy of their doctrines by the power of godliness.

There is no sadder spectacle than that of those who have been purchased by the blood of Christ, who have been intrusted with talents wherewith they may glorify God, turning to jest the messages graciously sent to them in the gospel, denying the divinity of Christ, and trusting to their own finite reasoning, and to arguments that have no foundation. When tested with affliction, when brought face to face with death, all these fallacies they have cherished will be melted away like frost before the sun.

How terrible it is to stand by the coffin of one who has rejected the appeals of divine mercy! How terrible to say: Here is a life lost! Here is one who might have reached the highest standard, and gained immortal life, but he surrendered his life to Satan, became ensnared by the vain philosophies of men, and was a plaything of the evil one! The Christian's hope is as an anchor to the soul, both sure and steadfast, and entereth into that which is within the veil, whither Christ the forerunner is for us entered. We have an individual work to do to prepare for the great events that are before us.

The Tempest Is Coming

The youth should seek God more earnestly. The tempest is coming, and we must get ready for its fury by having repentance toward God and faith toward our Lord Jesus Christ. The Lord will arise to shake terribly the earth. We shall see troubles on all sides. Thousands of ships will be hurled into the depths of the sea. Navies will go down, and human lives will be sacrificed by millions. Fires will break out unexpectedly, and no human effort will be able to quench them. The palaces of earth will be swept away in the fury of the flames.

Disasters by rail will become more and more frequent; confusion, collision, and death without a moment's warning will occur on the great lines of travel. The end is near, probation is closing. Oh, let us seek God while He may be found, call upon Him while He is near! The prophet says: "Seek ye the Lord, all ye meek of the earth, which have wrought His judgment; seek righteousness, seek meekness: it may be ye shall be hid in the day of the Lord's anger." *Signs of the Times*, April 21, 1890.

Daily Dependence on God

When you rise in the morning, do you feel your helplessness, and your need of strength from God? and do you humbly, heartily make known your wants to your heavenly Father? If so, angels mark your prayers, and if these prayers have not gone forth out of feigned lips, when you are in danger of unconsciously doing wrong, and exerting an influence which will lead others to do wrong, your guardian angel will be by your side, prompting you to a better course, choosing your words for you, and influencing your actions.

If you feel in no danger, and if you offer no prayer for help and strength to resist temptations, you will be sure to go astray; your neglect of duty will be marked in the book of God in heaven, and you will be found wanting in the trying day. *Testimonies for the Church*, Vol. 3, pp. 363, 364.

CHAPTER 23

One Weak Point

We may flatter ourselves that we are free from many things of which others are guilty; but if we have some strong points of character, and but one weak point, there is yet a communion between sin and the soul. The heart is divided in its service, and says, "Some of self and some of Thee." The child of God must search out the sin which he has petted and indulged himself in, and permit God to cut it out of his heart. He must overcome that one sin; for it is not a trifling matter in the sight of God.

One says, "I am not the least jealous, but then I do get provoked and say mean things, although I am always sorry after giving way to temper." Another says, "I have this fault or that, but then I just despise such and such meanness as is manifested by a certain person of my acquaintance." The Lord has not given us a list of graded sins, so that we may reckon some as of little consequence, and say that they will do but little harm, while others are of greater magnitude and will do much harm.

A chain is no stronger than is its weakest link. We might pronounce such a chain good on the whole, but if one link is weak the chain cannot be depended on. The work of overcoming is to be the study of every soul who enters the kingdom of God. That impatient word quivering on your lips must be left unspoken. That thought that your character is not rightly estimated must be put from you; for it weakens your influence, and works out the sure result, making you of light estimation in the minds of others. You should overcome the idea that you are a martyr, and lay claim to the promise of Christ, who says, "My grace is sufficient for thee." *Review and Herald*, August 1, 1893.

Thought Control

You should keep off from Satan's enchanted ground, and not allow your minds to be swayed from allegiance to God. Through Christ you may and should be happy, and should acquire habits of self-control. Even your thoughts must be brought into subjection to the will of God, and your feelings under the control of reason and religion. Your imagination was not given you to be allowed to run riot and have its own way, without any effort at restraint or discipline. If the thoughts are wrong, the feelings will be wrong; and the thoughts and feelings combined make up the moral character. When you decide that as Christians you are not required to restrain your thoughts and feelings, you are brought under the influence of evil angels, and invite their presence and their control. If you yield to your impressions, and allow your thoughts to run in a channel of suspicion, doubt, and repining, you will be among the most unhappy of mortals, and your lives will prove a failure. *Testimonies for the Church*, Vol. 5, p. 310.

SECTION III
Gaining Victories

Nothing is apparently more helpless, yet really more invincible, than the soul that feels its nothingness, and relies wholly on the merits of the Saviour. God would send every angel in heaven to the aid of such an one, rather than allow him to be overcome. Testimonies for the Church, *Vol. 7, p. 17.*

CHAPTER 24

Onward and Upward

I wish I could portray the beauty of the Christian life. Beginning in the morning of life, controlled by the laws of nature and of God, the Christian moves steadily onward and upward, daily drawing nearer his heavenly home, where await for him a crown of life, and a new name, "which no man knoweth saving he that receiveth it." Constantly he grows in happiness, in holiness, in usefulness. The progress of each year exceeds that of the past year.

God has given the youth a ladder to climb, a ladder that reaches from earth to heaven. Above this ladder is God, and on every round fall the bright beams of His glory. He is watching those who are climbing, ready, when the grasp relaxes and the steps falter, to send help. Yes, tell it in words full of cheer, that no one who perseveringly climbs the ladder will fail of gaining an entrance into the heavenly city.

Satan presents many temptations to the youth. He is playing the game of life for their souls, and he leaves no means untried to allure and ruin them. But God does not leave them to fight unaided against the tempter. They have an all-powerful Helper.

Stronger far than their foe is He who in this world and in human nature met and conquered Satan, resisting every temptation that comes to the youth today. He is their Elder Brother. He feels for them a deep and tender interest. He keeps over them a constant watch-care, and He rejoices when they try to please Him. As they pray, He mingles with their prayers the incense of His righteousness, and offers them to God as a fragrant sacrifice. In His strength the youth can endure hardness as good soldiers of the cross. Strengthened with His might, they are enabled to reach the high ideals before them. The sacrifice made on Calvary is the pledge of their victory.

God Not Unreasonable

The church of God is made up of vessels large and small. The Lord does not ask for anything unreasonable. He does not expect the smaller vessels to hold the contents of the larger ones. He looks for returns according to what a man has, not according to what he has not. Do your best, and God will accept your efforts. Take up the duty lying nearest you, and perform it with fidelity, and your work will be wholly acceptable to the Master. Do not, in your desire to do something great, overlook the smaller tasks awaiting you.

Beware how you neglect secret prayer and a study of God's Word. These are your weapons against him who is striving to hinder your progress heavenward. The first neglect of prayer and Bible study makes easier the second neglect. The first resistance to the Spirit's pleading prepares the way for the second resistance. Thus the heart is hardened, and the conscience seared.

On the other hand, every resistance of temptation makes resistance more easy. Every denial of self makes self-denial easier. Every victory gained prepares the way for a fresh victory. Each resistance of temptation, each self-denial, each triumph over sin, is a seed sown unto eternal life. Every unselfish action gives new strength to spirituality. No one can try to be like Christ without growing more noble and more true.

Develop Confidence

The Lord will recognize every effort you make to reach His ideal for you. When you make a failure, when you are betrayed into sin, do not feel that you cannot pray, that you are not worthy to come before the Lord. "My little children, these things write I unto you, that ye sin not. And if any man sin, we have an advocate with the Father, Jesus Christ the righteous." With outstretched arms He waits to welcome the prodigal. Go to Him, and tell Him about your mistakes and failures. Ask Him to strengthen you for fresh endeavor. He will never disappoint you, never abuse your confidence.

Trial will come to you. Thus the Lord polishes the roughness from your character. Do not murmur. You make the trial harder by repining. Honor God by cheerful submission. Patiently endure the pressure. Even though a wrong is done you, keep the love of God in the heart. "Keep thy tongue from evil, and thy lips from speaking guile. Depart from evil, and do good; seek peace, and pursue it. The eyes of the Lord are upon the righteous, and His ears are open unto their cry."

"Beware of desperate steps; the darkest day, Wait but tomorrow, will have passed away." "In quietness and in confidence shall be your strength." Christ knows the strength of your temptations and the strength of your power to resist. His hand is always stretched out in pitying tenderness to every suffering child. To the tempted, discouraged one he says, Child for whom I suffered and died, cannot you trust Me? "As thy days, so shall thy strength be." . . .

"Commit thy way unto the Lord; trust also in Him; and He shall bring it to pass." . . . He will be to you as the shadow of a great rock in a weary land. He says, "Come unto Me, . . . and I will give you rest"—rest that the world can neither give nor take away. . . .

Words cannot describe the peace and joy possessed by him who takes God at His Word. Trials do not disturb him, slights do not vex him. Self is crucified. Day by day his duties may become more taxing, his temptations stronger, his trials more severe; but he does not falter; for he receives strength equal to his need. *Youth's Instructor*, June 26, 1902.

Cost of Victory

Christ sacrificed everything for man, in order to make it possible for him to gain heaven. Now it is for fallen man to show what he will sacrifice on his own account, for Christ's sake, that he may win immortal glory. Those who have any just sense of the magnitude of salvation, and of its cost, will never murmur that their sowing must be in tears, and that conflict and self-denial are the Christian's portion in this life. *Signs of the Times*, March 4, 1880.

CHAPTER 25

Perfecting Character

Christ has given us no assurance that to attain perfection of character is an easy matter. A noble all-round character is not inherited. It does not come to us by accident. A noble character is earned by individual effort through the merits and grace of Christ. God gives the talents, the powers of the mind; we form the character. It is formed by hard, stern battles with self. Conflict after conflict must be waged against hereditary tendencies. We shall have to criticize ourselves closely, and allow not one unfavorable trait to remain uncorrected.

Let no one say, I cannot remedy my defects of character. If you come to this decision, you will certainly fail of obtaining everlasting life. The impossibility lies in your own will. If you will not, then you cannot overcome. The real difficulty arises from the corruption of an unsanctified heart, and an unwillingness to submit to the control of God.

Set Your Mark High

Many whom God has qualified to do excellent work accomplish very little, because they attempt little. Thousands pass through life as if they had no definite object for which to live, no standard to reach. Such will obtain a reward proportionate to their works.

Remember that you will never reach a higher standard than

you yourself set. Then set your mark high, and step by step, even though it be by painful effort, by self-denial and sacrifice, ascend the whole length of the ladder of progress. Let nothing hinder you. Fate has not woven its meshes about any human being so firmly that he need remain helpless and in uncertainty. Opposing circumstances should create a firm determination to overcome them. The breaking down of one barrier will give greater ability and courage to go forward. Press with determination in the right direction, and circumstances will be your helpers, not your hindrances.

Cultivate Every Grace of Character

Be ambitious, for the Master's glory, to cultivate every grace of character. In every phase of your character building you are to please God. This you may do; for Enoch pleased Him, though living in a degenerate age. And there are Enochs in this our day.

Stand like Daniel, that faithful statesman, a man whom no temptation could corrupt. Do not disappoint Him who so loved you that He gave His own life to cancel your sins. He says, "Without Me ye can do nothing." Remember this. If you have made mistakes, you certainly gain a victory if you see these mistakes, and regard them as beacons of warning. Thus you turn defeat into victory, disappointing the enemy, and honoring your Redeemer.

A character formed according to the divine likeness is the only treasure that we can take from this world to the next. Those who are under the instruction of Christ in this world will take every divine attainment with them to the heavenly mansions. And in heaven we are continually to improve. How important, then, is the development of character in this life.

His Biddings Are Enablings

The heavenly intelligences will work with the human agent who seeks with determined faith that perfection of character which will reach out to perfection in action. To every one engaged in this work Christ says, I am at your right hand to help you.

As the will of man cooperates with the will of God, it becomes omnipotent. Whatever is to be done at His command, may be accomplished in His strength. All His biddings are enablings. *Christ's Object Lessons*, pp. 331-333.

Our Constant Dependence

Those who fail to realize their constant dependence upon God will be overcome by temptation. We may now suppose that our feet stand secure, and that we shall never be moved. We may say with confidence, "I know in whom I have believed; nothing can shake my faith in God and in His Word." But Satan is planning to take advantage of our hereditary and cultivated traits of character, and to blind our eyes to our own necessities and defects. Only through realizing our own weakness, and looking steadfastly unto Jesus, can we walk securely. *The Desire of Ages*, p. 382.

CHAPTER 26

The Fight of Faith

Many of the youth have not a fixed principle to serve God. They sink under every cloud, and have no power of endurance. They do not grow in grace. They appear to keep the commandments of God, but they are not subject to the law of God, neither indeed can be. Their carnal hearts must be changed. They must see beauty in holiness: then they will pant after it as the hart panteth after the water-brooks; then they will love God and His law; then the yoke of Christ will be easy, and His burden light.

If your steps are ordered by the Lord, dear youth, you must not expect that your path will always be one of outward peace and prosperity. The path that leads to eternal day is not the easiest to travel, and at times it will seem dark and thorny. But you have the assurance that God's everlasting arms encircle you, to protect you from evil. He wants you to exercise earnest faith in Him, and learn to trust Him in the shadow as well as in the sunshine.

Living Faith

The follower of Christ must have faith abiding in the heart; for without this it is impossible to please God. Faith is the hand that takes hold of infinite help; it is the medium by which the renewed heart is made to beat in unison with the heart of Christ.

In her endeavors to reach her home, the eagle is often beaten down by the tempest to the narrow defiles of the mountains. The clouds, in black, angry masses sweep between her and the sunny heights where she secures her nest. For a while she seems bewildered, and dashes this way and that, beating her strong wings as if to sweep back the dense clouds. She awakens the doves of the mountains with her wild cry in her vain endeavors to find a way out of her prison. At last she dashes upward into the blackness, and gives a shrill scream of triumph as she emerges, a moment later, in the calm sunshine above. The darkness and tempest are all below her, and the light of heaven is shining about her. She reaches her loved home in the lofty crag, and is satisfied. It was through darkness that she reached the light. It cost her an effort to do this, but she is rewarded in gaining the object which she sought.

This is the only course we can pursue as followers of Christ. We must exercise that living faith, which will penetrate the clouds that, like a thick wall, separate us from heaven's light. We have heights of faith to reach, where all is peace and joy in the Holy Spirit.

A Lifelong Conflict

Have you ever watched a hawk in pursuit of a timid dove? Instinct has taught the dove that in order for the hawk to seize his prey, he must gain a loftier flight than his victim. So she rises higher and still higher in the blue dome of heaven, ever pursued by the hawk, which is seeking to obtain the advantage. But in vain. The dove is safe as long as she allows nothing to stop her in her flight, or draw her earthward; but let her once falter, and take a lower flight, and her watchful enemy will swoop down upon his victim. Again and again have we watched this scene with almost breathless interest, all our sympathies with the little dove. How sad we should have felt to see it fall a victim to the cruel hawk!

We have before us a warfare—a lifelong conflict with Satan and his seductive temptations. The enemy will use every argument, every deception, to entangle the soul; and in order to win the crown of life, we must put forth earnest, persevering effort. We must not lay off the armor or leave the battlefield until we have gained the victory, and can triumph in our Redeemer. As long as we continue to keep our eyes fixed upon the Author and Finisher of our faith, we shall be safe. But our affections must be placed upon things above, not on things of the earth. By faith we must rise higher and still higher in the attainment of the graces of Christ. By daily contemplating His matchless charms, we must grow more and more into His glorious image. While we thus live in communion with Heaven, Satan will lay his nets for us in vain. *Youth's Instructor*, May 12, 1898.

CHAPTER 27

Victory Appropriated

We have little idea of the strength that would be ours if we would connect with the source of all strength. We fall into sin again and again, and think it must always be so. We cling to our infirmities as if they were something to be proud of. Christ tells us that we must set our face as a flint if we would overcome. He has borne our sins in His own body on the tree; and through the power He has given us, we may resist the world, the flesh, and the devil. Then let us not talk of our weakness and inefficiency, but of Christ and His strength. When we talk of Satan's strength, the enemy fastens his power more firmly upon us. When we talk of the power of the Mighty One, the enemy is driven back. As we draw near to God, He draws near to us. . . .

Many of us fail to improve our privileges. We make a few feeble efforts to do right, and then go back to our old life of sin. If we ever enter the kingdom of God, we must enter with perfect characters, not having spot, or wrinkle, or any such thing. Satan works with increased activity as we near the close of time. He lays his snares, unperceived by us, that he may take possession of our minds. In every way he tries to eclipse the glory of God from the soul. It rests with us to decide whether he shall control our hearts and minds, or whether we shall have a place in the new earth, a title to Abraham's farm.

The power of God, combined with human effort, has wrought out a glorious victory for us. Shall we not appreciate this? All the riches of heaven were given to us in Jesus. God would not have the confederacy of evil say that He could do more than He has done. The worlds that He has created, the angels in heaven, could testify that He could do no more. God has resources of power of which we as yet know nothing, and from these He will supply us in our time of need. But our effort is ever to combine with the divine. Our intellect, our perceptive powers, all the strength of our being, must be called into exercise. . . . If we will rise to the emergency, and arm ourselves like men who wait for their Lord; if we will work to overcome every defect in our characters, God will give us increased light and strength and help. *Youth's Instructor*, January 4, 1900.

Faith and Duty

Faith is not feeling. Faith is the substance of things hoped for, the evidence of things not seen. There is a form of religion which is nothing more than selfishness. It takes pleasure in worldly enjoyment. It is satisfied with contemplating the religion of Christ, and knows nothing of its saving power. Those who possess this religion regard sin lightly because they do not know Jesus. While in this condition, they estimate duty very lightly. But a faithful performance of duty goes hand in hand with a right estimate of the character of God. *Review and Herald*, February 28, 1907.

CHAPTER 28

How to Be Strong

Christ has made every provision for us to be strong. He has given us His Holy Spirit, whose office is to bring to our remembrance all the promises that Christ has made, that we may have peace and a sweet sense of forgiveness. If we will but keep our eyes fixed on the Saviour, and trust in His power, we shall be filled with a sense of security; for the righteousness of Christ will become our righteousness. . . .

We dishonor Him by talking of our inefficiency. Instead of looking at ourselves, let us constantly behold Jesus, daily becoming more and more like Him, more and more able to talk of Him, better prepared to avail ourselves of His kindness and helpfulness, and to receive the blessings offered us.

As we thus live in communion with Him, we grow strong in His strength, a help and a blessing to those around us. If we would only do as the Lord desires us to, our hearts would become as sacred harps, every chord of which would sound forth praise and gratitude to the Redeemer sent by God to take away the sin of the world. . . .

Behold His Glory

When temptations assail you, as they surely will, when care and perplexity surround you, when, distressed and discouraged, you are almost ready to yield to despair, look, O look, to where with the eye of faith you last saw the light: and the darkness that encompasseth you will be dispelled by the bright shining of His glory. When sin struggles for the mastery in your soul, and burdens the conscience, when unbelief clouds the mind, go to the Saviour. His grace is sufficient to subdue sin. He will pardon us, making us joyful in God. . . .

Let us no longer talk of our inefficiency and lack of power. Forgetting the things that are behind, let us press forward in the heavenward way. Let us neglect no opportunity that, if improved, will make us more useful in God's service. Then like threads of gold, holiness will run through our lives, and the angels, beholding our consecration, will repeat the promise, "I will make a man more precious than fine gold; even a man than the golden wedge of Ophir." All heaven rejoices when weak, faulty human beings give themselves to Jesus, to live His life. *Review and Herald*, October 1, 1908.

Joy Through Repentance

The conditions of salvation for man are ordained of God. Self-abasement and cross-bearing are the provisions made for the repenting sinner to find comfort and peace. The thought that Jesus submitted to humiliation and sacrifice that man will never be called to endure, should hush every murmuring voice. The sweetest joy comes to man through his sincere repentance toward God because of the transgression of His law, and faith in Jesus Christ as the sinner's Redeemer and Advocate. *Signs of the Times*, March 4, 1880.

CHAPTER 29

The Victorious Life

Peace comes with dependence on divine power. As fast as the soul resolves to act in accordance with the light given, the Holy Spirit gives more light and strength. The grace of the Spirit is supplied to cooperate with the soul's resolve, but it is not a substitute for the individual exercise of faith. Success in the Christian life depends upon the appropriation of the light that God has given. It is not an abundance of light and evidence that makes the soul free in Christ; it is the rising of the powers and the will and the energies of the soul to cry out sincerely, "Lord, I believe; help Thou mine unbelief."

I rejoice in the bright prospects of the future, and so may you. Be cheerful, and praise the Lord for His lovingkindness. That which you cannot understand, commit to Him. He loves you, and pities your every weakness. He "hath blessed us with all spiritual blessings in heavenly places in Christ." It would not satisfy the heart of the infinite One to give those who love His Son a lesser blessing than He gives His Son.

Satan seeks to draw our minds away from the mighty Helper, to lead us to ponder over our degeneration of soul. But though Jesus sees the guilt of the past, He speaks pardon; and we should not dishonor Him by doubting His love. The feeling of guiltiness must be laid at the foot of the cross, or it will poison the springs of life. When Satan thrusts his threatenings upon you, turn from them, and comfort your soul with the promises of God. The cloud may be dark in itself, but when filled with the light of heaven, it turns to the brightness of gold; for the glory of God rests upon it.

God's children are not to be subject to feelings and emotions. When they fluctuate between hope and fear, the heart of Christ is hurt; for He has given them unmistakable evidence of His love. . . . He wants them to do the work He has given them; then their hearts will become in His hands as sacred harps, every chord of which will send forth praise and thanksgiving to the One sent by God to take away the sins of the world.

Christ's love for His children is as tender as it is strong. And it is stronger than death; for He died to purchase our salvation, and to make us one with Him, mystically and eternally one. So strong is His love that it controls all His powers, and employs the vast resources of heaven in doing His people good. It is without variableness or shadow of turning—the same yesterday, today, and forever. Although sin has existed for ages, trying to counteract this love and obstruct its flowing earthward, it still flows in rich currents to those for whom Christ died. *Testimonies to Ministers*, pp. 518, 519.

The Dominating Influence

Remember that in your life, religion is not merely one influence among others; it is to be an influence dominating all others. *Counsels to Teachers, Parents, and Students*, p. 489.

CHAPTER 30

Living Faith

Many who are sincerely seeking for holiness of heart and purity of life seem perplexed and discouraged. They are constantly looking to themselves, and lamenting their lack of faith; and because they have no faith, they feel that they cannot claim the blessing of God. These persons mistake feeling for faith. They look above the simplicity of true faith, and thus bring great darkness upon their souls. They should turn the mind from self, to dwell upon the mercy and goodness of God and to recount His promises, and then simply believe that He will fulfill His word.

We are not to trust in our faith, but in the promises of God. When we repent of our past transgressions of His law, and resolve to render obedience in the future, we should believe that God for Christ's sake accepts us, and forgives our sins.

Darkness and discouragement will sometimes come upon the soul, and threaten to overwhelm us; but we should not cast away our confidence. We must keep the eye fixed on Jesus, feeling or no feeling. We should seek to faithfully perform every known duty, and then calmly rest in the promises of God.

Do Not Depend on Feeling

At times a deep sense of our unworthiness will send a thrill of terror through the soul; but this is no evidence that God has changed toward us, or we toward God. No effort should be made to rein the mind up to a certain intensity of emotion. We may not feel today the peace and joy which we felt yesterday; but we should by faith grasp the hand of Christ, and trust Him as fully in the darkness as in the light.

Satan may whisper, "You are too great a sinner for Christ to save." While you acknowledge that you are indeed sinful and unworthy, you may meet the tempter with the cry, "By virtue of the atonement, I claim Christ as my Saviour. I trust not to my own merits, but to the precious blood of Jesus, which cleanses me. This moment I hang my helpless soul on Christ." The Christian life must be a life of constant, living faith. An unyielding trust, a firm reliance upon Christ, will bring peace and assurance to the soul.

Be Not Discouraged

Be not discouraged because your heart seems hard. Every obstacle, every internal foe, only increases your need of Christ. He came to take away the heart of stone, and give you a heart of flesh. Look to Him for special grace to overcome your peculiar faults. When assailed by temptation, steadfastly resist the evil promptings; say to your soul, "How can I dishonor my Redeemer? I have given myself to Christ; I cannot do the works of Satan." Cry to the dear Saviour for help to sacrifice every idol, and to put away every darling sin. Let the eye of faith see Jesus standing before the Father's throne, presenting His wounded hands as He pleads for you. Believe that strength comes to you through your precious Saviour.

Contemplation of Christ

By faith look upon the crowns laid up for those who shall overcome; listen to the exultant song of the redeemed, Worthy, worthy is the Lamb that was slain and hast redeemed us to God! Endeavor to regard these scenes as real. Stephen, the first Christian martyr, in his terrible conflict with principalities and powers, and spiritual wickedness in high places, exclaimed, "Behold, I see the heavens opened, and the Son of man standing on the right hand of God." The Saviour of the world was revealed to him as looking down from heaven upon him with the deepest interest; and the glorious light of Christ's countenance shone upon Stephen with such brightness that even his enemies saw his face shine like the face of an angel.

If we would permit our minds to dwell more upon Christ and the heavenly world, we should find a powerful stimulus and support in fighting the battles of the Lord. Pride and love of the world will lose their power as we contemplate the glories of that better land so soon to be our home. Beside the loveliness of Christ, all earthly attractions will seem of little worth.

Changing the Habits of Thought

Let none imagine that without earnest effort on their part they can obtain the assurance of God's love. When the mind has been long permitted to dwell only on earthly things, it is a difficult matter to change the habits of thought. That which the eye sees and the ear hears too often attracts the attention and absorbs the interest.

But if we would enter the city of God, and look upon Jesus in His glory, we must become accustomed to beholding Him with the eye of faith here. The words and the character of Christ should be often the subject of our thoughts and of our conversation; and each day some time should be especially devoted to prayerful meditation upon these sacred themes.

Sanctification a Daily Work

Sanctification is a daily work. Let none deceive themselves with the belief that God will pardon and bless them while they are trampling upon one of His requirements. The willful commission of a known sin silences the witnessing voice of the Spirit, and separates the soul from God. Whatever may be the ecstasies of religious feeling, Jesus cannot abide in the heart that disregards the divine law. God will honor those only who honor Him.

"To whom ye yield yourselves servants to obey, his servants ye are to whom ye obey." If we indulge anger, lust, covetousness, hatred, selfishness, or any other sin, we become servants of sin. "No man can serve two masters." If we serve sin, we cannot serve Christ. The Christian will feel the promptings of sin, for the flesh lusteth against the Spirit; but the Spirit striveth against the flesh, keeping up a constant warfare. Here is where Christ's help is needed. Human weakness becomes united to divine strength, and faith exclaims, "Thanks be to God, which giveth us the victory through our Lord Jesus Christ!"

If we would develop a character which God can accept, we must form correct habits in our religious life. Daily prayer is as essential to growth in grace, and even to spiritual life itself, as is temporal food to physical well-being. We should accustom ourselves to often lift the thoughts to God in prayer. If the mind wanders, we must bring it back; by persevering effort, habit will finally make it easy. We cannot for one moment separate ourselves from Christ with safety. We may have His presence to attend us at every step, but only by observing the conditions which He has Himself laid down.

Make Religion a Business

Religion must be made the great business of life. Everything else should be held subordinate to this. All our powers of soul, body, and spirit, must be engaged in the Christian warfare. We must look to Christ for strength and grace, and we shall gain the victory as surely as Jesus died for us. . . .

We must come nearer to the cross of Christ. Penitence at the foot of the cross is the first lesson of peace we have to learn. The love of Jesus—who can comprehend it? Infinitely more tender and self-denying than a mother's love! If we would know the value of a human soul, we must look in living faith upon the cross, and thus begin the study which shall be the science and the song of the redeemed through all eternity. The value of our time and our talents can be estimated only by the greatness of the ransom paid for our redemption. What ingratitude do we manifest toward God when we rob Him of His own by withholding from Him our affections and our service! Is it too much to give ourselves to Him who has sacrificed all for us? Can we choose the friendship of the world before the immortal honors which Christ proffers—"to sit with Me in My throne, even as I also overcame, and am set down with My Father in His throne"?

Sanctification, a Progressive Experience

Sanctification is a progressive work. The successive steps are set before us in the words of Peter: "Giving all diligence, add to your faith virtue; and to virtue knowledge; and to knowledge temperance; and to temperance patience; and to patience godliness; and to godliness brotherly kindness; and to brotherly kindness charity. For if these things be in you, and abound, they make you that ye shall neither be barren nor unfruitful in the knowledge of our Lord Jesus Christ." "Wherefore the rather, brethren, give diligence to make your calling and election sure; for if ye do these things, ye shall never fall; for so an entrance shall be ministered unto you abundantly into the everlasting kingdom of our Lord and Saviour Jesus Christ."

Here is a course by which we may be assured that we shall never fall. Those who are thus working upon the plan of addition in obtaining the Christian graces, have the assurance that God will work upon the plan of multiplication in granting them the gifts of His Spirit.

Peter addresses those who have obtained like precious faith: "Grace and peace be multiplied unto you through the knowledge of God, and of Jesus our Lord." By divine grace, all who will may climb the shining steps from earth to heaven, and at last, "with songs and everlasting joy," enter through the gates into the city of God. *Review and Herald*, Nov. 15, 1887.

Value of Trials

The trials of life are God's workmen, to remove the impurities and roughness from our characters. Their hewing, squaring, and chiseling, their burnishing and polishing, is a painful process, it is hard to be pressed down to the grinding wheel. But the stone is brought forth prepared to fill its place in the heavenly temple. Upon no useless material does the Master bestow such careful, thorough work. Only His precious stones are polished after the similitude of a palace. *Thoughts from the Mount of Blessing*, p. 10.

Secret Place of Power

To the secret place of the Most High, under the shadow of the Almighty, men now and then repair; they abide for a season, and the result is manifest in noble deeds; then their faith fails, the communion is interrupted, and the life work marred. But the life of Jesus was a life of constant trust, sustained by continual communion; and His service for heaven and earth was without failure or faltering.

As a man He supplicated the throne of God, till His humanity was charged with a heavenly current that connected humanity with divinity. Receiving life from God, He imparted life to men. *Education*, pp. 80, 81.

CHAPTER 31

Union With Christ

A union with Christ by living faith is enduring; every other union must perish. Christ first chose us, paying an infinite price for our redemption; and the true believer chooses Christ as first and last and best in everything. But this union costs us something. It is a union of utter dependence, to be entered into by a proud being. All who form this union must feel their need of the atoning blood of Christ. They must have change of heart. They must submit their own will to the will of God. There will be a struggle with outward and internal obstacles. There must be a painful work of detachment, as well as a work of attachment. Pride, selfishness, vanity, worldliness—sin in all its forms—must be overcome, if we would enter into a union with Christ. The reason why many find the Christian life so deplorably hard, why they are so fickle, so variable, is, they try to attach themselves to Christ without first detaching themselves from these cherished idols.

After the union with Christ has been formed, it can be preserved only by earnest prayer and untiring effort. We must resist, we must deny, we must conquer self. Through the grace of Christ, by courage, by faith, by watchfulness, we may gain the victory. *Testimonies for the Church*, Vol. 5, p. 231.

SECTION IV
Walking in the Light

The Saviour is bending over the purchase of His blood, saying with inexpressible tenderness and pity, "Wilt thou be made whole?" He bids you arise in health and peace. Do not wait to feel that you are made whole. Believe the Saviour's word. Put your will on the side of Christ. Will to serve Him, and in acting upon His word you will receive strength. Whatever may be the evil practice, the master passion which through long indulgence binds both soul and body, Christ is able and longs to deliver. He will impart life to the soul that is "dead in trespasses." He will set free the captive that is held by weakness and misfortune and the chains of sin. The Ministry of Healing, *pp. 84, 85.*

CHAPTER 32

Growing in Grace

"But grow in grace, and in the knowledge of our Lord and Saviour Jesus Christ." It is the privilege of the young, as they grow in Jesus, to grow in spiritual grace and knowledge. We may know more and more of Jesus through an interested searching of the Scriptures, and then following the ways of truth and righteousness therein revealed. Those who are ever growing in grace will be steadfast in the faith, and moving forward.

Growth Necessary to Steadfastness

There should be an earnest desire in the heart of every youth who has purposed to be a disciple of Jesus Christ to reach the highest Christian standard, to be a worker with Christ. If he makes it his aim to be of that number who shall be presented faultless before the throne of God, he will be continually advancing. The only way to remain steadfast is to progress daily in divine life. Faith will increase if, when brought in conflict with doubts and obstacles, it overcomes them. True sanctification is progressive. If you are growing in grace and the knowledge of Jesus Christ, you will improve every privilege and opportunity to gain more knowledge of the life and character of Christ.

Faith in Jesus will grow as you become better acquainted with your Redeemer by dwelling upon His spotless life and His infinite love. You cannot dishonor God more than to profess to be

His disciple while you keep at a distance from Him, and are not fed and nourished by His Holy Spirit. When you are growing in grace, you will love to attend religious meetings, and you will gladly bear testimony of the love of Christ before the congregation. God, by His grace, can make the young man prudent, and He can give to the children knowledge and experience. They can grow in grace daily. You should not measure your faith by your feelings.

Heart Examination

Closely examine your own heart, and the state of your affections toward God. Inquire, Have I devoted the precious moments of today in seeking to please myself, seeking for my own amusement? or have I made others happy? Have I helped those connected with me to greater devotion to God and to appreciate eternal things? Have I brought my religion into my home, and there revealed the grace of Christ in my words and in my deportment? By my respectful obedience, have I honored my parents, and thus kept the fifth commandment? Have I cheerfully taken up my little, everyday duties, performing them with fidelity, doing what I could to lighten the burdens of others? Have I kept my lips from evil, and my tongue from speaking guile? Have I honored Christ my Redeemer, who gave His precious life that eternal life might be within my reach?

Watch and Pray

At the beginning of the day, do not, dear youth, neglect to pray earnestly to Jesus that He will impart to you strength and grace to resist the temptations of the enemy in whatever form they may come; and if you pray earnestly, in faith and contrition of soul, the Lord will hear your prayer. But you must watch as well as pray. Jesus has said: "Ask, and it shall be given you; seek, and ye shall find; knock, and it shall be opened unto you: for every one that asketh receiveth; and he that seeketh findeth; and to him that knocketh it shall be opened. Or what man is there of you, whom, if his son ask bread, will he give him a stone? Or if he ask a fish, will he give him a serpent? If ye then, being evil, know how to give good gifts unto your children, how much more shall your Father which is in heaven give good things to them that ask Him?"

Children and youth may come to Jesus with their burdens and perplexities, and know that He will respect their appeals to Him, and give them the very things they need. Be earnest; be resolute. Present the promise of God, and then believe without a doubt. Do not wait to feel special emotions before you think the Lord answers. Do not mark out some particular way that the Lord must work for you before you believe you receive the things you ask of Him; but trust His word, and leave the whole matter in the hands of the Lord, with full faith that your prayer will be honored, and the answer will come at the very time and in the very way your heavenly Father sees is for your good; and then live out your prayers. Walk humbly and keep moving forward.

"For the Lord God is a sun and shield: the Lord will give grace and glory: no good thing will He withhold from them that walk uprightly." Psalm 84:11.

"O fear the Lord, ye His saints: for there is no want to them that fear Him. The young lions do lack, and suffer hunger: but they that seek the Lord shall not want any good thing." Psalm 34:9, 10.

"Keep thy tongue from evil, and thy lips from speaking guile. Depart from evil, and do good; seek peace, and pursue it. The eyes of the Lord are upon the righteous, and His ears are open unto their cry. The face of the Lord is against them that do evil, to cut off the remembrance of them from the earth. The righteous cry, and the Lord heareth, and delivereth them out of all their troubles. The Lord is nigh unto them that are of a broken heart; and saveth such as be of a contrite spirit." Psalm 34:13-18.

Here are promises, rich and abundant, upon conditions that you cease to do evil and learn to do well. Then set your aim in life high, as did Joseph and Daniel and Moses; and take into consideration the cost of character-building, and then build for time and for eternity. . . .

We are weak and without wisdom, but God has said: "If any of you lack wisdom, let him ask of God, that giveth to all men liberally, and upbraideth not; and it shall be given him." James 1:5. Only learn to be thorough, never to let go your hold upon God, to persevere in His service, and you will be an overcomer through the blood of the Lamb.

Limitless Possibilities for Good

In doing this work for yourself you are having an influence on many others with whom you associate. Words spoken in season, how good are they! How much strength a word of hope, courage, and determination in a right course will give one who is inclined to slide into habits that are demoralizing! The firm purpose you may possess in carrying out good principles will have an influence to balance souls in the right direction.

There is no limit to the good you may do. If you make the word of God the rule of your life, and govern your actions by its precepts, making all your purposes and exertions in the fulfilling of your duty a blessing and not a curse to others, success will crown your efforts. You have placed yourself in connection with God; you have become a channel of light to others. You are honored by becoming co-laborers with Jesus; and no higher honor can you receive than the blessed benediction from the lips of the Saviour: "Well done, good and faithful servant, enter thou into the joy of thy Lord." *Youth's Instructor*, September 1, 1886.

Self-surrender

The Redeemer will not accept divided service. Daily the worker for God must learn the meaning of self-surrender. He must study the Word of God, learning its meaning and obeying its precepts. Thus he may reach the standard of Christian excellence. Day by day God works with him, perfecting the character that is to stand in the time of final test. And day by day the believer is working out before men and angels a sublime experiment, showing what the gospel can do for fallen human beings. *Gospel Workers,* p. 113.

CHAPTER 33

Conformity to the World

Those who travel in the narrow way are talking of the joy and happiness they will have at the end of the journey. Their countenances are often sad, yet often beam with holy, sacred joy. They do not dress like the company in the broad road, or talk like them, or act like them. A Pattern has been given them. A Man of sorrows and acquainted with grief opened that road for them, and traveled it Himself. His followers see His footsteps and are comforted and cheered. He went through safely; so can they, if they follow His footsteps.

The Broad Way

In the broad road all are occupied with their persons, their dress, and the pleasures in the way. They indulge freely in hilarity and glee, and think not of their journey's end, of the certain destruction at the end of the path. Every day they approach nearer their destruction; yet they madly rush on faster and faster. Oh, how dreadful this looked to me!

I saw many traveling in this broad road who had written upon them, "Dead to the world. The end of all things is at hand. Be ye also ready." They looked just like all the vain ones around them, except a shade of sadness which I noticed upon their countenances. Their conversation was just like that of the gay, thoughtless ones around them; but they would occasionally point with great satisfaction to the letters on their garments, calling for the others to have the same upon theirs. They were in the broad way, yet they professed to be of that number who were traveling the narrow way. Those around them would say, "There is no distinction between us. We are all alike; we dress and talk and act alike." . . .

I was shown the conformity of some professed Sabbathkeepers to the world. Oh, I saw that it is a disgrace to their profession, a disgrace to the cause of God. They give the lie to their profession. They think they are not like the world, but they are so near like them in dress, in conversation, and actions, that there is no distinction. I saw them decorating their poor mortal bodies, which are liable at any moment to be touched by the finger of God, and laid upon a bed of anguish. Oh, then, as they approach their last change, mortal anguish racks their frames, and the great inquiry then is, "Am I prepared to die? prepared to appear before God in judgment, and pass the grand review?"

Ask them then how they feel about decorating their bodies, and if they have any sense of what it is to be prepared to appear before God, they will tell you that if they could take back and live over the past, they would correct their lives, shun the follies of the world, its vanity, its pride, and would adorn the body with modest apparel, and set an example to all around them. They would live to the glory of God.

Why is it so hard to lead a self-denying, humble life? Because professed Christians are not dead to the world. It is easy living after we are dead. But many are longing for the leeks and onions of Egypt. They have a disposition to dress and act as much like the world as possible, and yet go to heaven. Such climb up some other way. They do not enter through the strait gate and narrow way. . . .

Such will have no excuse. Many dress like the world to have an influence. But here they make a sad and fatal mistake. If they would have a true and saving influence, let them live out their profession, show their faith by their righteous works, and make the distinction great between the Christian and the world. I saw that the words, the dress, and actions should tell for God. Then a holy influence will be shed upon all, and all will take knowledge of them that they have been with Jesus. Unbelievers will see that the truth we profess has a holy influence, and that faith in Christ's coming affects the character of the man or woman. If any wish to have their influence tell in favor of the truth, let them live it out, and thus imitate the humble Pattern.

Preparation for Jesus' Coming

I saw that God hates pride, and that all the proud, and all that do wickedly, shall be stubble, and the day that cometh shall burn them up. I saw that the third angel's message must yet work like leaven upon many hearts that profess to believe it, and purge away their pride, selfishness, covetousness, and love of the world.

Jesus is coming, and will He find a people conformed to the world? and will he acknowledge them as His people that He has purified unto Himself? Oh, no. None but the pure and holy will He acknowledge as His. Those who have been purified and made white through suffering, and have kept themselves separate, unspotted from the world, He will own as His.

As I saw the dreadful fact that God's people were conformed to the world, with no distinction, except in name, between many of the professed disciples of the meek and lowly Jesus, and unbelievers, my soul felt deep anguish. I saw that Jesus was wounded and put to an open shame. Said the angel, as with sorrow he saw the professed people of God loving the world, partaking of its spirit, and following its fashions, "Cut loose! Cut loose! lest He appoint you your portion with hypocrites and unbelievers outside the city. Your profession will only cause you greater anguish, and your punishment will be greater, because ye knew His will, but did it not."

Those who profess to believe the third angel's message often wound the cause of God by lightness, joking, and trifling. I was shown that this evil was all through our ranks. I saw that there should be a humbling before the Lord. The Israel of God should rend the heart, and not the garment. Childlike simplicity is rarely seen; the approbation of man is more thought of than the displeasure of God.

Said the angel, "Set your heart in order, lest He visit you in judgment, and the brittle thread of life be cut, and you lie down in the grave unsheltered, unprepared for the judgment. Or if ye do not make your bed in the grave, unless ye soon make your peace with God, and tear yourselves from the world, your hearts will grow harder, and ye will lean upon a false prop, a supposed preparation, and find out your mistake too late to secure a well-grounded hope." *Testimonies for the Church*, Vol. 1, pp. 127-134.

What Shall It Profit?

Christ calls upon every one to consider. Make an honest reckoning. Put into one scale Jesus, which means eternal treasure, life, truth, heaven, and the joy of Christ in souls redeemed; put into the other every attraction the world can offer. Into one scale put the loss of your own soul, and the souls of those whom you might have been instrumental in saving; into the other, for yourself and for them, a life that measures with the life of God. Weigh for time and for eternity. While you are thus engaged, Christ speaks; "What shall it profit a man, if he shall gain the whole world, and lose his own soul?"

God desires us to choose the heavenly in place of the earthly. He opens before us the possibilities of a heavenly investment. He would give encouragement to our loftiest aims, security to our choicest treasure. He declares, "I will make a man more precious than fine gold; even a man than the golden wedge of Ophir." When the riches that moth devours and rust corrupts shall be swept away, Christ's followers can rejoice in their heavenly treasure, the riches that are imperishable. *Christ's Object Lessons*, p. 374.

CHAPTER 34

Genuine Christian Experience

I saw that unless there is an entire change in the young, a thorough conversion, they may despair of heaven. From what has been shown me, there are not more than half of the young who profess religion and the truth, who have been truly converted. If they had been converted, they would bear fruit to the glory of God. Many are leaning upon a supposed hope, without a true foundation. The fountain is not cleansed, therefore the streams proceeding from that fountain are not pure. Cleanse the fountain, and the streams will be pure.

If the heart is right, your words, your dress, your acts will all be right. True godliness is lacking. I would not dishonor my Master so much as to admit that a careless, trifling, prayerless person is a Christian. No; a Christian has victory over his besetments, over his passions. There is a remedy for the sin-sick soul. That remedy is in Jesus. Precious Saviour! His grace is sufficient for the weakest; and the strongest must also have His grace or perish.

Saving Grace

I saw how this grace could be obtained. Go to your closet, and there alone plead with God: "Create in me a clean heart, O God; and renew a right spirit within me." Be in earnest, be sincere. Fervent prayer availeth much. Jacob-like, wrestle in prayer. Agonize. Jesus in the garden sweat great drops of blood; you must make an effort. Do not leave your closet until you feel strong in

God; then watch, and just as long as you watch and pray you can keep these evil besetments under, and the grace of God can and will appear in you.

God forbid that I should cease to warn you. Young friends, seek the Lord with all your heart. Come with zeal, and when you sincerely feel that without the help of God you perish, when you pant after Him as the hart panteth after the water-brooks, then will the Lord strengthen you speedily. Then will your peace pass all understanding. If you expect salvation, you must pray. Take time. Be not hurried and careless in your prayers. Beg of God to work in you a thorough reformation, that the fruits of His Spirit may dwell in you, and you shine as lights in the world. Be not a hindrance or curse to the cause of God; you can be a help, a blessing. Does Satan tell you that you cannot enjoy salvation, full and free? Believe him not.

The First Steps

It is the privilege of every Christian to enjoy the deep movings of the Spirit of God. A sweet, heavenly peace will pervade the mind, and you will love to meditate upon God and heaven. You will feast upon the glorious promises of His Word. But know first that you have begun the Christian course. Know that the first steps are taken in the road to everlasting life. Be not deceived. I fear, yea, I know that many of you know not what religion is. You have felt some excitement, some emotion, but have never seen sin in its enormity. You have never felt your undone condition, and turned from your evil ways with bitter sorrow. You have never died to the world. You still love its pleasures; you love to engage in conversation on worldly matters. But when the truth of God is introduced, you have nothing to say. Why so silent! Why so talkative upon worldly things, and so silent upon the subject that should most concern you—a subject that should engage your whole soul? The truth of God does not dwell in you. *Testimonies for the Church*, Vol. 1, pp. 158, 159.

Opening the Way for God's Blessing

There is nothing that Satan fears so much as that the people of God shall clear the way by removing every hindrance, so that the Lord can pour out His Spirit upon a languishing church and an impenitent congregation. If Satan had his way, there would never be another awakening, great or small, to the end of time. But we are not ignorant of his devices. It is possible to resist his power. When the way is prepared for the Spirit of God, the blessing will come. Satan can no more hinder a shower of blessing from descending upon God's people than he can close the windows of heaven that rain cannot come upon the earth. Wicked men and devils cannot hinder the work of God, or shut out His presence from the assemblies of His people, if they will, with subdued, contrite hearts, confess and put away their sins, and in faith claim His promises. *Review and Herald*, March 22, 1887.

CHAPTER 35

Self-discipline

"He that is slow to anger is better than the mighty; and he that ruleth his spirit than he that taketh a city." He has conquered self—the strongest foe man has to meet.

The highest evidence of nobility in a Christian is self-control. He who can stand unmoved amid a storm of abuse is one of God's heroes.

To rule the spirit is to keep self under discipline; to resist evil; to regulate every word and deed by God's great standard of righteousness. He who has learned to rule his spirit will rise above the slights, the rebuffs, the annoyances, to which we are daily exposed, and these will cease to cast a gloom over his spirit.

It is God's purpose that the kingly power of sanctified reason, controlled by divine grace, shall bear sway in the lives of human beings. He who rules his spirit is in possession of this power.

Power of Self-control

In childhood and youth the character is most impressible. The power of self-control should then be acquired. By the fireside and at the family board influences are exerted the results of which are as enduring as eternity. More than any natural endowment, the habits established in early years will decide whether a man shall be victorious or vanquished in the battle of life.

In the use of language, there is, perhaps, no error that old and young are more ready to pass over lightly in themselves than hasty, impatient speech. They think it is a sufficient excuse to plead, "I was off my guard, and did not really mean what I said." But God's Word does not treat it lightly. The Scripture says: "Seest thou a man that is hasty in his words? there is more hope of a fool than of him." "He that hath no rule over his own spirit is like a city that is broken down, and without walls."

The largest share of life's annoyances, its heartaches, its irritations, is due to uncontrolled temper. In one moment, by hasty, passionate, careless words, may be wrought evil that a whole lifetime's repentance cannot undo. Oh, the hearts that are broken, the friends estranged, the lives wrecked, by the harsh, hasty words of those who might have brought help and healing!

Overwork sometimes causes a loss of self-control. But the Lord never compels hurried, complicated movements. Many gather to themselves burdens that the merciful Heavenly Father did not place on them. Duties He never designed them to perform chase one another wildly. God desires us to realize that we do not glorify His name when we take so many burdens that we are overtaxed, and, becoming heart-weary and brain-weary, chafe and fret and scold. We are to bear only the responsibilities that the Lord gives us, trusting in Him, and thus keeping our hearts pure and sweet and sympathetic.

Ruling the Spirit

There is a wonderful power in silence. When impatient words are spoken to you, do not retaliate. Words spoken in reply to one who is angry usually act as a whip, lashing the temper into greater fury. But anger met by silence quickly dies away. Let the Christian bridle his tongue, firmly resolving not to speak harsh, impatient words. With the tongue bridled, he may be victorious in every trial of patience through which he is called to pass.

In his own strength man cannot rule his spirit. But through Christ he may gain self-control. In His strength he may bring his thoughts and words into subjection to the will of God. The religion of Christ brings the emotions under the control of reason and disciplines the tongue. Under its influence the hasty temper is subdued, and the heart is filled with patience and gentleness.

Hold firmly to the One who has all power in heaven and in earth. Though you so often fail to reveal patience and calmness, do not give up the struggle. Resolve again, this time more firmly, to be patient under every provocation. And never take your eyes off your divine Example. *Review and Herald*, October 31, 1907.

No Excuse for Sinning

The tempter's agency is not to be accounted an excuse for one wrong act. Satan is jubilant when he hears the professed followers of Christ making excuses for their deformity of character. It is these excuses that lead to sin. There is no excuse for sinning. A holy temper, a Christlike life, is accessible by every repenting, believing child of God. *The Desire of Ages*, p. 311.

CHAPTER 36

A Living Experience

The Lord of life and glory clothed His divinity with humanity to demonstrate to man that God through the gift of Christ would connect us with Him. Without a connection with God no one can possibly be happy. Fallen man is to learn that our Heavenly Father cannot be satisfied until His love embraces the repentant sinner, transformed through the merits of the spotless Lamb of God.

The work of all the heavenly intelligences is to this end. Under the command of their General they are to work for the reclaiming of those who by transgression have separated themselves from their Heavenly Father. A plan has been devised whereby the wondrous grace and love of Christ shall stand revealed to the world. In the infinite price paid by the Son of God to ransom man, the love of God is revealed. This glorious plan of redemption is ample in its provisions to save the whole world. Sinful and fallen man may be made complete in Jesus through the forgiveness of sin and the imputed righteousness of Christ.

Power of the Cross

Jesus Christ laid hold on humanity, that with His human arm He might encircle the race, while with His divine arm He grasped the throne of the Infinite. He planted His cross midway between earth and heaven, and said, "I, if I be lifted up from the earth, will draw all men unto Me." The cross was to be the center of attraction.

It was to speak to all men, and draw them across the gulf that sin had made, to unite finite man with the infinite God. It is the power of the cross alone that can separate man from the strong confederacy of sin. Christ gave Himself for the saving of the sinner. Those whose sins are forgiven, who love Jesus, will be united with Him. They will bear the yoke of Christ. This yoke is not to hamper them, not to make their religious life one of unsatisfying toil. No; the yoke of Christ is to be the very means by which the Christian life is to become one of pleasure and joy. The Christian is to be joyful in contemplation of that which the Lord has done in giving His only-begotten Son to die for the world, "that whosoever believeth in Him should not perish, but have everlasting life.

Loyalty to Christ

Those who stand under the blood-stained banner of Prince Immanuel should be faithful soldiers in Christ's army. They should never be disloyal, never be untrue. Many of the young will volunteer to stand with Jesus, the Prince of life. But if they would continue to stand with Him they must constantly look unto Jesus, their Captain, for His orders. They cannot be soldiers of Christ, and yet engage with the confederacy of Satan, and help on his side, for then they would be enemies of Christ. They would betray sacred trusts. They would form a link between Satan and the true soldiers, so that through these living agencies the enemy would be constantly working to steal away the hearts of Christ's soldiers.

I ask you, dear youth, who profess to be soldiers of Jesus Christ, what battles have you fought? What have been your engagements? When the Word of God has plainly revealed your work, have you refused to do it because it did not suit your inclination? Has the attraction of the world allured you from the service of Christ? Satan is employed in devising specious allurements; and by transgression in what seem little matters he draws you away from Jesus. Then larger attractions are presented to seduce you fully from God.

You may have your name upon the church books and claim to be a child of God, yet your example, your influence, misrepresents the character of Christ, and you lead others away from Him. There is no happiness, no peace or joy, to a professed believer whose whole soul is not enlisted in the work the Lord has given him to do. He is constantly bringing the world into the church, not by repentance and confession and surrender to God, but by surrendering more and more to the world, and engaging on Satan's side in the battle rather than on Christ's side.

Experimental Knowledge Needed

I would appeal to the youth to cut the finest thread which binds you in practice and in spirit with the world. "Come out from among them, and be ye separate, saith the Lord, and touch not the unclean thing; and I will receive you, and will be a Father unto you, and ye shall be My sons and daughters, saith the Lord Almighty."

Will our youth heed this voice of invitation? How little do our young people realize the necessity of setting before their youthful associates a Christlike example in their life and character. Many of our youth understand the theory of the truth, but how few understand by experimental knowledge the practical bearing of the truth upon their every action. Where are youthful missionaries doing any work that presents itself to them in the great harvest field? Where are those who are daily learners in the school of Christ? Let them never feel that they are prepared to graduate. Let them wait in the courts of the Lord, that they may be directed as to how to work in unison with the heavenly intelligences. Dear youth, I wish to speak decidedly to you because I want you to be saved. Lose no more time. You cannot serve God and mammon. You may apparently be Christians, but when temptations come, when sorely tried, do you not generally yield?

Christian Fellowship

The conflict in which you have to take an active part is found in your everyday life. Will you not in times of trial lay your desires by the side of the written Word, and in earnest prayer seek Jesus for counsel? Many declare that it is certainly no harm to go to a concert and neglect the prayer-meeting, or absent themselves from meetings where God's servants are to declare a message from heaven. It is safe for you to be just where Christ has said He would be.

Those who appreciate the words of Christ will not turn

aside from the prayer meeting, or from the meeting where the Lord's messenger has been sent to tell them concerning things of eternal interest. Jesus has said, "Where two or three are gathered together in My name, there am I in the midst of them." Can you afford to choose your pleasure and miss the blessing? It is indulgence in these things that has a telling influence not only on your own life and character, but upon the life and character of your associates.

If all who profess to be followers of Christ would be so in deed and in truth, they would have the mind of Christ, and would work the works of God. They would resist temptation to indulge self, and would show that they do not enjoy the frivolous pleasure of the world more than the privilege of meeting with Christ in the social meeting. They would then have a decided influence upon others, and lead them to follow their example.

Actions speak louder than words, and those who are lovers of pleasure do not appreciate the rich blessings of being in the assembly of the people of God. They do not appreciate the privilege of influencing their associates to go with them, hoping that their hearts will be touched by the Spirit of the Lord. Who goes with them into these worldly gatherings? Jesus is not there to bless those assembled. But Satan will bring to the mind many things to crowd out matters of eternal interest. It is his opportunity to confuse the right by mixing it up with the wrong.

Through attendance at worldly gatherings a taste is created for exciting amusements, and moral power is weakened. Those who love pleasure may keep up a form of godliness, but they have no vital connections with God. Their faith is dead, their zeal has departed. They feel no burden to speak a word in season to souls who are out of Christ, and to urge them to give their hearts to the Lord. *Youth's Instructor*, April 23, 1912, also in *Youth's Instructor*, March 30, 1893.

Religion Not a Sentiment

Pure and undefiled religion is not a sentiment, but the doing of works of mercy and love. This religion is necessary to health and happiness. It enters the polluted soul-temple, and with a scourge drives out the sinful intruders. Taking the throne, it consecrates all by its presence, illuminating the heart with the bright beams of the Sun of Righteousness. It opens the windows of the soul heavenward, letting in the sunshine of God's love. With it comes serenity and composure. Physical, mental, and moral strength increase, because the atmosphere of heaven, as a living, active agency, fills the soul. Christ is formed within, the hope of glory. *Review and Herald*, October 15, 1901.

CHAPTER 37

Faithful in That Which Is Least

"He that is faithful in that which is least is faithful also in much."

It is conscientious attention to what the world terms "little things" that makes life a success. Little deeds of charity, little acts of self-denial, speaking simple words of helpfulness, watching against little sins—this is Christianity. A grateful acknowledgment of daily blessings, a wise improvement of daily opportunities, a diligent cultivation of intrusted talents—this is what the Master calls for.

He who faithfully performs small duties will be prepared to answer the demands of larger responsibilities. The man who is kind and courteous in the daily life, who is generous and forbearing in his family, whose constant aim it is to make home happy, will be the first to deny self and make sacrifices when the Master calls.

A Well-balanced Character

We may be willing to give our property to the cause of God, but this will not count unless we give Him also a heart of love and gratitude. Those who would be true missionaries in foreign fields must first be true missionaries in the home. Those who desire to work in the Master's vineyard must prepare themselves for this by a careful cultivation of the little piece of vineyard He has intrusted to their care.

As a man "thinketh in his heart, so is he." Many thoughts make up the unwritten history of a single day; and these thoughts have much to do with the formation of character. Our thoughts are to be strictly guarded; for one impure thought makes a deep impression on the soul. An evil thought leaves an evil impress on the mind. If the thoughts are pure and holy, the man is better for having cherished them. By them the spiritual pulse is quickened, and the power for doing good is increased. And as one drop of rain prepares the way for another in moistening the earth, so one good thought prepares the way for another.

The longest journey is performed by taking one step at a time. A succession of steps brings us to the end of the road. The longest chain is composed of separate links. If one of these links is faulty, the chain is worthless. Thus it is with character. A well-balanced character is formed by single acts well performed. One defect, cultivated instead of being overcome, makes the man imperfect, and closes against him the gate of the Holy City. He who enters heaven must have a character that is without spot or wrinkle or any such thing. Naught that defileth can ever enter there. In all the redeemed host not one defect will be seen.

Faithfulness in Everyday Life

God's work is perfect as a whole because it is perfect in every part, however minute. He fashions the tiny spear of grass with as much care as He would exercise in making a world. If we desire to be perfect, even as our Father in heaven is perfect, we must be faithful in doing little things. That which is worth doing at all is worth doing well. Whatever your work may be, do it faithfully. Speak the truth in regard to the smallest matters. Each day do loving deeds and speak cheerful words. Scatter smiles along the pathway of life. As you work in this way, God will place His approval on you, and Christ will one day say to you, "Well done, thou good and faithful servant."

At the day of judgment, those who have been faithful in their everyday life, who have been quick to see their work and do it, not thinking of praise or profit, will hear the words, "Come, ye blessed of My Father, inherit the kingdom prepared for you from the foundation of the world." Christ does not commend them for the eloquent orations they have made, the intellectual power they have displayed, or the liberal donations they have given. It is for doing little things which are generally overlooked that they are rewarded. "I was an hungered, and ye gave Me meat," He says. "Inasmuch as ye have done it unto one of the least of these My brethren, ye have done it unto Me." *Youth's Instructor*, January 17, 1901.

CHAPTER 38

Accountability for Light

Young men and women, you are accountable to God for the light that He has given you. This light and these warnings, if not heeded will rise up in the judgment against you. Your dangers have been plainly stated; you have been cautioned and guarded on every side, hedged in with warnings. In the house of God you have listened to the most solemn, heart-searching truths presented by the servants of God in demonstration of the Spirit. What weight do these solemn appeals have upon your hearts? What influence do they have upon your characters? You will be held responsible for every one of these appeals and warnings. They will rise up in the judgment to condemn those who pursue a life of vanity, levity, and pride.

Dear young friends, that which you sow you will also reap. Now is the sowing time for you. What will the harvest be? What are you sowing? Every word you utter, every act you perform, is a seed which will bear good or evil fruit, and will result in joy or sorrow to the sower. As is the seed sown, so will be the crop. God has given you great light and many privileges. After this light has been given, after your dangers have been plainly presented before you, the responsibility becomes yours. The manner in which you treat the light that God gives you will turn the scale for happiness or woe. You are shaping your destinies for yourselves. *Testimonies for the Church*, Vol. 3, p. 363.

CHAPTER 39

Earnestness of Purpose

When the four Hebrew youth were receiving an education for the king's court in Babylon, they did not feel that the blessing of the Lord was a substitute for the taxing effort required of them. They were diligent in study; for they discerned that through the grace of God their destiny depended upon their own will and action. They were to bring all their ability to the work; and by close, severe taxation of their powers they were to make the most of their opportunities for study and labor.

Cooperation With God

While these youth were working out their own salvation, God was working in them to will and to do of His good pleasure. Here are revealed the conditions of success. To make God's grace our own, we must act our part. The Lord does not propose to perform for us either the willing or the doing. His grace is given to work in us to will and to do, but never as a substitute for our effort. Our souls are to be aroused to cooperate. The Holy Spirit works in us, that we may work out our own salvation. This is the practical lesson the Holy Spirit is striving to teach us. "It is God which worketh in you both to will and to do of His good pleasure."

The Lord will cooperate with all who earnestly strive to be faithful in His service, as He cooperated with Daniel and his three companions. Fine mental qualities and a high tone of moral character are not the result of accident. God gives opportunities; success depends upon the use made of them. The openings of Providence must be quickly discerned and eagerly entered. There are many who might become mighty men, if, like Daniel, they would depend upon God for grace to be overcomers, and for strength and efficiency to do their work.

Whole-hearted Service

I address you, young men: Be faithful. Put heart into your work. Imitate none who are slothful, and who give divided service. Actions, often repeated, form habits, habits form character. Patiently perform the little duties of life. So long as you undervalue the importance of faithfulness in the little duties, your character-building will be unsatisfactory. In the sight of Omnipotence, every duty is important. The Lord has said, "He that is faithful in that which is least is faithful also in much." In the life of a true Christian there are no non-essentials.

Many who claim to be Christians are working at cross-purposes with God. Many are waiting for some great work to be brought to them. Daily they lose opportunities for showing their faithfulness to God; daily they fail of discharging with whole-heartedness the little duties of life, which seem to them uninteresting. While waiting for some great work in which they may exercise their supposedly great talents, and thus satisfy their ambitious longings, their life passes away.

My dear young friends, do the work that lies nearest at hand. Turn your attention to some humble line of effort within your reach. Put mind and heart into the doing of this work. Force your thoughts to act intelligently on the things that you can do at home. Thus you will be fitting yourself for greater usefulness. Remember that of King Hezekiah it is written: "In every work that he began, . . . he did it with all his heart, and prospered."

The Value of Concentration

The ability to fix the thoughts on the work in hand is a great blessing. God-fearing youth should strive to discharge their duties with thoughtful consideration, keeping the thoughts in the right channel, and doing their best. They should recognize their present duties, and fulfill them without allowing the mind to wander. This kind of mental discipline will be helpful and beneficial throughout life. Those who learn to put thought into everything they undertake, however small the work may appear, will be of use in the world.

Dear youth, be earnest, be persevering. "Gird up the loins of your mind." Stand like Daniel, the faithful Hebrew, who purposed in his heart to be true to God. Do not disappoint your parents and friends. And there is Another to be remembered. Do not disappoint Him who so loved you that He gave His life to make it possible for you to be co-laborers with God.

The Highest Motive

The desire to honor God should be to us the most powerful of all motives. It should lead us to make every exertion to improve the privileges and opportunities provided for us, that we may understand how to use wisely the Lord's goods. It should lead us to keep brain, bone, muscle, and nerve in the most healthful condition, that our physical strength and mental clearness may make us faithful stewards. Selfish interest, if given room to act, dwarfs the mind and hardens the heart; if allowed to control, it destroys moral power. Then disappointment comes. . . .

True success is given to men and women by the God who gave success to Daniel. He who read the heart of Daniel looked with pleasure upon His servant's purity of motive, his determination to honor the Lord. Those who in their life fulfill God's purpose must put forth painstaking effort, applying themselves closely and earnestly to the accomplishment of whatever He gives them to do. *Youth's Instructor*, August 20, 1903.

Abiding Joy

And all the way up the steep road leading to eternal life are wellsprings of joy to refresh the weary. Those who walk in wisdom's ways are, even in tribulation, exceeding joyful; for He whom their soul loveth walks, invisible, beside them. At each upward step they discern more distinctly the touch of His hand; at every step brighter gleamings of glory from the Unseen fall upon their path; and their songs of praise, reaching ever a higher note, ascend to join the songs of angels before the throne. *Thoughts from the Mount of Blessing*, p. 140.

CHAPTER 40

Exercise of the Will

Pure religion has to do with the will. The will is the governing power in the nature of man, bringing all the other faculties under its sway. The will is not the taste or the inclination, but it is the deciding power, which works in the children of men unto obedience to God, or unto disobedience.

Instability and Doubt

You are a young man of intelligence; you desire to make your life such as will fit you for heaven at last. You are often discouraged at finding yourself weak in moral power, in slavery to doubt, and controlled by the habits and customs of your old life in sin. You find your emotional nature untrue to yourself, to your best resolutions, and to your most solemn pledges. Nothing seems real. Your own instability leads you to doubt the sincerity of those who would do you good. The more you struggle in doubt, the more unreal everything looks to you, until it seems that there is no solid ground for you anywhere. Your promises are like ropes of sand, and you regard in the same unreal light the words and works of those in whom you should trust.

Strength Through Yielding the Will

You will be in constant peril until you understand the true force of the will. You may believe and promise all things, but your promises or your faith are of no value until you put your will on the side of faith and action. If you fight the fight of faith with all your will-power, you will conquer. Your feelings, your impressions, your emotions, are not to be trusted, for they are not reliable, especially with your perverted ideas; and the knowledge of your broken promises and your forfeited pledges weakens your confidence in yourself, and the faith of others in you.

But you need not despair. You must be determined to believe, although nothing seems true and real to you. I need not tell you it is yourself that has brought you into this unenviable position. You must win back your confidence in God and in your brethren. It is for you to yield up your will to the will of Jesus Christ; and as you do this, God will immediately take possession, and work in you to will and to do of His good pleasure. Your whole nature will then be brought under the control of the Spirit of Christ; and even your thoughts will be subject to Him.

You cannot control your impulses, your emotions, as you may desire, but you can control the will, and you can make an entire change in your life. By yielding up your will to Christ, your life will be hid with Christ in God, and allied to the power which is above all principalities and powers. You will have strength from God that will hold you fast to His strength; and a new light, even the light of living faith, will be possible to you. But your will must cooperate with God's will, not with the will of associates through whom Satan is constantly working to ensnare and destroy you.

Will you not, without delay, place yourself in right relation to God? Will you not say, "I will give my will to Jesus, and I will do it now," and from this moment be wholly on the Lord's side? Disregard custom, and the strong clamoring of appetite and passion. Give Satan no chance to say, "You are a wretched hypocrite." Close the door, so that Satan will not thus accuse and dishearten you. Say, "I will believe, I do believe that God is my helper," and you will find that you are triumphant in God. By steadfastly keeping the will on the Lord's side, every emotion will be brought into captivity to the will of Jesus. You will then find your feet on solid rock. It will take, at times, every particle of will-power that you possess, but it is God that is working for you, and you will come forth from the molding process a vessel unto honor.

God's Will and Man's Will United

Talk faith. Keep on God's side of the line. Set not your foot on the enemy's side, and the Lord will be your Helper. He will do for you that which it is not possible for you to do for yourself. The result will be that you will become like a "cedar of Lebanon." Your life will be noble, and your works will be wrought in God. There will be in you a power, an earnestness, and a simplicity that will make you a polished instrument in the hands of God.

You need to drink daily at the fountain of truth, that you may understand the secret of pleasure and joy in the Lord. But you must remember that your will is the spring of all your actions. This will, that forms so important a factor in the character of man, was at the fall given into the control of Satan; and he has ever since been working in man to will and to do of his own pleasure, but to the utter ruin and misery of man.

But the infinite sacrifice of God in giving Jesus, His beloved Son, to become a sacrifice for sin, enables Him to say, without violating one principle of His government, "Yield yourself up to Me; give Me that will; take it from the control of Satan, and I will take possession of it; then I can work in you to will and to do of My good pleasure." When He gives you the mind of Christ, your will becomes as His will, and your character is transformed to be like Christ's character. Is it your purpose to do God's will? Do you wish to obey the Scriptures? "If any man will come after Me, let him deny himself, and take up his cross, and follow Me."

There is no such thing as following Christ unless you refuse to gratify inclination and determine to obey God. It is not your feelings, your emotions, that make you a child of God, but the doing of God's will. A life of usefulness is before you, if your will becomes God's will. Then you may stand in your God-given manhood, an example of good works. You will then help to maintain rules of discipline, instead of helping to break them down. You will then help to maintain order, instead of despising it, and inciting to irregularity of life by your own course of action.

I tell you in the fear of God, I know what you may be, if your will is placed on the side of God. "We are laborers together with God," You may be doing your work for time and eternity in such a manner that it will stand the test of the judgment. Will you try? Will you now turn square about? You are the object of Christ's love and intercession. Will you now surrender to God, and help those who are placed as sentinels to guard the interests of His work, instead of causing them grief and discouragement? *Testimonies for the Church*, Vol. 5, pp. 513-516.

Special Effort Essential

God has appointed means, if we will use them diligently and prayerfully, that no vessel shall be shipwrecked, but outride the tempest and storm, and anchor in the haven of bliss at last. But if we despise and neglect these appointments and privileges, God will not work a miracle to save any of us, and we will be lost as were Judas and Satan.

Do not think that God will work a miracle to save those weak souls who cherish evil, who practice sin; or that some supernatural element will be brought into their lives, lifting them out of self into a higher sphere, where it will be comparatively easy work, without any special effort, any special fighting, without any crucifixion of self; because all who dally on Satan's ground for this to be done will perish with the evildoers. They will be suddenly destroyed, and that without remedy. *Testimonies to Ministers*, p. 453.

CHAPTER 41

Divine Guidance

There are three ways in which the Lord reveals His will to us, to guide us. . . .

God reveals His will to us in His Word, the Holy Scriptures.

His voice is also revealed in His providential workings; and it will be recognized if we do not separate our souls from Him by walking in our own ways, doing according to our own wills, and following the promptings of an unsanctified heart, until the senses have become so confused that eternal things are not discerned, and the voice of Satan is so disguised that it is accepted as the voice of God.

Another way in which God's voice is heard, is through the appeals of His Holy Spirit, making impressions upon the heart, which will be wrought out in the character.

If you are in doubt upon any subject, you must first consult the Scriptures. If you have truly begun the life of faith, you have given yourself to the Lord, to be wholly His, and He has taken you to mold and fashion according to His purpose, that you may be a vessel unto honor. You should have an earnest desire to be pliable in His hands, and to follow whithersoever He may lead you. You are then trusting Him to work out His designs, while at the same time you are cooperating with Him by working out your own salvation with fear and trembling. *Testimonies for the Church*, Vol. 5, p. 512.

CHAPTER 42

Silent Working of the Holy Spirit

The Christian's life is not a modification or improvement of the old, but a transformation of nature. There is a death to self and sin, and a new life altogether. This change can be brought about only by the effectual working of the Holy Spirit.

Nicodemus was still perplexed, and Jesus used the wind to illustrate His meaning: "The wind bloweth where it listeth, and thou hearest the sound thereof, but canst not tell whence it cometh, and whither it goeth: so is every one that is born of the Spirit."

The wind is heard among the branches of the trees, rustling the leaves and flowers; yet it is invisible, and no man knows whence it comes or whither it goes. So with the work of the Holy Spirit upon the heart. It can no more be explained than can the movements of the wind. A person may not be able to tell the exact time or place, or to trace all the circumstances in the process of conversion; but this does not prove him to be unconverted. By an agency as unseen as the wind, Christ is constantly working upon the heart. Little by little, perhaps unconsciously to the receiver, impressions are made that tend to draw the soul to Christ. These may be received through meditating upon Him, through reading the Scriptures, or through hearing the Word from the living preacher. Suddenly, as the Spirit comes with more direct appeal, the soul gladly surrenders itself to Jesus. By many this is called sudden conversion; but it is the result of long wooing by the Spirit of God—a patient, protracted process.

While the wind is itself invisible, it produces effects that are seen and felt. So the work of the Spirit upon the soul will reveal itself in every act of him who has felt its saving power. When the Spirit of God takes possession of the heart, it transforms the life. Sinful thoughts are put away, evil deeds are renounced; love, humility, and peace take the place of anger, envy, and strife. Joy takes the place of sadness, and the countenance reflects the light of heaven. No one sees the hand that lifts the burden, or beholds the light descend from the courts above. The blessing comes when, by faith, the soul surrenders itself to God. . . .

It is impossible for finite minds to comprehend the work of redemption. Its mystery exceeds human knowledge; yet he who passes from death to life realizes that it is a divine reality. The beginning of redemption we may know here through a personal experience. Its results reach through the eternal ages. *The Desire of Ages*, pp. 172, 173.

Evidence of Divine Aid

If you have a sense of need in your soul, if you hunger and thirst after righteousness, this is an evidence that Christ has wrought upon your heart in order that He may be sought unto to do for you, through the endowment of the Holy Spirit, those things which it is impossible for you to do for yourself. *Thoughts from the Mount of Blessing*, p. 19.

CHAPTER 43

The Indwelling Christ

If we are rooted and grounded in love, we shall be "able to comprehend with all saints what is the breadth, and length, and depth, and height; and to know the love of Christ, which passeth knowledge." O precious possibilities and encouragement! In the human heart cleansed from all moral impurity dwells the precious Saviour, ennobling, sanctifying the whole nature, and making the man a temple for the Holy Spirit. . . .

His Response to Our Faith

We are abiding in Christ by a living faith. He is abiding in our hearts by our individual appropriating of faith. We have the companionship of the divine presence, and as we realize this presence our thoughts are brought into captivity to Jesus Christ. Our spiritual exercises are in accordance with the vividness of our sense of this companionship. Enoch walked with God in this way; and Christ is dwelling in our hearts by faith when we will consider what He is to us, and what a work He has wrought out for us in the plan of redemption. We shall be most happy in cultivating a sense of this great gift of God to our world and to us personally.

These thoughts have a controlling power upon the whole character. I want to impress upon your mind that you may have a divine companion with you, if you will, always. "And what agreement hath the temple of God with idols? for ye are the temple of the living God; as God hath said, I will dwell in them, and walk in them; and I will be their God, and they shall be My people."

Molded by His Love

As the mind dwells upon Christ, the character is molded after the divine similitude. The thoughts are pervaded with a sense of His goodness, His love. We contemplate His character, and thus He is in all our thoughts. His love encloses us. If we gaze even a moment upon the sun in its meridian glory, when we turn away our eyes the image of the sun will appear in everything upon which we look.

Thus it is when we behold Jesus; everything we look upon reflects His image, the Sun of Righteousness. We cannot see anything else, or talk of anything else. His image is imprinted upon the eye of the soul, and affects every portion of our daily life, softening and subduing our whole nature. By beholding, we are conformed to the divine similitude, even the likeness of Christ. To all with whom we associate we reflect the bright and cheerful beams of His righteousness. We have become transformed in character; for heart, soul, mind, are irradiated by the reflection of Him who loved us and gave Himself for us. Here again there is the realization of a personal, living influence dwelling in our hearts by faith.

When His words of instruction have been received, and have taken possession of us, Jesus is to us an abiding presence, controlling our thoughts and ideas and actions. We are imbued with the instruction of the greatest teacher the world ever knew. A sense of human accountability and of human influence, gives character to our views of life and of daily duties.

Jesus Christ is everything to us—the first, the last, the best in everything. Jesus Christ, His Spirit, His character, colors everything; it is the warp and woof, the very texture of our entire being. The words of Christ are spirit and life. We cannot, then, center our thoughts upon self; it is no more we that live, but Christ that liveth in us, and He is the hope of glory. Self is dead, but Christ is a living Saviour. Continuing to look unto Jesus, we reflect His image to all around us. We cannot stop to consider our disappointments, or even to talk of them; for a more pleasant picture attracts our sight—the precious love of Jesus. He dwells in us by the word of truth. *Testimonies to Ministers*, pp. 387-390.

The Pearl of Great Price

We are to give ourselves to Christ, to live a life of willing obedience to all His requirements. All that we are, all the talents and capabilities we possess, are the Lord's to be consecrated to His service. When we thus give ourselves wholly to Him, Christ, with all the treasures of heaven, gives Himself to us. We obtain the pearl of great price. *Christ's Object Lessons*, p. 116.

CHAPTER 44

Self-denial

Jesus emptied Himself, and in all that He did self did not appear. He subordinated all things to the will of His Father. When His mission on earth was about to close, He could say, "I have glorified Thee on the earth: I have finished the work which Thou gavest Me to do." And He bids us, "Learn of Me; for I am meek and lowly in heart." "If any man will come after Me, let him deny himself"; let self be dethroned, and no longer hold the supremacy of the soul.

He who beholds Christ in His self-denial, His lowliness of heart, will be constrained to say, as did Daniel when he beheld One like the sons of men, "My comeliness was turned in me into corruption." . . . Human nature is ever struggling for expression, ready for contest; but he who learns of Christ is emptied of self, of pride, of love of supremacy, and there is silence in the soul. Self is yielded to the disposal of the Holy Spirit. Then we are not anxious to have the highest place. We have no ambition to crowd and elbow ourselves into notice; but we feel that our highest place is at the feet of our Saviour. We look to Jesus, waiting for His hand to lead, listening for His voice to guide. The apostle Paul had this experience, and he said, "I am crucified with Christ: nevertheless I live; yet not I, but Christ liveth in me; and the life which I now live in the flesh, I live by the faith of the Son of God, who loved me, and gave Himself for me." *Thoughts from the Mount of Blessing*, pp. 14, 15.

CHAPTER 45

The Character That God Approves

The youth need to be instructed, carefully and prayerfully, that they may build their characters upon the abiding foundation. The reason so many make grievous blunders is that they do not heed the teachings of experience. The counsel of parents and teachers is lost upon them, and they yield to the temptations of the enemy. God loves the youth. He sees in them great possibilities for good, if they will realize their need of Christ, and build upon the sure foundation. He also knows their trials. He knows that they will have to battle against the powers of darkness that strive to gain control of the human mind; and He has opened the way by which young men and young women may become partakers of the divine nature. . . .

Persevering Effort Required

Character does not come by chance. It is not determined by one outburst of temper, one step in the wrong direction. It is the repetition of the act that causes it to become habit, and molds the character either for good or for evil. Right characters can be formed only by persevering, untiring effort, by improving every intrusted talent and capability to the glory of God. Instead of doing this, many allow themselves to drift wherever impulse or circumstances may carry them. This is not because they are lacking in good material, but because they do not realize that in their youth God wants them to do their very best.

If the youth today would stand as Daniel stood, they must put to the stretch every spiritual nerve and muscle. The Lord does not desire that they shall remain novices. He wishes them to reach the highest point of excellence. He desires them to reach the very highest round of the ladder, that they may step from it into the kingdom of God.

Influence of Associates

The youth who leave their homes, and are no longer under the watch-care of their parents, are to a large extent left to choose their own associates. They should remember that the eye of their Heavenly Father is upon them, and that He sees their every necessity, their every temptation. There are always to be found in schools some youth who, by their course of action, reveal that their minds are cast in an inferior mold. Through unwise training in childhood, they have developed one-sided characters; and as they have advanced in years these defects have remained to mar their experience. By precept and example, these souls lead astray those who are weak in moral power.

Time is golden, dear youth. You must not imperil your souls by sowing wild oats. You cannot afford to be careless in regard to the companions you choose. Dwell upon that which is noble in the characters of others, and these traits will become to you a moral power in resisting the evil and choosing the good. Set your mark high. Your parents and teachers, who love and fear God, may follow you with their prayers day and night, they may entreat and warn you; but all this will be in vain if you choose reckless associates. If you see no real danger, and think you can do right as well as wrong, just as you choose, you will not discern that the leaven of wickedness is insidiously tainting and corrupting your mind.

Christ Our Only Hope

Christ was afflicted, insulted, abused; on the right hand and on the left He was assailed by temptation, yet He sinned not, but presented to God a perfect obedience that was entirely satisfactory. By this He removed forever every semblance of excuse for disobedience. He came to show man how to obey, how to keep all the commandments. He laid hold of divine power, and this is the sinner's only hope. He gave his life that man might be a partaker of the divine nature, having escaped the corruption that is in the world through lust. . . .

God has given the youth talents to improve for His glory; but many apply these gifts to unsanctified, unholy purposes. Many have abilities which, if cultivated, would yield a rich harvest of mental, moral, and physical acquirements. But they do not stop to consider. They do not count the cost of their course of action. They encourage a recklessness and folly that will not listen to counsel or reproof. This is a terrible mistake. Young men would be sober-minded if they realized that God's eye is upon them, that angels of God are watching the development of character, and weighing moral worth. *Youth's Instructor*, July 27, 1899.

CHAPTER 46

Abiding Presence of Christ

The religion of Christ means more than the forgiveness of sin; it means taking away our sins, and filling the vacuum with the graces of the Holy Spirit. It means divine illumination, rejoicing in God. It means a heart emptied of self, and blessed with the abiding presence of Christ. When Christ reigns in the soul there is purity, freedom from sin. The glory, the fullness, the completeness of the gospel plan is fulfilled in the life. The acceptance of the Saviour brings a glow of perfect peace, perfect love, perfect assurance. The beauty and fragrance of the character of Christ, revealed in the life, testifies that God has indeed sent His Son into the world to be its Saviour. . . .

To His faithful followers Christ has been a daily companion and familiar friend. They have lived in close contact, in constant communion with God. Upon them the glory of the Lord has risen. In them the light of the knowledge of the glory of God in the face of Jesus Christ has been reflected. Now they rejoice in the undimmed rays of the brightness and glory of the King in His majesty. They are prepared for the communion of heaven; for they have heaven in their hearts. *Christ's Object Lessons*. pp. 419-421.

SECTION V
Preparation for the Life Work

True education means more than taking a certain course of study. It is broad. It includes the harmonious development of all the physical powers and the mental faculties. It teaches the love and fear of God, and is a preparation for the faithful discharge of life's duties. Counsels to Teachers, Parents, and Students, *p. 64.*

True education is the preparation of the physical, mental, and moral powers for the performance of every duty; it is the training of body, mind, and soul for divine service. This is the education that will endure unto eternal life. Christ's Object Lessons, *p. 330.*

CHAPTER 47

Christian Education

The human mind is susceptible of the highest cultivation. A life devoted to God should not be a life of ignorance. Many speak against education because Jesus chose uneducated fishermen to preach His gospel. They assert that He showed preference for the uneducated. Many learned and honorable men believed His teaching. Had these fearlessly obeyed the convictions of their consciences, they would have followed Him. Their abilities would have been accepted, and employed in the service of Christ, had they offered them. But they had not moral power, in face of the frowning priests and jealous rulers, to confess Christ and venture their reputation in connection with the humble Galilean.

He who knew the hearts of all, understood this. If the educated and noble would not do the work they were qualified to do, Christ would select men who would be obedient and faithful in doing His will. He chose humble men and connected them with Himself, that He might educate them to carry forward the great work on earth when He should leave it.

Christ the Great Educator

Christ was the light of the world. He was the fountain of all knowledge. He was able to qualify the unlearned fishermen to receive the high commission He would give them. The lessons of truth given these lowly men were of mighty significance. They were to move the world. It seemed but a simple thing for Jesus to connect these humble persons with Himself; but it was an event productive of tremendous results. Their words and their works were to revolutionize the world.

Jesus did not despise education. The highest culture of the mind, if sanctified through the love and the fear of God, receives His fullest approval. The humble men chosen by Christ were with Him three years, subject to the refining influence of the Majesty of heaven. Christ was the greatest educator the world ever knew.

God will accept the youth with their talent and their wealth of affection, if they will consecrate themselves to him. They may reach to the highest point of intellectual greatness; and if balanced by religious principle they can carry forward the work which Christ came from heaven to accomplish, and in thus doing be co-workers with the Master.

The students at our College have valuable privileges, not only of obtaining a knowledge of the sciences, but also of learning how to cultivate and practice virtues which will give them symmetrical characters. They are God's responsible moral agents. The talents of wealth, station, and intellect are given of God in trust to man for his wise improvement. These varied trusts He has distributed proportionately to the known powers and capacities of His servants, to every one his work. *Review and Herald*, June 21, 1877.

CHAPTER 48

True Education

True education is the inculcation of those ideas that will impress the mind and heart with the knowledge of God the Creator and Jesus Christ the Redeemer. Such an education will renew the mind and transform the character. It will strengthen and fortify the mind against the deceptive whisperings of the adversary of souls, and enable us to understand the voice of God. It will fit the learned to become a co-worker with Christ.

If our youth gain this knowledge, they will be able to gain all the rest that is essential; but if not, all the knowledge they may acquire from the world will not place them in the ranks of the Lord. They may gather all the knowledge that books can give, and yet be ignorant of the first principles of that righteousness which could give them a character approved of God.

Those who are seeking to acquire knowledge in the schools of earth should remember that another school also claims them as students—the school of Christ. From this school the students are never graduated. Among the pupils are both old and young. Those who give heed to the instructions of the divine Teacher are constantly gaining more wisdom and nobility of soul, and thus they are prepared to enter that higher school, where advancement will continue throughout eternity.

Infinite Wisdom sets before us the great lessons of life—the lessons of duty and happiness. These are often hard to learn, but without them we can make no real progress. They may cost us effort, tears, and even agony; but we must not falter nor grow weary. It is in this world, amid its trials and temptations, that we are to gain a fitness for the society of the pure and holy angels. Those who become so absorbed in less important studies that they cease to learn in the school of Christ, are meeting with infinite loss.

Every faculty, every attribute, with which the Creator has endowed the children of men is to be employed for His glory; and in this employment is found its purest, noblest, happiest exercise. The principles of heaven should be made paramount in the life, and every advance step taken in the acquirement of knowledge or in the culture of the intellect should be a step toward the assimilation of the human to the divine. *Fundamentals of Christian Education*, pp. 543, 544.

The Essential in Education

The most essential education for our youth today to gain, and that which will fit them for the higher grades of the school above, is an education that will teach them how to reveal the will of God to the world. *Review and Herald*, October 24, 1907.

The Highest Education

Those who give themselves to learn the way and will of God are receiving the highest education that it is possible for mortals to receive. They are building their experience, not on the sophistries of the world, but upon principles that are eternal. *Counsels to Teachers, Parents, and Students*, p. 36.

CHAPTER 49

The Need of Christian Education

God requires the training of the mental faculties. He designs that His servants shall possess more intelligence and clearer discernment than the worldling, and He is displeased with those who are too careless or too indolent to become efficient, well-informed workers. The Lord bids us love Him with all the heart, and with all the soul, and with all the strength, and with all the mind. This lays upon us the obligation of developing the intellect to its fullest capacity, that with all the mind we may know and love our Creator.

If placed under the control of His Spirit, the more thoroughly the intellect is cultivated the more effectively it can be used in the service of God. The uneducated man who is consecrated to God and who longs to bless others can be, and is, used by the Lord in His service. But those who, with the same spirit of consecration, have had the benefit of a thorough education, can do a much more extensive work for Christ. They stand on vantage ground.

Training for Higher Service

The Lord desires us to obtain all the education possible, with the object in view of imparting our knowledge to others. None can know where or how they may be called to labor or to speak for God. Our Heavenly Father alone sees what He can make of men. There are before us possibilities which our feeble faith does not discern. Our minds should be so trained that if necessary we can present the truths of His Word before the highest earthly authorities in such a way as to glorify His name. We should not let slip even one opportunity of qualifying ourselves intellectually to work for God.

An All-round Education

Let the youth who need an education set to work with a determination to obtain it. Do not wait for an opening; make one for yourselves. Take hold in any small way that presents itself. Practice economy. Do not spend your means for the gratification of appetite or in pleasure-seeking. Be determined to become as useful and efficient as God calls you to be. Be thorough and faithful in whatever you undertake. Procure every advantage within your reach for strengthening the intellect. Let the study of books be combined with useful manual labor, and by faithful endeavor, watchfulness, and prayer, secure the wisdom that is from above. This will give you an all-round education. Thus you may rise in character and gain an influence over other minds, enabling you to lead them in the path of uprightness and holiness.

Far more might be accomplished in the work of self-education if we were awake to our own opportunities and privileges. True education means more than the colleges can give. While the study of the sciences is not to be neglected, there is a higher training to be obtained through a vital connection with God. Let every student take his Bible, and place himself in communion with the great Teacher. Let the mind be trained and disciplined to wrestle with hard problems in the search for divine truth.

Knowledge and Self-discipline

Those who hunger for knowledge that they may bless their fellow men will themselves receive blessing from God. Through the study of His Word their mental powers will be aroused to earnest activity. There will be an expansion and development of the faculties, and the mind will acquire power and efficiency.

Self-discipline must be practiced by every one who would be a worker for God. This will accomplish more than eloquence or the most brilliant talents. *Christ's Object Lessons*, pp. 334, 335.

Meeting Expectations of Parents

It is always best and safe to do right because it is right. Will you not now do some serious thinking? Right thinking lies at the foundation of right action. Make up your mind that you will respond to the expectations your parents have of you, that you will make faithful efforts to excel, that you will see to it that the money expended for you has not been misapplied and misused. Have a determined purpose to cooperate with the efforts made by parents and teachers, and reach a high standard of knowledge and character. Be determined not to disappoint those who love you well enough to trust you. It is manly to do right, and Jesus will help you to do right, if you seek to do it because it is right. *Fundamentals of Christian Education*, p. 248.

CHAPTER 50

Education for Eternity

John writes: "I have written unto you, young men, because ye are strong, and the word of God abideth in you, and ye have overcome the wicked one." And Paul exhorts Timothy to bid the young men to "be sober-minded." Elevate your soul to be as was Daniel, a loyal, steadfast servant of the Lord of hosts. Ponder well the path of your feet; for you are standing on holy ground, and the angels of God are about you.

It is right that you should feel that you must climb to the highest round of the educational ladder. Philosophy and history are important studies; but your sacrifice of time and money will avail nothing if you do not use your attainments for the honor of God and the good of humanity. Unless the knowledge of science is a stepping-stone to the attainment of the highest purposes, it is worthless.

The education that does not furnish knowledge as enduring as eternity is of no purpose. Unless you keep heaven and the future, immortal life before you, your attainments are of no permanent value. But if Jesus is your teacher, not simply on one day of the week, but every day, every hour, you may have His smile upon you in the pursuit of literary acquirements. *Fundamentals of Christian Education*, pp. 191, 192.

CHAPTER 51

A Practical Training

Useful manual labor is a part of the gospel plan. The great Teacher, enshrouded in the pillar of cloud, gave directions to Israel that every youth should be taught some line of useful employment. Therefore it was the custom of the Jews, the wealthy as well as the poorer classes, to teach their sons and daughters some useful trade, so that, should adverse circumstances arise, they would not be dependent upon others, but would be able to provide for their own necessities. They might be instructed in literary lines, but they must also be trained to some craft. This was deemed an indispensable part of their education.

Symmetrical Education

Now, as in the days of Israel, every youth should be instructed in the duties of practical life. Each should acquire a knowledge of some branch of manual labor by which, if need be, he may obtain a livelihood. This is essential, not only as a safeguard against the vicissitudes of life, but from its bearing upon physical, mental, and moral development. Even if it were certain that one would never need to resort to manual labor for support, still he should be taught to work. Without physical exercise no one can have a sound constitution and vigorous health; and the discipline of well-regulated labor is no less essential to the securing of a strong, active mind and a noble character.

Students who have gained book knowledge without gaining a knowledge of practical work cannot lay claim to a symmetrical education. The energies that should have been devoted to business of various lines have been neglected. Education does not consist in using the brain alone. Physical employment is a part of the training essential for every youth. An important phase of education is lacking if the student is not taught how to engage in useful labor.

The healthful exercise of the whole being will give an education that is broad and comprehensive. Every student should devote a portion of each day to active labor. Thus habits of industry will be formed and a spirit of self-reliance encouraged, while the youth will be shielded from many evil and degrading practices that are so often the result of idleness. And this is all in keeping with the primary object of education; for in encouraging activity, diligence, and purity, we are coming into harmony with the Creator.

Benefit of Useful Work

The greatest benefit is not gained from exercise that is taken as play or exercise merely. There is some benefit in being in the fresh air, and also from the exercise of the muscles; but let the same amount of energy be given to the performance of useful work, and the benefit will be greater. A feeling of satisfaction will be realized; for such exercise carries with it the sense of helpfulness and the approval of conscience for duty well done.

Students should go forth from our schools with educated

efficiency, so that when thrown upon their own resources they will have knowledge which they can use, and which is needful to success in life. Diligent study is essential, so also is diligent hard work. Play is not essential. Devotion of the physical powers to amusement is not most favorable to a well-balanced mind. If the time employed in physical exercise which, step by step leads on to excess, were used in working in Christ's lines, the blessing of God would rest upon the worker.

The discipline for practical life that is gained by physical labor combined with mental taxation is sweetened by the reflection that it is qualifying mind and body better to perform the work that God designs men to do. The more perfectly the youth understand how to perform the duties of practical life, the greater will be their enjoyment day by day in being of use to others. The mind educated to enjoy useful labor becomes enlarged; through training and discipline it is fitted for usefulness; for it has acquired the knowledge essential to make its possessor a blessing to others.

I cannot find an instance in the life of Christ where He devoted time to play and amusement. He was the great educator for the present and the future life; yet I have not been able to find one instance where He taught the disciples to engage in amusement in order to gain physical exercise. . . .

Learn How to Cook

Both young men and women should be taught how to cook economically, and to dispense with everything in the line of flesh food. Let no encouragement be given to the preparation of dishes which are composed in any degree of flesh food, for this is pointing to the darkness and ignorance of Egypt, rather than to the purity of health reform.

Women especially should learn how to cook. What part of the education of a girl is so important as this? Whatever may be her circumstances in life, here is knowledge that she may put to practical use. . . .

In the Mission Field

Culture on all points of practical life will make our youth useful after they leave the school to go to foreign countries. They will not then have to depend upon the people to whom they go to cook and sew for them, or to build their habitations. And they will be much more influential if they show that they can educate the ignorant how to labor with the best methods and to produce the best results. A smaller fund will be required to sustain such missionaries, because they have put to the very best use their physical powers in useful, practical labor combined with their studies. This will be appreciated where means are difficult to obtain. They will reveal that missionaries can become educators in teaching how to labor. And wherever they may go, all that they have gained in this line will give them standing room. *Counsels to Teachers, Parents, and Students*, pp. 307-314.

CHAPTER 52

Student Loyalty

Those students who profess to love God and obey the truth should possess that degree of self-control and strength of religious principle that will enable them to remain unmoved amid temptations, and to stand up for Jesus in the college, at their boarding houses, or wherever they may be. Religion is not to be worn merely as a cloak in the house of God; religious principles should characterize the entire life.

Character and Deportment

Those who are drinking at the fountain of life will not, like the worldling, manifest a longing desire for change and pleasure. In their deportment and character will be seen the rest and peace and happiness that they have found in Jesus by daily laying their perplexities and burdens at His feet. They will show that in the path of obedience and duty there is contentment and even joy. Such ones will exert an influence over their fellow students which will tell upon the entire school. . . .

One earnest, conscientious, faithful young man in a school is an inestimable treasure. Angels of heaven look lovingly upon him, and in the ledger of heaven is recorded every work of righteousness, every temptation resisted, every evil overcome. He is laying up a good foundation against the time to come, that he may lay hold on eternal life.

Upon Christian youth depend in a great measure the preservation and perpetuity of the institutions which God has devised as a means by which to advance His work. Never was there a period when results so important depended upon a generation of men. Then how important that the young should be qualified for this great work, that God may use them as His instruments! Their Maker has claims upon them which are paramount to all others. . . .

Value of School Discipline

The wild, reckless character of many of the youth in this age of the world is heart-sickening. If the youth could see that in complying with the laws and regulations of our institutions they are only doing that which will improve their standing in society, elevate the character, ennoble the mind, and increase their happiness, they would not rebel against just rules and wholesome requirements, nor engage in creating suspicion and prejudice against these institutions.

With energy and fidelity our youth should meet the demands upon them; and this will be a guarantee of success. Young men who have never made a success in the temporal duties of life will be equally unprepared to engage in the higher duties. A religious experience is gained only through conflict, through disappointment, through severe discipline of self, through earnest prayer. The steps to heaven must be taken one at a time; and every advance step gives strength for the next. *Counsels to Teachers, Parents, and Students*, pp, 98-100.

CHAPTER 53

Student Opportunities

Students, cooperate with your teachers. As you do this, you give them hope and courage. You are helping them, and at the same time you are helping yourselves to advance. Remember that it rests largely with you whether your teachers stand on vantage ground, their work an acknowledged success. In the highest sense you are to be learners, seeing God behind the teacher, and the teacher cooperating with Him.

Your opportunities for work are fast passing. You have no time to spend in self-pleasing. Only as you strive earnestly to succeed will you gain true happiness. Precious are the opportunities offered you during the time you spend in school. Make your student life as perfect as possible. You will pass over the way but once. And it rests with you yourself whether your work shall be a success or a failure. As you succeed in gaining a knowledge of the Bible, you are storing up treasures to impart.

Helping Others

If you have a fellow student who is backward, explain to him the lesson that he does not understand. This will aid your own understanding. Use simple words; state your ideas in language that is clear and easy to be understood.

By helping your fellow student, you help your teachers. And often one whose mind is apparently stolid will catch ideas more quickly from a fellow student than from a teacher. This is the cooperation that Christ commends. The great Teacher stands beside you, helping you to help the one who is backward.

In your school life you may have opportunity to tell the poor and ignorant of the wonderful truths of God's Word. Improve every such opportunity. The Lord will bless every moment spent in this way. *Testimonies for the Church*, Vol. 7, pp. 275, 276.

Thorough Mastery of Fundamentals

Never rest satisfied with a low standard. In attending school, be sure that you have in view a noble, holy object. Go because you desire to fit yourselves for service in some part of the Lord's vineyard. Do all that you can to attain this object. You can do more for yourselves than any one can do for you. And if you do all that you can for yourselves, what a burden you will lift from the principal and the teachers!

Before attempting to study the higher branches of literary knowledge, be sure that you thoroughly understand the simple rules of English grammar, and have learned to read and write and spell correctly. . . .

Do not spend time in learning that which will be of little use to you in your after life. Instead of reaching out for a knowledge of the classics, learn first to speak the English language correctly. Learn how to keep accounts. Gain a knowledge of those lines of study that will help you to be useful wherever you are. *Counsels to Teachers, Parents, and Students*, pp. 218, 219.

CHAPTER 54

Training for Service

Considering the light that God has given, it is marvelous that there are not scores of young men and women inquiring, "Lord, what wilt Thou have me to do?" It is a perilous mistake to imagine that unless a young man has decided to give himself to the ministry, no special effort is required to fit him for the work of God. Whatever may be your calling, it is essential that you improve your abilities by diligent study.

Young men and women should be urged to appreciate the heaven-sent blessings of opportunities to become well-disciplined and intelligent. They should take advantage of the schools that have been established for the purpose of imparting the best of knowledge. It is sinful to be indolent and negligent in regard to obtaining an education. Time is short, and therefore, because the Lord is soon to come to close the scenes of earth's history, there is all the greater necessity of improving present opportunities and privileges.

Consecrate Ability to God

Young men and young women should place themselves in our schools, in the channel where knowledge and discipline may be obtained. They should consecrate their ability to God, become diligent Bible students, that they may be fortified against erroneous doctrine, and not be led away by the error of the wicked; for it is by diligent searching of the Bible that we obtain a knowledge of what is truth. By the practice of the truth we already know, increased light will shine upon us from the holy Scriptures. . . .

Those who are truly consecrated to God will not enter the work prompted by the same motive which leads men to engage in worldly business, merely for the sake of a livelihood, but they will enter the work allowing no worldly consideration to control them, realizing that the cause of God is sacred.

Preparation for Future Contingencies

The world is to be warned, and no soul should rest satisfied with a superficial knowledge of truth. You know not to what responsibility you may be called. You know not where you may be called upon to give your witness of truth. Many will have to stand in the legislative courts; some will have to stand before kings and before the learned of the earth, to answer for their faith.

Those who have only a superficial understanding of truth will not be able clearly to expound the Scriptures, and give definite reasons for their faith. They will become confused, and will not be workmen that need not to be ashamed. Let no one imagine that he has no need to study because he is not to preach in the sacred desk. You know not what God may require of you.

It is a lamentable fact that the advancement of the cause is hindered by the dearth of educated laborers who have fitted themselves for positions of trust. The Lord will accept of thousands to labor in His great harvest field, but many have failed to fit themselves for the work. But every one who has espoused the cause of Christ, who has offered himself as a soldier in the Lord's army, should place himself where he may have faithful drill. Religion has meant altogether too little to the professed followers of Christ; for it is not the will of God that any one should remain ignorant when wisdom and knowledge have been placed within reach. *Fundamentals of Christian Education*, pp. 216, 217.

Balanced by Right Principles

It is not true that brilliant young men always make the greatest success. How often men of talent and education have been placed in positions of trust, and have proved failures. Their glitter had the appearance of gold, but when it was tried it proved to be but tinsel and dross. They made a failure of their work through unfaithfulness. They were not industrious and persevering, and did not go to the bottom of things. They were not willing to begin at the bottom of the ladder, and with patient toil ascend round after round till they reached the top. They walked in the sparks (their bright flashes of thought) of their own kindling. They did not depend on the wisdom which God alone can give. Their failure was not because they did not have a chance, but because they were not sober-minded. They did not feel that their educational advantages were of value to them, and so did not advance as they might have advanced in the knowledge of religion and science. Their mind and character were not balanced by high principles of right. *Fundamentals of Christian Education*, p. 193.

CHAPTER 55

Aspiration for Improvement

If each one realized his accountability to God for his personal influence, he would in no case be an idler, but would cultivate his ability and train every power that he might serve Him who has purchased him with His own blood.

The youth especially should feel that they must train their minds, and take every opportunity to become intelligent, that they may render acceptable service to Him who has given His precious life for them. And let no one make the mistake of regarding himself as so well educated as to have no more need of studying books or nature. Let every one improve every opportunity with which in the providence of God he is favored, to acquire all that is possible in revelation or science.

We should learn to place the proper estimate on the powers that God has given us. If a youth has to begin at the lowest round of the ladder, he should not be discouraged, but be determined to climb round after round until he shall hear the voice of Christ saying, "Child, come up higher. Well done, thou good and faithful servant: thou hast been faithful over a few things, I will make thee ruler over many things: enter thou into the joy of thy Lord." *Fundamentals of Christian Education*, p. 213.

CHAPTER 56

True Wisdom

Young men and young women may obtain the highest earthly education, and yet may be ignorant of the first principles that would make them subjects of the kingdom of God. Human learning cannot qualify any one for the heavenly kingdom. The subjects of Christ's kingdom are not made thus by forms and ceremonies, or by long study of books. "This is life eternal, that they might know Thee the only true God, and Jesus Christ, whom Thou hast sent." . . .

The Bible and Science

The Old and the New Testament Scriptures need to be studied daily. The knowledge of God and the wisdom of God come to the student who is a constant learner of His ways and works. The Bible is to be our light, our educator. When the youth learn to believe that God sends the dew, the rain, and the sunshine from heaven, causing vegetation to flourish; when they realize that all blessings come from Him, and that thanksgiving and praise are due to Him, they will be led to acknowledge God in all their ways, and discharge with fidelity their duties day by day; God will be in all their thoughts. . . .

Many young men, in talking about science, are wise above that which is written; they seek to explain by something that meets their finite comprehension the ways and work of God; but it is all a miserable failure. True science and Inspiration are in perfect harmony. False science is something independent of God. It is pretentious ignorance.

One of the greatest evils that has attended the quest of knowledge, the investigation of science, is that those who engage in these researches too often lose sight of the divine character of pure and unadulterated religion. The worldly-wise have attempted to explain, on scientific principles, the influence of the Spirit of God upon the heart. The least advance in this direction will lead the mind into the mazes of skepticism. The religion of the Bible is simply the mystery of godliness; no human mind can fully understand it, and it is utterly incomprehensible to the unregenerate heart.

Taught of God

The youth will not become weak-minded or inefficient by consecrating themselves to the service of God. To many, education means a knowledge of books; but "the fear of the Lord is the beginning of wisdom." The youngest child who loves and fears God is greater in His sight than the most talented and learned man who neglects the matter of personal salvation. The youth who consecrate their hearts and lives to God are placing themselves in connection with the Fountain of all wisdom and excellence.

If the youth will but learn of the heavenly Teacher, as Daniel did, they will know for themselves that the fear of the Lord is indeed the beginning of wisdom. Having thus laid a sure foundation, they may, like Daniel, turn every privilege and opportunity to the very best account, and may rise to any height in intellectual attainments. Consecrated to God, and having the protection of His grace and the quickening influence of His Holy Spirit, they will manifest deeper intellectual power than the mere worldling.

To learn science through the interpretation that men have placed on it is to obtain a false education. To learn of God, and of Jesus Christ whom He has sent, is to learn the science of the Bible. The pure in heart see God in every providence, in every phase of true education. They recognize the first approach of the light that radiates from God's throne. Communications from heaven are made to those who will catch the first gleams of spiritual knowledge.

The students in our schools are to regard the knowledge of God as above everything else. Only by searching the Scriptures can this knowledge be attained. "The preaching of the cross is to them that perish foolishness; but unto us which are saved it is the power of God. For it is written, I will destroy the wisdom of the wise, and will bring to nothing the understanding of the prudent. . . . The foolishness of God is wiser than men; and the weakness of God is stronger than men. . . . But of Him are ye in Christ Jesus, who of God is made unto us wisdom, and righteousness, and sanctification, and redemption: that, according as it is written, He that glorieth, let him glory in the Lord." *Youth's Instructor*, Nov. 24, 1903.

CHAPTER 57

Set a High Standard

God desires us to make use of every opportunity for securing a preparation for His work. He expects us to put all our energies into its performance, and to keep our hearts alive to its sacredness and its fearful responsibilities.

Many who are qualified to do excellent work accomplish little because they attempt little. Thousands pass through life as if they had no great object for which to live, no high standard to reach. One reason of this is the low estimate which they place upon themselves. Christ paid an infinite price for us, and according to the price paid He desires us to value ourselves.

Be not satisfied with reaching a low standard. We are not what we might be, or what it is God's will that we should be. God has given us reasoning powers, not to remain inactive, or to be perverted to earthly and sordid pursuits, but that they may be developed to the utmost, refined, sanctified, ennobled, and used in advancing the interests of His kingdom.

Maintain Personality

None should consent to be mere machines, run by another man's mind. God has given us ability to think and to act, and it is by acting with carefulness, looking to Him for wisdom, that you will become capable of bearing burdens. Stand in your God-given personality. Be no other person's shadow. Expect that the Lord will work in and by and through you.

Never think that you have learned enough, and that you may now relax your efforts. The cultivated mind is the measure of the man. Your education should continue during your lifetime; every day you should be learning, and putting to practical use the knowledge gained.

Remember that in whatever position you may serve, you are revealing motive, developing character. Whatever your work, do it with exactness, with diligence; overcome the inclination to seek an easy task.

Whole-hearted Service

The same spirit and principles that one brings into the daily labor will be brought into the whole life. Those who desire a fixed amount to do and a fixed salary, and who wish to prove an exact fit without the trouble of adaptation or training, are not the ones whom God calls to work in His cause. Those who study how to give as little as possible of their physical, mental, and moral power are not the workers upon whom He can pour out abundant blessings. Their example is contagious. Self-interest is the ruling motive. Those who need to be watched, and who work only as every duty is specified to them, are not the ones who will be pronounced good and faithful. Workers are needed who manifest energy, integrity, diligence, those who are willing to do anything that needs to be done.

Many become inefficient by evading responsibilities for fear of failure. Thus they fail of gaining that education which results from experience, and which reading and study and all the advantages otherwise gained cannot give them.

Man can shape circumstances, but circumstances should not be allowed to shape the man. We should seize upon circumstances as instruments by which to work. We are to master them, but should not permit them to master us.

Men of power are those who have been opposed, baffled, and thwarted. By calling their energies into action, the obstacles they meet prove to them positive blessings. They gain self-reliance. Conflict and perplexity call for the exercise of trust in God, and for that firmness which develops power. *The Ministry of Healing*, pp. 498-500.

Making the Most of Life

While a good education is a great benefit if combined with consecration in its possessor, still those who do not have the privilege of gaining high literary attainments need not think they cannot advance in intellectual and spiritual life. If they will make the most of the knowledge they have, if they will seek to gather something to their store every day, and will overcome all perverseness of temper through the studious cultivation of Christlike traits of character, God will open channels of wisdom to them, and it may be said of them as it was said of old concerning the Hebrew children, God gave them wisdom and understanding. *Fundamentals of Christian Education*, pp. 192, 193.

SECTION VI
Service

With such an army of workers as our youth, rightly trained, might furnish, how soon the message of a crucified, risen, and soon-coming Saviour might be carried to the whole world! How soon might the end come—the end of suffering and sorrow and sin! How soon, in place of a possession here, with its blight of sin and pain, our children might receive their inheritance where "the righteous shall inherit the land, and dwell therein forever"; where "the inhabitant shall not say, I am sick," and "the voice of weeping shall be no more heard." Counsels to Teachers, Parents, and Students, *p. 555.*

CHAPTER 58

The Youth Called to Be Laborers

There are many Christian youth that can do a good work if they will learn lessons in the school of Christ from the great Teacher. Even though pastors, evangelists, and teachers should neglect the seeking of the lost, let not the children and youth neglect to be doers of the Word. . . .

Let young men, and women, and children go to work in the name of Jesus. Let them unite together upon some plan and order of action. Cannot you form a band of workers, and have set times to pray together and ask the Lord to give you His grace, and put forth united action? You should consult with men who love and fear God, and who have experience in the work, that under the movings of the Spirit of God you may form plans and develop methods by which you may work in earnest and for certain results. The Lord will help those who will use their God-intrusted capabilities to His name's glory. Will our young men and young women who believe the truth become living missionaries?. . .

Work in Faith

As you labor for others, the divine power of the Spirit will work upon their souls; for they have been purchased by the blood of the only-begotten Son of God. We can be successful in winning souls for whom Christ has died only as we shall depend on the grace and power of God to do the work of convincing and converting the heart. While you are presenting to them the truth of God, unbelief and uncertainty will strive to hold the mind; but let the pledged word of God expel doubt from your hearts.

Take God at His word, and work in faith. Satan will come with his suggestions to make you distrust the word of your heavenly Father; but consider, "Whatsoever is not of faith is sin." Press your faith through the dark shadow of Satan, and lodge it upon the mercy seat, and let not one doubt be entertained. This is the only way in which you will gain an experience, and find the evidence so essential for your peace and confidence.

As your experience grows, you will have increased ardor of soul and warmer love for the service of God, because you have oneness of purpose with Jesus Christ. Your sympathies are begotten of the Holy Spirit. You wear the yoke with Christ, and are laborers together with God. *Youth's Instructor*, August 9, 1894.

Call for Volunteers

The Lord calls for volunteers who will take their stand firmly on His side, and will pledge themselves to unite with Jesus of Nazareth in doing the very work that needs to be done now, just now. *Fundamentals of Christian Education*, p. 488.

CHAPTER 59

Responsibility for Soul Winning

Upon the youth there rest grave responsibilities. God expects much from the young men who live in this generation of increased light and knowledge. He desires to use them in dispelling the error and superstition that cloud the minds of many. They are to discipline themselves by gathering up every jot and tittle of knowledge and experience. God holds them responsible for the opportunities given them. The work before them is waiting for their earnest efforts, that it may be carried forward from point to point as the time demands.

If the youth will consecrate mind and heart to the Lord's service, they may reach a high standard of efficiency and usefulness. This is the standard that the Lord expects the youth to attain. To do less than this is to refuse to make the most of God-given opportunities. This will be looked upon as treason against God—a failure to work for the good of humanity.

What are you doing, dear youth, to make known to others how important it is to take the Word of God for a guide, to keep the commandments of Jehovah? Are you by precept and example declaring that it is only by obedience to the Word of God that men can be saved. If you will do what you can, you will be a blessing to others. As you labor according to the best of your ability, ways and opportunities will open before you to do more. *Youth's Instructor*, January 1, 1907.

CHAPTER 60

Witnessing for Christ

All who are on the Lord's side are to confess Christ. "Ye are My witnesses, saith the Lord." The faith of the genuine believer will be made manifest in purity and holiness of character. Faith works by love and purifies the soul, and with faith there will be corresponding obedience, a faithful doing of the words of Christ. Christianity is always intensely practical, adapting itself to all the circumstances of actual life. "Ye are My witnesses." To whom? To the world; for you are to bear about with you a holy influence. Christ is to abide in your soul, and you are to talk of Him and make manifest the charms of His character.

Our Conversation

The fashionable religion of the time has so molded character that youth who make a profession of Christ scarcely mention His name to their associates. They converse of many subjects, but the precious plan of redemption is not made a theme of conversation. Suppose that as practical Christians we should change this order of things, and "show forth the praises of Him who hath called us out of darkness into His marvelous light." If Christ is abiding in the heart by faith, you cannot keep silent. If you have found Jesus, you will be a true missionary. You are to be enthusiastic in this matter, and let those know who do not appreciate Jesus that you have found Him precious to your soul, that He has put a new song in your mouth, even praise to God.

My young friends, will you begin your Christian life as those whose hearts are warmed with the love of Jesus? You will never know how much good you may do by speaking tenderly sensible, serious words regarding their souls' salvation to those who do not claim to be children of God. On the other hand you may never know until the judgment how many opportunities to be Christ's witnesses you have left unimproved. You may never know in this world the mischief you have done to some soul by your little acts of frivolity, your cheap talk, your levity, which was wholly inconsistent with your holy faith.

Winning Loved Ones

It is true, you may feel a sort of anxiety for the souls of those you love. You may seek to open to them the treasures of truth, and in your earnestness shed tears for their salvation; but when your words seem to make but little impression, and there is no apparent response to your prayers, you almost feel like casting reflection upon God that your labors bear no fruit. You feel that your dear ones have special hardness of heart, and that they do not respond to your efforts. But have you thought seriously that the fault may lie in your own self? Have you thought that you are pulling down with one hand that which you are striving to build up with the other?

At times you have permitted the Spirit of God to have a controlling power over you, and at other times you have denied your faith by your practice, and have destroyed your labor for your loved ones; for your efforts in their behalf have been made of none effect by your practice. Your temper, your unspoken language, your manners, the repining state of your mind, your want of Christian fragrance, your want of spirituality, the very expression of your countenance, has witnessed against you. . . .

Never underrate the importance of little things. Little things supply the actual discipline of life. It is by them that the soul is trained that it may grow into the likeness of Christ, or bear the likeness of evil. God helps us to cultivate habits of thought, word, look, and action that will testify to all about us that we have been with Jesus and learned of Him! *Youth's Instructor*, March 9, 1893.

Earnestness

A life spent in active work for God is a blessed one. Multitudes who are wasting their time in trifles, in idle regrets, and in unprofitable murmurings, might have altogether a different experience if they would appreciate the light God has given them, and let it shine upon others; and many make life miserable by their own selfishness and love of ease. By a diligent activity, their lives might become as bright rays of sunshine to guide those who are in the dark road to death into the pathway to heaven. If they take this course, their own hearts will be filled with peace and joy in Jesus Christ. *Review and Herald*, October 25, 1881.

CHAPTER 61

Personal Work

The work of Christ was largely composed of personal interviews. He had a faithful regard for the one-soul audience; and that one soul has carried to thousands the intelligence received.

The most successful toilers are those who will cheerfully work to serve God in small things. Every human being is to work with his own individual thread, weave it into the fabric that composes the web, and complete the pattern. . . .

Educate the youth to help the youth; and in seeking to do this work each will gain experience that will qualify him to become a consecrated worker in a larger sphere. Thousands of hearts can be reached in the most simple way.

The most intellectual, those who are looked upon and praised as the world's great and gifted men and women, are often refreshed by the most humble, simple words spoken by one who loves God, who can speak of that love as naturally as worldlings can speak of those things which their minds contemplate and feed upon. Words, even if well prepared and studied, have little influence; but the true, honest work of a son or a daughter of God in words, or in a service of little things, done in natural simplicity, will unbolt the door, which has long been locked, to many souls. *Review and Herald*, May 9, 1899.

CHAPTER 62

Young People as Soul Winners

Satan is a vigilant foe, intent upon his purpose of leading the youth to a course of action entirely contrary to that which God would approve. He well knows that there is no other class that can do as much good as young men and young women who are consecrated to God. The youth, if right, could sway a mighty influence. Preachers, or laymen advanced in years, cannot have one-half the influence upon the young that the youth, devoted to God, can have upon their associates. They ought to feel that a responsibility rests upon them to do all they can to save their fellow mortals, even at a sacrifice of their pleasure and natural desires. Time, and even means, if required, should be consecrated to God.

All who profess godliness should feel the danger of those who are out of Christ. Soon their probation will close. Those who might have exerted an influence to save souls, had they stood in the counsel of God, yet failed to do their duty through selfishness, indolence, or because they were ashamed of the cross of Christ, will not only lose their own souls, but will have the blood of poor sinners upon their garments. Such will be required to render an account for the good that they could have done had they been consecrated to God, but did not do because of their unfaithfulness.

Those who have really tasted the sweets of redeeming love will not, cannot, rest until all with whom they associate are made acquainted with the plan of salvation. The young should inquire, "Lord, what wilt Thou have me to do? How can I honor and glorify Thy name upon the earth?" Souls are perishing all around us, and yet what burden do the youth bear to win souls to Christ?

Solicitude for Others

Those who attend school could have an influence for the Saviour; but who name the name of Christ? and who are seen pleading with tender earnestness with their companions to forsake the ways of sin and choose the path of holiness?

This is the course which the believing young should take, but they do not; it is more congenial to their feelings to unite with the sinner in sport and pleasure. The young have a wide sphere of usefulness, but they see it not. Oh that they would now exert their powers of mind in seeking ways to approach perishing sinners, that they might make known to them the path of holiness, and by prayer and entreaty win even one soul to Christ!

What a noble enterprise? One soul to praise God through eternity! One soul to enjoy happiness and everlasting life! One gem in their crown to shine as a star forever and ever! But even more than one can be brought to turn from error to truth, from sin to holiness. Says the Lord by the prophet, "And they that turn many to righteousness shall shine as the stars forever and ever." Then those who engage with Christ and angels in the work of saving perishing souls are richly rewarded in the kingdom of heaven.

I saw that many souls might be saved if the young were where they ought to be, devoted to God and to the truth; but they generally occupy a position where constant labor must be bestowed upon them or they will become of the world themselves. They are a source of constant anxiety and heartache. Tears flow on their account, and agonizing prayers are wrung from the hearts of parents in their behalf. Yet they move on, reckless of the pain which their course of action causes. They plant thorns in the breasts of those who would die to save them, and have them become what God designed they should, through the merits of the blood of Christ. . . .

A Work to Do

Young men and young women, I saw that God has a work for you to do; take up your cross and follow Christ, or you are unworthy of Him. While you remain in listless indifference, how can you tell what is the will of God concerning you? and how do you expect to be saved, unless as faithful servants you do your Lord's will. Those who possess eternal life will all have done well. The King of glory will exalt them to His right hand, while He says to them, "Well done, good and faithful servants." How can you tell how many souls you might save from ruin, if, instead of studying your own pleasure, you were seeking what work you could do in the vineyard of your Master? How many souls have these gatherings for conversation and the practice of music been the means of saving? If you cannot point to one soul thus saved, turn, oh, turn to a new course of action. Begin to pray for souls, come near to Christ, close to His bleeding side. Let a meek and quiet spirit adorn your lives, and let your earnest, broken, humble petitions ascend to Him for wisdom that you may have success in saving not only your own soul, but the souls of others.

Pray more than you sing. Do you not stand in greater need of prayer than of singing? Young men and women, God calls upon you to work, work for Him. Make an entire change in your course of action. You can do a work that those who minister in word and doctrine cannot do. You can reach a class whom the minister cannot affect. *Testimonies for the Church*, Vol. 1, pp. 511-513.

Where to Begin

Let those who desire to work for God begin at home, in their own household, in their own neighborhood, among their own friends. Here they will find a favorable missionary field. This home missionary work is a test, revealing their ability or inability for service in a wider field. *Testimonies for the Church*, Vol. 6, p. 428.

The Most Successful Way

In our work, individual effort will accomplish more than can be estimated. It is for the want of this that souls are perishing. One soul is of infinite value; Calvary speaks its worth. One soul won to Christ will be instrumental in winning others, and there will be an ever-increasing result of blessing and salvation. *Gospel Workers*, p. 184.

CHAPTER 63

Service in Different Lines

God calls for ministers, Bible workers, and canvassers. Let our young men and young women go forth as canvassers, evangelists, and Bible workers, in company with laborers of experience, who can show them how to labor successfully. Let canvassers carry our publications from house to house. When opportunity offers, let them speak of the truth for this time to those whom they meet, and let them sing and pray with them. When in our work for God right methods are energetically followed, a harvest of souls will be gathered.

There is room in the work of God for all who are filled with the spirit of self-sacrifice. God is calling for men and women who are willing to deny self for the sake of others, willing to consecrate all they have and are to His work. Men are needed who, when they encounter difficulties, will move steadily on, saying, We will not fail or become discouraged. Men are needed who will strengthen and build up the work that others are trying to do. *Review and Herald*, April 28, 1904.

Gaining Efficiency

In this work, as in every other, skill is gained in the work itself. It is by training in the common duties of life and in ministry to the needy and suffering that efficiency is assured. *Education*, p. 268.

CHAPTER 64

Unselfish Service

Those who, so far as it is possible, engage in the work of doing good to others by giving practical demonstration of their interest in them, are not only relieving the ills of human life in helping them bear their burdens, but are at the same time contributing largely to their own health of soul and body. Doing good is a work that benefits both giver and receiver. If you forget self in your interest for others, you gain a victory over your infirmities. The satisfaction you will realize in doing good will aid you greatly in the recovery of the healthy tone of the imagination.

The pleasure of doing good animates the mind and vibrates through the whole body. While the faces of benevolent men are lighted up with cheerfulness, and their countenances express the moral elevation of the mind, those of selfish, stingy men are dejected, cast down, and gloomy. Their moral defects are seen in their countenances. Selfishness and self-love stamp their own image upon the outward man.

That person who is actuated by true disinterested benevolence is a partaker of the divine nature, having escaped the corruption that is in the world through lust; while the selfish and avaricious have cherished their selfishness until it has withered their social sympathies, and their countenances reflect the image of the fallen foe rather than that of purity and holiness. *Testimonies for the Church*, Vol. 2, p. 534.

CHAPTER 65

The Reward of Diligence

Let the youth remember that the indolent forfeit the invaluable experience gained by a faithful performance of the daily duties of life. He who is indolent and willingly ignorant places in his pathway that which will always be an obstruction. He refuses the culture that comes from honest toil. By failing to put forth a helping hand in behalf of humanity, he robs God. His career is very different from the career which God marked out for him; for to despise useful employment encourages the lower tastes and effectually paralyzes the most useful energies of the being.

Not a few, but thousands, of human beings exist only to consume the benefits which God in His mercy bestows on them. They forget to bring the Lord gratitude offerings for the riches He has intrusted to them in giving them the fruit of the earth. They forget that God desires them, by trading wisely on the talents lent them, to be producers as well as consumers. If they had a realization of the work the Lord desires them to do as His helping hand, they would not feel it a privilege to shun all responsibility and be waited on.

The Blessing of Labor

Real happiness is found only in being good and doing good. The purest, highest enjoyment comes to those who faithfully fulfill their appointed duties. No honest work is degrading. It is ignoble sloth which leads human beings to look down on the simple, everyday duties of life. The refusal to perform these duties causes a mental and moral deficiency which will one day be keenly felt. At some time in the life of the slothful his deformity will stand out clearly defined. Over his life-record is written the words, A consumer, but not a producer.

From all the vocations of life, useful spiritual lessons may be learned. Those who till the soil may, as they work, study the meaning of the words, "Ye are God's husbandry." In the human heart the seeds of truth are to be sown, that the life may bear the beautiful fruit of the Spirit. God's impress on the mind is to mold it into graceful symmetry. The crude energies, both physical and mental, are to be trained for the Master's service. . . .

To all Christ has given the work of ministry. He is the King of glory, yet He declared, "The Son of man came not to be ministered unto, but to minister." He is the Majesty of heaven, yet He willingly consented to come to this earth to do the work laid upon Him by His Father. He has ennobled labor. That He might set us an example of industry, He worked with His hands at the carpenter's trade. From a very early age, He acted His part in sustaining the family. He realized that He was a part of the family firm, and willingly bore His share of the burdens.

Helping in the Home

Children and youth should take pleasure in making lighter the cares of father and mother, showing an unselfish interest in the home. As they cheerfully lift the burdens that fall to their share, they are receiving a training which will fit them for positions of trust and usefulness. Each year they are to make steady advancement, gradually but surely laying aside the inexperience of boyhood and girlhood for the experience of manhood and womanhood. In the faithful performance of the simple duties of the home, boys and girls lay the foundation for mental, moral, and spiritual excellence.

The Web of Destiny

Remember, dear young friends, that each day, each hour, each moment, you are weaving the web of your own destiny. Each time the shuttle is thrown, there is drawn into the web a thread which either mars or beautifies the pattern. If you are careless and indolent, you spoil the life which God designed should be bright and beautiful. If you choose to follow your own inclinations, unchristlike habits will bind you with bands of steel. And as you walk away from Christ, your example will be followed by many who, because of your wrong course, will never enjoy the glories of heaven. But if you make brave efforts to overcome selfishness, allowing no opportunity to pass for helping those around you, the light of your example will guide others to the cross. *Youth's Instructor*, December 5, 1901.

CHAPTER 66

The Dignity of Labor

It was God's purpose to alleviate by toil the evil brought into the world by man's disobedience. By toil the temptations of Satan might be made ineffectual, and the tide of evil stayed. And though attended with anxiety, weariness, and pain, labor is still a source of happiness and development, and a safeguard against temptation. Its discipline places a check on self-indulgence, and promotes industry, purity, and firmness. Thus it becomes a part of God's great plan for our recovery from the fall.

Manual Labor Versus Games

The public feeling is that manual labor is degrading, yet men may exert themselves as much as they choose at cricket, baseball, or in pugilistic contests, without being regarded as degraded. Satan is delighted when he sees human beings using their physical and mental powers in that which does not educate, which is not useful, which does not help them to be a blessing to those who need their help. While the youth are becoming expert in games that are of no real value to themselves or to others, Satan is playing the game of life for their souls, taking from them the talents that God has given them, and placing in their stead his own evil attributes. It is his effort to lead men to ignore God. He seeks to engross and absorb the mind so completely that God will find no place in the thoughts. He does not wish people to have a knowledge of their Maker, and he is well pleased if he can set in operation games and theatrical performances that will so confuse the senses of the youth that God and heaven will be forgotten.

One of the surest safeguards against evil is useful occupation, while idleness is one of the greatest curses; for vice, crime, and poverty follow in its wake. Those who are always busy, who go cheerfully about their daily tasks, are the useful members of society. In the faithful discharge of the various duties that lie in their pathway, they make their lives a blessing to themselves and to others. Diligent labor keeps them from many of the snares of him who "finds some mischief still for idle hands to do."

A stagnant pool soon becomes offensive; but a flowing brook spreads health and gladness over the land. The one is a symbol of the idle, the other of the industrious. . . .

Christ's Example

The path of toil appointed to the dwellers on earth may be hard and wearisome, but it is honored by the footprints of the Redeemer, and he is safe who follows in this sacred way. By precept and example, Christ has dignified useful labor. From His earliest years He lived a life of toil. The greater part of His earthly life was spent in patient work in the carpenter's shop at Nazareth. In the garb of a common laborer the Lord of life trod the streets of the little town in which He lived, going to and returning from His humble toil; and ministering angels attended Him as He walked side by side with peasants and laborers, unrecognized and unhonored. . . .

Judicious labor is a healthful tonic for the human race. It makes the feeble strong, the poor rich, the wretched happy. Satan lies in ambush, ready to destroy those whose leisure gives him opportunity to approach them under some attractive disguise. He is never more successful than when he comes to men in their idle hours.

The Lesson of Contented Industry

Among the evils resulting from wealth, one of the greatest is the fashionable idea that work is degrading. The prophet Ezekiel declares: "Behold, this was the iniquity of thy sister Sodom, pride, fullness of bread, and abundance of idleness was in her and in her daughters, neither did she strengthen the hand of the poor and needy." Ezekiel 16:49. Here are presented before us the terrible results of idleness, which enfeebles the mind, debases the soul, and perverts the understanding, making a curse of that which was given as a blessing. It is the working man or woman who sees something great and good in life, and who is willing to bear its responsibilities with faith and hope.

The essential lesson of contented industry in the necessary duties of life, is yet to be learned by many of Christ's followers. It requires more grace, more stern discipline of character, to work for God in the capacity of mechanic, merchant, lawyer, or farmer, carrying the precepts of Christianity into the ordinary business of life, than to labor as an acknowledged missionary in the open field. It requires a strong spiritual nerve to bring religion into the workshop and the business office, sanctifying the details of everyday life, and ordering every transaction according to the standard of God's Word. But this is what the Lord requires.

The apostle Paul regarded idleness as a sin. He learned the trade of tent-making in its higher and lower branches, and during his ministry he often worked at this trade to support himself and others. Paul did not regard as lost the time thus spent. As he worked, the apostle had access to a class of people whom he could not otherwise have reached. He showed his associates that skill in the common arts is a gift from God. He taught that even in everyday toil God is to be honored. His toil-hardened hands detracted nothing from the force of his pathetic appeals as a Christian minister.

God designs that all shall be workers. The toiling beast of burden answers the purpose of its creation better than does the indolent man. God is a constant worker. The angels are workers; they are ministers of God to the children of men. Those who look forward to a heaven of inactivity will be disappointed; for the economy of heaven provides no place for the gratification of indolence. But to the weary and heavy-laden rest is promised. It is the faithful servant who will be welcomed from his labors to the joy of his Lord. He will lay off his armor with rejoicing, and will forget the noise of battle in the glorious rest prepared for those who conquer through the cross of Christ. *Counsels to Teachers, Parents, and Students*, pp. 274-280.

CHAPTER 67

Sowing Beside All Waters

The Lord is calling upon His people to take up different lines of missionary work, to sow beside all waters. We do but a small part of the work that He desires us to do among our neighbors and friends. By kindness to the poor, the sick, or the bereaved we may obtain an influence over them, so that divine truth will find access to their hearts. No such opportunity for service should be allowed to pass unimproved. It is the highest missionary work that we can do. The presentation of the truth in love and sympathy from house to house is in harmony with the instruction of Christ to His disciples when He sent them out on their first missionary tour.

The Gift of Song

Those who have the gift of song are needed. Song is one of the most effective means of impressing spiritual truth upon the heart. Often by the words of sacred song the springs of penitence and faith have been unsealed. Church members, young and old, should be educated to go forth to proclaim this last message to the world. If they go in humility, angels of God will go with them, teaching them how to lift up the voice in prayer, how to raise the voice in song, and how to proclaim the gospel message for this time.

Young men and women, take up the work to which God calls you. Christ will teach you to use your abilities to good purpose. As you receive the quickening influence of the Holy Spirit, and seek to teach others, your minds will be refreshed, and you will be able to present words that are new and strangely beautiful to your hearers. . . .

Medical Missionary Work

The medical missionary work presents many opportunities for service. Intemperance in eating and ignorance of nature's laws are causing much of the sickness that exists, and are robbing God of the glory due Him. Because of a failure to deny self, many of God's people are unable to reach the high standard of spirituality He sets before them. Teach the people that it is better to know how to keep well than to know how to cure disease. We should be wise educators, warning all against self-indulgence. As we see the wretchedness, deformity, and disease that have come into the world as a result of ignorance, how can we refrain from doing our part to enlighten the ignorant and relieve the suffering?

Because the avenues to the soul have been closed by the tyrant Prejudice, many are ignorant of the principles of healthful living. Good service can be done by teaching the people how to prepare healthful food. This line of work is as essential as any that can be taken up. More cooking schools should be established, and some should labor from house to house, giving instruction in the art of cooking wholesome foods. Many, many will be rescued from physical, mental, and moral degeneracy through the influence of health reform. *Review and Herald*, June 6, 1912.

CHAPTER 68

Many Lines of Work

The church is organized for service, and in a life of service to Christ connection with the church is one of the first steps. Loyalty to Christ demands the faithful performance of church duties. This is an important part of one's training; and in a church imbued with the Master's life it will lead directly to effort for the world without. There are many lines in which the youth can find opportunity for helpful effort. *Education*, pp. 268, 269.

Each Has His Place

Each has his place in the eternal plan of heaven. Each is to work in cooperation with Christ for the salvation of souls. Not more surely is the place prepared for us in the heavenly mansions than is the special place designated on earth where we are to work for God. *Christ's Object Lessons*, pp. 326, 327.

The Sabbath School Work

The Lord calls for young men and women to gird themselves for lifelong, earnest labor in the Sabbath-school work. . . . The Lord would have teachers in the Sabbath-school work who can give whole-hearted service, who will increase their talent by exercise, and make improvement on what has already been attained. *Testimonies on Sabbath School Work*, p. 53.

Bible Work

The idea of holding Bible readings is a heaven-born idea, and opens the way to put hundreds of young men and women into the field to do an important work, which otherwise could not have been done.

The Bible is unchained. It can be carried to every man's door, and its truths may be presented to every man's conscience. There are many who, like the noble Bereans, will search the Scriptures daily for themselves, when the truth is presented, to see whether or not these things are so. Christ has said, "Search the Scriptures; for in them ye think ye have eternal life: and they are they which testify of Me." Jesus, the world's Redeemer, bids men not only to read, but to "search the Scriptures." This is a great and important work, and it is committed to us, and in doing this we shall be greatly benefited; for obedience to Christ's command will not go unrewarded. He will crown with especial tokens of His favor this act of loyalty in following the light revealed in His Word. *Testimonies on Sabbath School Work*, pp. 29, 30.

Canvassing

The Lord calls upon our youth to labor as canvassers and evangelists, to do house-to-house work in places that have not yet heard the truth. He speaks to our young men, saying, "Ye are not your own; for ye are bought with a price; therefore glorify God in your body, and in your spirit, which are God's." Those who will go forth to the work under God's direction will be wonderfully blessed. *Testimonies for the Church*, Vol. 8, p. 229.

One of the very best ways in which young men can obtain a fitness for the ministry is by entering the canvassing field. Let them go into towns and cities to canvass for the books which contain the truth for this time. In this work they will find opportunity to speak the words of life, and the seeds of truth they sow will spring up to bear fruit. By meeting the people and presenting to them our publications, they will gain an experience that they could not gain by preaching. . . .

All who desire an opportunity for true ministry, and who will give themselves unreservedly to God, will find in the canvassing work opportunity to speak upon many things pertaining to the future immortal life. *Gospel Workers*, p. 96.

Teaching

The very best talent that can be secured is needed to educate and mould the minds of the young, and to carry on successfully the many lines of work that will need to be done by the teacher in our church schools. . . .

Teachers are needed, especially for the children, who are calm and kind, manifesting forbearance and love for the very ones who most need it. . . . Our church schools need teachers who have high moral qualities; those who can be trusted; those who are sound in the faith, and who have tact and patience; those who walk with God, and abstain from the very appearance of evil. *Testimonies for the Church*, Vol. 6, pp. 200, 201.

Business

The Lord desires to have in His service intelligent men, men qualified for various lines of work. There is need of business men who will weave the grand principles of truth into all their transactions. And their talents should be perfected by most thorough study and training. If men in any line of work need to improve their opportunities to become wise and efficient, it is those who are using their ability in building up the kingdom of God in our world. Of Daniel we learn that in all his business transactions, when subjected to the closest scrutiny, not one fault or error could be found. He was a sample of what every business man may be. His history shows what may be accomplished by one who consecrates the strength of brain and bone and muscle, of heart and life, to the service of God. *Christ's Object Lessons*, pp. 350, 351.

Medical Work

There is no missionary field more important than that occupied by the faithful, God-fearing physician. There is no field where a man may accomplish greater good, or win more jewels to shine in the crown of his rejoicing. He may carry the grace of Christ, as a sweet perfume, into all the sick-rooms he enters; he may carry the true healing balm to the sin-sick soul. He can point the sick and dying to the Lamb of God that taketh away the sin of the world. He should not listen to the suggestion that it is dangerous to speak of their eternal interests to those who lives are in peril, lest it should make them worse; for in nine cases out of ten the knowledge of a sin-pardoning Saviour would make them better both in mind and body. Jesus can limit the power of Satan. He is the physician in whom the sin-sick soul may trust to heal the maladies of the body as well as of the soul. *Testimonies for the Church*, Vol. 5, pp. 448, 449.

In almost every community there are large numbers who do not listen to the preaching of God's Word or attend any religious service. If they are reached by the gospel, it must be carried to their homes. Often the relief of their physical needs is the only avenue by which they can be approached. Missionary nurses who care for the sick and relieve the distress of the poor will find many opportunities to pray with them, to read to them from God's Word, and to speak of the Saviour. They can pray with and for the helpless ones who have not strength of will to control the appetites that passion has degraded. They can bring a ray of hope into the lives of the defeated and disheartened. Their unselfish love, manifested in acts of disinterested kindness, will make it easier for the suffering ones to believe in the love of Christ. *The Ministry of Healing*, pp. 144, 145.

The Ministry

There must be no belittling of the gospel ministry. No enterprise should be so conducted as to cause the ministry of the Word to be looked upon as an inferior matter. It is not so. Those who belittle the ministry are belittling Christ. The highest of all work is ministry in its various lines, and it should be kept before the youth that there is no work more blessed of God than that of the gospel minister.

Let not our young men be deterred from entering the ministry. There is danger that through glowing representations some will be drawn away from the path where God bids them walk. Some have been encouraged to take a course of study in medical lines who ought to be preparing themselves to enter the ministry. The Lord calls for more ministers to labor in His vineyard. The words were spoken, "Strengthen the outposts; have faithful sentinels in every part of the world." God calls for you, young men. He calls for whole armies of young men who are large-hearted and large-minded, and who have a deep love for Christ and the truth. *Testimonies for the Church*, Vol. 6, p. 411.

Foreign Mission Work

Young men are wanted. God calls them to missionary fields. Being comparatively free from care and responsibilities, they are more favorably situated to engage in the work than are those who must provide for the training and support of a large family. Furthermore, young men can more readily adapt themselves to new climates and new society, and can better endure inconveniences and hardships. By tact and perseverance, they can reach the people where they are. *Testimonies for the Church*, Vol. 5, p. 393.

Young men should be qualifying themselves by becoming familiar with other languages, that God may use them as mediums to communicate His saving truth to those of other nations. These young men may obtain a knowledge of other languages even while engaged in laboring for sinners. If they are economical of their time, they can be improving their minds and qualifying themselves for more extended usefulness. If young women who have borne but little responsibility would devote themselves to God, they could qualify themselves for usefulness by studying and becoming familiar with other languages. They could devote themselves to the work of translating. *Testimonies for the Church*, Vol. 3, p. 204.

Youthful Service

Children can be acceptable missionary workers in the home and in the church. God desires them to be taught that they are in this world for useful service, not merely for play. In the home they can be trained to do missionary work that will prepare them for wider spheres of usefulness. Parents, help your children to fulfill God's purpose for them. *Review and Herald*, December 8, 1910.

CHAPTER 69

Acceptable Service

In His infinite mercy and love God has given us light from His Word, and Christ says to us, "Freely ye have received, freely give." Let the light God has given you shine forth to those in darkness. As you do this, heavenly angels will be beside you, helping you win souls for Christ. . . .

Dear young friends, remember that it is not necessary to be an ordained minister in order to serve the Lord. There are many ways of working for Christ. Human hands may never have been laid on you in ordination, but God can give you fitness for His service. He can work through you to the saving of souls. If, having learned in the school of Christ, you are meek and lowly in heart, He will give you words to speak for Him. . . .

Our Relation to Mistakes

Do all in your power to gain perfection; but do not think that because you make mistakes you are excluded from God's service. The Lord knows our frame; He remembers that we are dust. As you use faithfully the talents God has given you, you will gain knowledge that will make you dissatisfied with self. You will see the need of sifting away harmful habits, lest by a wrong example you injure others.

Work diligently, giving to others the truth so precious to you. Then when there are vacancies to be filled, you will hear the words, "Come up higher." You may be reluctant to respond; but move forward in faith, bringing into God's work a fresh, honest zeal.

The secret of winning souls can be learned only from the great Teacher. As the dew and the still showers fall gently on the withering plant, so our words are to fall gently and lovingly on the souls we are seeking to win. We are not to wait till opportunities come to us; we are to seek for them, keeping the heart uplifted in prayer that God may help us to speak the right word at the right time. When an opportunity presents itself, let no excuse lead you to neglect it; for its improvement may mean the salvation of a soul from death. *Youth's Instructor*, February 6, 1902.

The Highest Work

The work above all work—the business above all others which should draw and engage the energies of the soul—is the work of saving souls for whom Christ has died. Make this the main, the important work of your life. Make it your special life work. Cooperate with Christ in this grand and noble work, and become home and foreign missionaries. Be ready and efficient to work at home or in far-off climes for the saving of souls. Work the works of God and demonstrate your faith in your Saviour by toiling for others. O that young and old were thoroughly converted to God, and would take up the duty that lies next them, and work as they have opportunity, becoming laborers together with God! *Youth's Instructor*, May 4, 1893.

CHAPTER 70

Faithfulness in Service

Those who are unfaithful in the least of temporal affairs will be unfaithful in responsibilities of greater importance. They will rob God, and fail of meeting the claims of the divine law. They will not realize that their talents belong to God and should be devoted to His service. Those who do nothing for their employers except that which is commanded them, when they know that the prosperity of the work depends on some extra exertion on their part, will fail to be accounted faithful servants. There are many things not specified that wait to be done, that come directly under the notice of the one employed.

Leaks and losses occur that might be prevented if painstaking diligence and unselfish effort were manifested, if the principles of love enjoined upon us by Jesus were carried out in the life of those who profess His name. But many are working in the cause of God who are registered as "eye-servants."

Unfaithfulness Recorded

It is the most abhorrent form of selfishness that leads the worker to neglect the improvement of time, the care of property, because he is not directly under the eye of the master. But do such workers imagine that their neglects are not noticed, their unfaithfulness not recorded? Could their eyes be opened, they would see that a Watcher looks on, and all their carelessness is recorded in the books of heaven.

Those who are unfaithful to the work of God are lacking in principle; their motives are not of a character to lead them to choose the right under all circumstances. The servants of God are to feel at all times that they are under the eye of their employer. He who watched the sacrilegious feast of Belshazzar is present in all our institutions, in the counting-room of the merchant, in the private workshop; and the bloodless hand is as surely recording your neglect as it recorded the awful judgment of the blasphemous king. Belshazzar's condemnation was written in words of fire, "Thou art weighed in the balances, and art found wanting"; and if you fail to fulfill your God-given obligations your condemnation will be the same.

True Motives in Service

There are many who profess to be Christians who are not united with Christ. Their daily life, their spirit, testifies that Christ is not formed within, the hope of glory. They cannot be depended upon, they cannot be trusted. They are anxious to reduce their service to the minimum of effort, and at the same time exact the highest of wages. The name "servant" applies to every man; for we are all servants, and it will be well for us to see what mold we are taking on. Is it the mold of unfaithfulness, or of fidelity?

Is it the disposition generally among servants to do as much as possible? Is it not rather the prevalent fashion to slide through the work as quickly, as easily, as possible, and obtain the wages at as little cost to themselves as they can? The object is not to be as thorough as possible but to get the remuneration. Those who profess to be the servants of Christ should not forget the injunction of the apostle Paul, "Servants, obey in all things your masters according to the flesh; not with eyeservice, as menpleasers; but in singleness of heart, fearing God: and whatsoever ye do, do it heartily, as to the Lord, and not unto men; knowing that of the Lord ye shall receive the reward of the inheritance: for ye serve the Lord Christ."

Those who enter the work as "eye-servants," will find that their work cannot bear the inspection of men or of angels. The thing essential for successful work is a knowledge of Christ; for this knowledge will give sound principles of right, impart a noble, unselfish spirit, like that of our Saviour whom we profess to serve. Faithfulness, economy, care-taking, thoroughness, should characterize all our work, wherever we may be, whether in the kitchen, in the workshop, in the office of publication, in the sanitarium, in the college, or wherever we are stationed in the vineyard of the Lord. "He that is faithful in that which is least is faithful also in much: and he that is unjust in the least is unjust also in much." *Review and Herald*, September 22, 1891.

SECTION VII
Health and Efficiency

Since the mind and the soul find expression through the body, both mental and spiritual vigor are in great degree dependent upon physical strength and activity; whatever promotes physical health promotes the development of a strong mind and a well-balanced character. Without health, no one can as distinctly understand or as completely fulfill his obligations to himself, to his fellow-beings, or to his Creator. Therefore the health should be as faithfully guarded as the character. A knowledge of physiology and hygiene should be the basis of all educational effort. Education, *p. 195.*

CHAPTER 71

The Science of Living

What can be done to stay the tide of disease and crime that is sweeping our race down to ruin and to death? As the great cause of the evil is to be found in the indulgence of appetite and passion, so the first and great work of reform must be to learn and practice the lessons of temperance and self-control.

To effect a permanent change for the better in society, the education of the masses must begin in early life. The habits formed in childhood and youth, the tastes acquired, the self-control gained, the principles inculcated from the cradle, are almost certain to determine the future of the man or woman. The crime and corruption occasioned by intemperance and lax morals might be prevented by the proper training of the youth.

Health and Self-control

One of the greatest aids in perfecting pure and noble characters in the young, strengthening them to control appetite and refrain from debasing excesses, is sound physical health. And, on the other hand, these very habits of self-control are essential to the maintenance of health.

It is of the highest importance that men and women be instructed in the science of human life, and the best means of preserving and acquiring health. Especially is youth the time to lay up a stock of knowledge to be put in daily practice through life.

Youth is the time to establish good habits, to correct wrong ones already contracted, to gain and to hold the power of self-control, and to lay the plan, and accustom one's self to the practice, of ordering all the acts of life with reference to the will of God and the welfare of our fellow-creatures. . . .

Jesus did not ignore the claims of the body. He had respect for the physical condition of man, and went about healing the sick and restoring their faculties to those suffering from their loss. . . .

Life a Trust

The young should be shown that they are not at liberty to do as they please with their lives. Now is their day of trust, and by and by will come their day of reckoning. God will not hold them guiltless for treating lightly His precious gifts; the world's Redeemer has paid an infinite price for them, and their lives and talents belong to Him; and they will finally be judged according to the faithful or unfaithful stewardship of the capital which God has intrusted to their care. They should be taught that the greater their endowment of means and opportunities the more heavily does the responsibility of God's work rest upon them, and the more are they required to do. If the youth are thus brought up to feel their responsibility to the Creator, and the important trust given them in their own lives, they will hesitate to plunge into the vortex of dissipation and crime that swallows up so many of the promising young men of our age. *Review and Herald*, December 13, 1881.

CHAPTER 72

Safeguarding the Health

Health is a blessing of which few appreciate the value; yet upon it the efficiency of our mental and physical powers largely depends. Our impulses and passions have their seat in the body, and it must be kept in the best condition physically and under the most spiritual influences in order that our talents may be put to the highest use. Anything that lessens physical strength enfeebles the mind, and makes it less capable of discriminating between right and wrong.

The misuse of our physical powers shortens the time in which our lives can be used for the glory of God, and it unfits us to accomplish the work God has given us to do. By allowing ourselves to form wrong habits, by keeping late hours, by gratifying appetite at the expense of health, we lay the foundation for feebleness. . . .

Those who thus shorten their lives and unfit themselves for service by disregarding nature's laws, are guilty of robbery toward God. And they are robbing their fellow men also. The opportunity of blessing others, the very work for which God sent them into the world, has by their own course of action been cut short. And they have unfitted themselves to do even that which in a briefer period of time they might have accomplished. The Lord holds us guilty when by our injurious habits we thus deprive the world of good. *Review and Herald*, June 20, 1912.

CHAPTER 73

Sacredness of Health

Satan comes to man with his temptations as an angel of light, as he came to Christ. He has been working to bring man into a condition of physical and moral weakness, that he may overcome him with his temptations, and then triumph over his ruin. And he has been successful in tempting man to indulge appetite, regardless of the result. He well knows that it is impossible for man to discharge his obligations to God and to his fellow-men, while he impairs the faculties God has given him. The brain is the capital of the body. If the perceptive faculties become benumbed through intemperance of any kind, eternal things are not discerned.

Relation of Health to Character Building

God gives no permission to man to violate the laws of his being. But man, through yielding to Satan's temptations to indulge intemperance, brings the higher faculties into subjection to the animal appetites and passions. When these gain the ascendency, man, who was created a little lower than the angels, with faculties susceptible of the highest cultivation, surrenders to be controlled by Satan. And he gains easy access to those who are in bondage to appetite. Through intemperance, some sacrifice one-half, and others two-thirds, of their physical, mental and moral powers and become playthings for the enemy.

Those who would have clear minds to discern Satan's

devices must have their physical appetites under the control of reason and conscience. The moral and vigorous action of the higher powers of the mind are essential to the perfection of Christian character. And the strength or the weakness of the mind has very much to do with our usefulness in this world, and with our final salvation. The ignorance that has prevailed in regard to God's law in our physical nature is deplorable. Intemperance of any kind is a violation of the laws of our being. Imbecility is prevailing to a fearful extent. Sin is made attractive by the covering of light which Satan throws over it, and he is well pleased when he can hold the Christian world in their daily habits under the tyranny of custom, like the heathen, and allow appetite to govern them.

Intemperance Degrading

If men and women of intelligence have their moral powers benumbed through intemperance of any kind, they are, in many of their habits, elevated but little above the heathen. Satan is constantly drawing the people from saving light to custom and fashion, irrespective of physical, mental, and moral health. The great enemy knows that if appetite and passion predominate, health of body and strength of intellect are sacrificed upon the altar of self-gratification, and man is brought to speedy ruin. If enlightened intellect holds the reins, controlling the animal propensities, keeping them in subjection to the moral powers, Satan well knows that his power to overcome with his temptations is very small. . . .

A large share of the Christian world have no right to call themselves Christians. Their habits, their extravagance, and general treatment of their own bodies, are in violation of physical law and contrary to the Bible standard. They are working out for themselves, in their course of life, physical suffering, mental and moral feebleness. *Review and Herald*, September 8, 1874.

Self-mastery a Duty

The body is to be brought into subjection. The higher powers of the being are to rule. The passions are to be controlled by the will, which is itself to be under the control of God. The kingly power of reason, sanctified by divine grace, is to bear sway in our lives.

The requirements of God must be brought home to the conscience. Men and women must be awakened to the duty of self-mastery, the need of purity, freedom from every depraving appetite and defiling habit. They need to be impressed with the fact that all their powers of mind and body are the gift of God, and are to be preserved in the best possible condition for His service. *The Ministry of Healing*, p. 130.

CHAPTER 74

A Balanced Education

The time spent in physical exercise is not lost. The student who is constantly poring over his books, while he takes but little exercise in the open air, does himself an injury. A proportionate exercise of the various organs and faculties of the body is essential to the best work of each. When the brain is constantly taxed, while the other organs are left inactive, there is a loss of physical and mental strength. The physical powers are robbed of their healthy tone, the mind loses its freshness and vigor, and a morbid excitability is the result.

In order for men and women to have well-balanced minds, all the powers of the being should be called into use and developed. There are in this world many who are one-sided because only one set of faculties has been cultivated, while others are dwarfed from inaction. The education of many youth is a failure. They overstudy, while they neglect that which pertains to the practical life. That the balance of the mind may be maintained, a judicious system of physical work should be combined with mental work, that there may be a harmonious development of all the powers. *Counsels to Teachers, Parents, and Students*, pp. 295, 296.

CHAPTER 75

Education Obtained at Expense of Health

Some students put the whole being into their studies, and concentrate their minds upon the object of obtaining an education. They work the brain, but allow the physical powers to remain inactive. Thus the brain is overworked, and the muscles become weak because they are not exercised. When these students are graduated, it is evident that they have obtained their education at the expense of life. They have studied day and night, year after year, keeping their minds continually upon the stretch, while they have failed to exercise their muscles sufficiently. . . .

Young ladies frequently give themselves up to study, to the neglect of other branches of education even more essential for practical life than the study of books. And after having obtained their education, they are often invalids for life. They have neglected their health by remaining too much indoors, deprived of the pure air of heaven and of the God-given sunlight. These young women might have come from school in health had they combined with their studies household labor and exercise in the open air.

Health is a great treasure. It is the richest possession that mortals can have. Wealth, honor, or learning is dearly purchased if it be at the loss of the vigor of health. None of these attainments can secure happiness if health is wanting. *Counsels to Teachers, Parents, and Students*, pp. 285, 286.

CHAPTER 76

The Insignia of Nobility

During their three years of training, Daniel and his associates maintained their abstemious habits, their allegiance to God, and their constant dependence upon His power. When the time came for their abilities and acquirements to be tested by the king, they were examined with other candidates for the service of the kingdom. But "among them all was found none like Daniel, Hananiah, Mishael, and Azariah." Their keen apprehension, their choice and exact language, their extensive knowledge, testified to the unimpaired strength and vigor of their mental power. Therefore they stood before the king. "And in all matters of wisdom and understanding, that the king inquired of them, he found them ten times better than all the magicians and astrologers that were in all his realm."

God always honors the right. The most promising youths from all the lands subdued by the great conqueror had been gathered at Babylon, yet amid them all the Hebrew captives were without a rival. The erect form, the firm, elastic step, the fair countenance, the undimmed senses, the untainted breath—all these were insignia of the nobility with which nature honors those who are obedient to her laws.

Effect of Physical Habits on the Mind

The lesson here presented is one that we would do well to ponder. A strict compliance with the Bible requirements will be a blessing both to body and soul. The fruit of the Spirit is not only love, joy, and peace, but temperance also. We are enjoined not to defile our bodies; for they are the temples of the Holy Spirit.

The Hebrew captives were men of like passions with ourselves. Amid the seductive influences of the luxurious courts of Babylon, they stood firm. The youth of today are surrounded with allurements to self-indulgence. Especially in our large cities, every form of sensual gratification is made easy and inviting. Those who, like Daniel, refuse to defile themselves, will reap the reward of temperate habits. With their greater physical stamina and increased power of endurance, they have a bank of deposit upon which to draw in case of emergency.

Right physical habits promote mental superiority. Intellectual power, physical stamina, and length of life depend upon immutable laws. Nature's God will not interfere to preserve men from the consequences of violating nature's requirements. He who strives for the mastery must be temperate in all things. Daniel's clearness of mind and firmness of purpose, his power in acquiring knowledge and in resisting temptation, were due in a great degree to the plainness of his diet, in connection with his life of prayer.

Shaping Our Own Destiny

There is much sterling in the adage, "Every man is the architect of his own fortune." While parents are responsible for the stamp of character, as well as for the education and training, of their sons and daughters, it is still true that our position and usefulness in the world depend, to a great degree, upon our own course of action.

Daniel and his companions enjoyed the benefits of correct training and education in early life, but these advantages alone would not have made them what they were. The time came when they must act for themselves—when their future depended upon their own course. Then they decided to be true to the lessons given them in childhood. The fear of God, which is the beginning of wisdom, was the foundation of their greatness.

The history of Daniel and his youthful companions has been recorded on the pages of the inspired word for the benefit of the youth of all succeeding ages. Through the record of their fidelity to the principles of temperance, God is speaking today to young men and young women, bidding them gather up the precious rays of light He has given on the subject of Christian temperance, and place themselves in right relation to the laws of health.

Temperance Richly Rewarded

There is now need of men who, like Daniel, will do and dare. A pure heart and a strong, fearless hand are wanted in the world today. God designed that man should be constantly improving, daily reaching a higher point in the scale of excellence. He will help us if we seek to help ourselves. Our hope of happiness in two worlds depends upon our improvement in one. At every point we should be guarded against the first approach to intemperance.

Dear youth, God calls upon you to do a work which through His grace you can do. "Present your bodies a living sacrifice, holy, acceptable unto God, which is your reasonable service." Stand forth in your God-given manhood and womanhood. Show a purity of tastes, appetite, and habits that bears comparison with Daniel's. God will reward you with calm nerves, a clear brain, an unimpaired judgment, keen perceptions. The youth of today whose principles are firm and unwavering will be blessed with health of body, mind, and soul. *Youth's Instructor*, July 9, 1903.

Religion and Health

"The fear of the Lord is the beginning of wisdom." When men of wrong habits and sinful practices yield to the power of divine truth, the entrance of God's Word gives light and understanding to the simple. There is an application of truth to the heart; and moral power, which seemed to have been paralyzed, revives. The receiver is possessed of stronger, clearer understanding than before. He has riveted his soul to the Eternal Rock. Health improves, in the very sense of his security in Christ. Thus religion and the laws of health go hand in hand. *Testimonies for the Church*, Vol. 4, pp. 553, 554.

SECTION VIII
The Devotional Life

God's holy, educating Spirit is in His Word. A light, a new and precious light, shines forth from every page. Truth is there revealed, and words and sentences are made bright and appropriate for the occasion, as the voice of God speaking to the soul.

The Holy Spirit loves to address the youth, and to discover to them the treasures and beauties of God's Word. The promises spoken by the great Teacher will captivate the senses and animate the soul with a spiritual power that is divine. There will grow in the fruitful mind a familiarity with divine things that will be as a barricade against temptation. Christ's Object Lessons, *p. 132.*

CHAPTER 77

Prayer Our Stronghold

Amid the perils of these last days, the only safety of the youth lies in ever-increasing watchfulness and prayer. The youth who finds his joy in reading the Word of God, and in the hour of prayer, will be constantly refreshed by drafts from the fountain of life. He will attain a height of moral excellence and a breadth of thought of which others cannot conceive. Communion with God encourages good thoughts, noble aspirations, clear perceptions of truth, and lofty purposes of action. Those who thus connect themselves with God are acknowledged by Him as His sons and daughters. They are constantly reaching higher and still higher, obtaining clearer views of God and of eternity, until the Lord makes them channels of light and wisdom to the world.

How to Pray

But prayer is not understood as it should be. Our prayers are not to inform God of something He does not know. The Lord is acquainted with the secrets of every soul. Our prayers need not be long and loud. God reads the hidden thoughts. We may pray in secret, and He who sees in secret will hear, and will reward us openly.

The prayers that are offered to God to tell Him of all our wretchedness, when we do not feel wretched at all, are the prayers of hypocrisy. It is the contrite prayer that the Lord regards. "For thus saith the high and lofty One that inhabiteth eternity, whose name is Holy; I dwell in the high and holy place, and with him also that is of a contrite and humble spirit, to revive the spirit of the humble, and to revive the heart of the contrite ones."

Prayer is not intended to work any change in God; it brings us into harmony with God. It does not take the place of duty. Prayer offered ever so often and ever so earnestly will never be accepted by God in the place of our tithe. Prayer will not pay our debts to God. . . .

Prayer Brings Power

The strength acquired in prayer to God will prepare us for our daily duties. The temptations to which we are daily exposed make prayer a necessity. In order that we may be kept by the power of God through faith, the desires of the mind should be continually ascending in silent prayer. When we are surrounded by influences calculated to lead us away from God, our petitions for help and strength must be unwearied. Unless this is so, we shall never be successful in breaking down pride and overcoming the power of temptation to sinful indulgences which keep us from the Saviour. The light of truth, sanctifying the life, will discover to the receiver the sinful passions of his heart which are striving for the mastery, and which make it necessary for him to stretch every nerve and exert all his powers to resist Satan that he may conquer through the merits of Christ. *Youth's Instructor*, August 18, 1898.

CHAPTER 78

The Power of Prayer

It was in the mount with God that Moses beheld the pattern of that wonderful building which was to be the abiding-place of His glory. It is in the mount with God—the secret place of communion—that we are to contemplate His glorious ideal for humanity. Thus we shall be enabled so to fashion our character-building that to us may be fulfilled the promise, "I will dwell in them, and walk in them; and I will be their God, and they shall be My people."

While engaged in our daily work, we should lift the soul to heaven in prayer. These silent petitions rise like incense before the throne of grace; and the enemy is baffled. The Christian whose heart is thus stayed upon God cannot be overcome. No evil arts can destroy his peace. All the promises of God's Word, all the power of divine grace, all the resources of Jehovah, are pledged to secure his deliverance. It was thus that Enoch walked with God. And God was with him, a present help in every time of need.

In Touch With the Infinite

Prayer is the breath of the soul. It is the secret of spiritual power. No other means of grace can be substituted and the health of the soul be preserved. Prayer brings the heart into immediate contact with the Wellspring of life, and strengthens the sinew and muscle of the religious experience. Neglect the exercise of prayer, or engage in prayer spasmodically, now and then, as seems convenient, and you lose your hold on God. The spiritual faculties lose their vitality, the religious experience lacks health and vigor. . . .

It is a wonderful thing that we can pray effectually, that unworthy, erring mortals possess the power of offering their requests to God. What higher power can man desire than this—to be linked with the infinite God? Feeble, sinful man has the privilege of speaking to his Maker. We may utter words that reach the throne of the Monarch of the universe. We may speak with Jesus as we walk by the way, and He says, I am at thy right hand.

Every Sincere Prayer Answered

We may commune with God in our hearts; we may walk in companionship with Christ. When engaged in our daily labor, we may breathe out our heart's desire, inaudible to any human ear; but that word cannot die away into silence, nor can it be lost. Nothing can drown the soul's desire. It rises above the din of the street, above the noise of machinery. It is God to whom we are speaking, and our prayer is heard.

Ask, then; ask, and ye shall receive. Ask for humility, wisdom, courage, increase of faith. To every sincere prayer an answer will come. It may not come just as you desire, or at the time you look for it; but it will come in the way and at the time that will best meet your need. The prayers you offer in loneliness, in weariness, in trial, God answers, not always according to your expectations, but always for your good. *Gospel Workers*, pp. 254-258.

CHAPTER 79

Our Attitude In Prayer

Both in public and in private worship, it is our privilege to bow on our knees before the Lord when we offer our petitions to Him. Jesus, our example, "kneeled down, and prayed." Of His disciples it is recorded that they, too, "kneeled down, and prayed." Paul declared, "I bow my knees unto the Father of our Lord Jesus Christ." In confessing before God the sins of Israel, Ezra knelt. Daniel "kneeled upon his knees three times a day, and prayed, and gave thanks before his God."

True reverence for God is inspired by a sense of His infinite greatness and a realization of His presence. With this sense of the Unseen, every heart should be deeply impressed. The hour and place of prayer are sacred, because God is there; and as reverence is manifested in attitude and demeanor, the feeling that inspires it will be deepened. "Holy and reverend is His name," the psalmist declares. Angels, when they speak that name, veil their faces. With what reverence, then, should we, who are fallen and sinful, take it upon our lips!

Well would it be for old and young to ponder those words of Scripture that show how the place marked by God's special presence should be regarded. "Put off thy shoes from off thy feet," He commanded Moses at the burning bush," for the place whereon thou standest is holy ground." Jacob, after beholding the vision of the angels, exclaimed, "The Lord is in this place; and I knew it not. . . ." *Gospel Workers*, pp. 178, 179.

CHAPTER 80

Faith and Prayer

Through faith in Christ, every deficiency of character may be supplied, every defilement cleansed, every fault corrected, every excellence developed.

"Ye are complete in Him."

Prayer and faith are closely allied, and they need to be studied together. In the prayer of faith there is a divine science; it is a science that every one who would make his life work a success must understand. Christ says, "What things soever ye desire, when ye pray, believe that ye receive them, and ye shall have them." He makes it plain that our asking must be according to God's will; we must ask for the things that He has promised, and whatever we receive must be used in doing His will. The conditions met, the promise is unequivocal.

For the pardon of sin, for the Holy Spirit, for a Christlike temper, for wisdom and strength to do His work, for any gift He has promised, we may ask; then we are to believe that we receive, and return thanks to God that we have received.

We need look for no outward evidence of the blessing. The gift is in the promise, and we may go about our work assured that what God has promised He is able to perform, and that the gift, which we already possess, will be realized when we need it most. *Education*, pp. 257, 258.

CHAPTER 81

The Value of Bible Study

The study of the Bible is superior to all other study in strengthening the intellect. What fields of thought the youth may find to explore in the Word of God! The mind may go deeper and still deeper in its research, gathering strength with every effort to comprehend truth; and yet there is an infinity beyond.

Those who profess to love God and reverence sacred things, and yet allow the mind to come down to the superficial and unreal, are placing themselves on Satan's ground, and are doing his work. If the young would study the glorious works of God in nature, and His majesty and power as revealed in His Word, they would come from every such exercise with faculties quickened and elevated. A vigor would be received, having no kin to arrogance. By a contemplation of the marvels of divine power, the mind will learn that hardest but most useful of all lessons, that human wisdom, unless connected with the Infinite and sanctified by the grace of Christ, is foolishness.

The Mediatorial Work of Christ

The work of God's dear Son in undertaking to link the created with the Uncreated, the finite with the Infinite, in His own divine person, is a subject that may well employ our thoughts for a lifetime. This work of Christ was to confirm the beings of other worlds in their innocency and loyalty, as well as to save the lost and perishing of this world. He opened a way for the disobedient to return to their allegiance to God, while by the same act He placed a safeguard around those who were already pure, that they might not become polluted.

While we rejoice that there are worlds which have never fallen, these worlds render praise and honor and glory to Jesus Christ for the plan of redemption to save the fallen sons of Adam, as well as to confirm themselves in their position and character of purity. The arm that raised the human family from the ruin which Satan has brought upon the race through his temptations, is the arm which has preserved the inhabitants of other worlds from sin. Every world throughout immensity engages the care and support of the Father and the Son; and this care is constantly exercised for fallen humanity. Christ is mediating in behalf of man, and the order of unseen worlds also is preserved by His mediatorial work. Are not these themes of sufficient magnitude and importance to engage our thoughts, and call forth our gratitude and adoration to God?

Intellectual Development

Open the Bible to our youth, draw their attention to its hidden treasures, teach them to search for its jewels of truth, and they will gain a strength of intellect such as the study of all that philosophy embraces could not impart. The grand subjects upon which the Bible treats, the dignified simplicity of it inspired utterances, the elevated themes which it presents to the mind, the light, sharp and clear, from the throne of God, enlightening the understanding, will develop the powers of the mind to an extent that can scarcely be comprehended, and never fully explained.

The Bible presents a boundless field for the imagination, as much higher and more ennobling in character than the superficial creations of the unsanctified intellect as the heavens are higher than the earth. The inspired history of our race is placed in the hands of every individual. All may now begin their research. They may become acquainted with our first parents as they stood in Eden, in holy innocency, enjoying communion with God and sinless angels. They may trace the introduction of sin and its results upon the race, and follow, step by step, down the track of sacred history, as it records the disobedience and impenitence of man and the just retribution for sin.

The Highest Culture

The reader may hold converse with patriarchs and prophets; he may move through the most inspiring scenes; he may behold Christ, who was Monarch in heaven, equal with God, coming down to humanity, and working out the plan of redemption, breaking off from man the chains wherewith Satan had bound him, and making it possible for him to regain his godlike manhood. Christ taking upon Himself humanity, and preserving the level of man for thirty years, and then making His soul an offering for sin, that man might not be left to perish, is a subject for the deepest thought and the most concentrated study. . . .

Let the mind grasp the stupendous truths of revelation,

and it will never be content to employ its powers upon frivolous themes; it will turn with disgust from the trashy literature and idle amusements that are demoralizing the youth of today. Those who have communed with the poets and sages of the Bible, and whose souls have been stirred by the glorious deeds of the heroes of faith, will come from the rich fields of thought far more pure in heart and elevated in mind than if they had been occupied in studying the most celebrated secular authors, or in contemplating and glorifying the exploits of the Pharaohs and Herods and Caesars of the world.

The powers of the youth are mostly dormant, because they do not make the fear of God the beginning of wisdom. The Lord gave Daniel wisdom and knowledge, because he would not be influenced by any power that would interfere with his religious principles. The reason why we have so few men of mind, of stability and solid worth, is that they think to find greatness while disconnecting from Heaven.

God is not feared, and loved, and honored, by the children of men. Religion is not lived out, as well as professed. The Lord can do but little for man, because he is so easily exalted, is so ready to think himself of consequence. God would have us enlarge our capabilities, and avail ourselves of every privilege to unfold, to cultivate, to strengthen the understanding. Man was born for a higher, nobler life than that which he develops. The period of our mortal existence is preparatory to the life which measures with the life of God.

The Bible the Greatest Teacher

What subjects are presented in the Sacred Scriptures for the mind to dwell upon! Where can be found higher themes for contemplation? Where are themes so intensely interesting? In what sense are all the researches of human science comparable in sublimity and mystery with the science of the Bible? Where is anything that will so call out the strength of the intellect in deep and earnest thought?

If we will let it speak to us, the Bible will teach us what nothing else can teach. But alas! everything else is dwelt upon except the Word of God. Worthless literature, fictitious stories, are greedily devoured, while the Bible, with all its treasures of sacred truth, lies neglected upon our tables. The Sacred Word, if made the rule of life, will refine, elevate, and sanctify. It is the voice of God to man. Will we heed it?

"The entrance of Thy words giveth light; it giveth understanding unto the simple." Angels stand beside the searcher of the Scriptures, to impress and illuminate the mind. The command of Christ comes to us with the same force today as when addressed to the first disciples eighteen hundred years ago: "Search the Scriptures; for in them ye think ye have eternal life: and they are they which testify of Me." *Review and Herald*, January 11, 1881.

CHAPTER 82

Search the Scriptures for Yourself

Young men should search the Scriptures for themselves. They are not to feel that it is sufficient for those older in experience to find out the truth; that the younger ones can accept it from them as authority. The Jews perished as a nation because they were drawn from the truth of the Bible by their rulers, priests, and elders. Had they heeded the lessons of Jesus, and searched the Scriptures for themselves, they would not have perished. . . .

It is impossible for any mind to comprehend all the richness and greatness of even one promise of God. One catches the glory of one point of view, another the beauty and grace from another point, and the soul is filled with the heavenly light. If we saw all the glory, the spirit would faint. But we can bear far greater revelations from God's abundant promises than we now enjoy. It makes my heart sad to think how we lose sight of the fullness of blessing designed for us. We content ourselves with momentary flashes of spiritual illumination, when we might walk day by day in the light of His presence. *Testimonies to Ministers*, pp. 109, 111.

CHAPTER 83

Persevering Effort in Bible Study

"Search the Scriptures; for in them ye think ye have eternal life." To search means to look diligently for something which has been lost. Search for the hidden treasures in God's Word. You cannot afford to be without them. Study the difficult passages, comparing verse with verse, and you will find that Scripture is the key which unlocks Scripture.

Those who prayerfully study the Bible go from each search wiser than they were before. Some of their difficulties have been solved; for the Holy Spirit has done the work spoken of in the fourteenth chapter of John: "The Comforter, which is the Holy Ghost, whom the Father will send in My name, He shall teach you all things, and bring all things to your remembrance, whatsoever I have said unto you."

Nothing worth having is obtained without earnest, persevering effort. In business, only those who have a will to do see successful results. Without earnest toil we cannot expect to obtain a knowledge of spiritual things. Those who obtain the jewels of truth must dig for them as a miner digs for the precious ore hidden in the earth.

Those who work indifferently and half-heartedly will never succeed. Young and old should read the Word of God; and not only should they read it, but they should study it with diligent earnestness, praying, believing, and searching. Thus they will find the hidden treasure; for the Lord will quicken their understanding.

Open-mindedness

In your study of the Word, lay at the door of investigation your preconceived opinions and your hereditary and cultivated ideas. You will never reach the truth if you study the Scriptures to vindicate your own ideas. Leave these at the door, and with a contrite heart go in to hear what the Lord has to say to you. As the humble seeker for truth sits at Christ's feet, and learns of Him, the Word gives him understanding. To those who are too wise in their own conceit to study the Bible, Christ says, You must become meek and lowly in heart if you desire to become wise unto salvation.

Do not read the Word in the light of former opinions; but, with a mind free from prejudice, search it carefully and prayerfully. If, as you read, conviction comes, and you see that your cherished opinions are not in harmony with the Word, do not try to make the Word fit these opinions. Make your opinions fit the Word. Do not allow what you have believed or practiced in the past to control your understanding. Open the eyes of your mind to behold wondrous things out of the law. Find out what is written, and then plant your feet on the eternal Rock.

The Knowledge of God's Will

Our salvation depends upon our knowledge of God's will as it is contained in His Word. Never cease asking and searching for Truth. You need to know your duty. You need to know what you must do to be saved. And it is God's will that you shall know what He has said to you. But you must exercise faith. As you search the Scriptures, you must believe that God is, and that He rewards those who diligently seek Him.

O search the Bible with a heart hungry for spiritual food! Dig into the Word as a miner digs into the earth to find the veins of gold. Do not give up your search till you have learned your relation to God and His will concerning you. *Youth's Instructor*, July 24, 1902.

Reverence in Bible Study

We should come with reverence to the study of the Bible, feeling that we are in the presence of God. All lightness and trifling should be laid aside. While some portions of the Word are easily understood, the true meaning of other parts is not so readily discerned. There must be patient study and meditation, and earnest prayer. Every student, as he opens the Scriptures, should ask for the enlightenment of the Holy Spirit; and the promise is sure that it will be given.

The spirit in which you come to the investigation of the Scriptures will determine the character of the assistant at your side. Angels from the world of light will be with those who in humility of heart seek for divine guidance. But if the Bible is opened with irreverence, with a feeling of self-sufficiency, if the heart is filled with prejudice, Satan is beside you, and he will set the plain statements of God's Word in a perverted light. *Testimonies to Ministers*, pp. 107-108.

CHAPTER 84

The Reward of Diligent Bible Study

The search for truth will reward the seeker at every turn, and each discovery will open up richer fields for his investigation. Men are changed in accordance with what they contemplate. If commonplace thoughts and affairs take up the attention, the man will be commonplace. If he is too negligent to obtain anything but a superficial understanding of God's truth, he will not receive the rich blessings that God would be pleased to bestow upon him. It is a law of the mind, that it will narrow or expand to the dimensions of the things with which it becomes familiar.

The mental powers will surely become contracted, and will lose their ability to grasp the deep meanings of the Word of God, unless they are put vigorously and persistently to the task of searching for truth. The mind will enlarge, if it is employed in tracing out the relation of the subjects of the Bible, comparing scripture with scripture, and spiritual things with spiritual. Go below the surface; the richest treasures of thought are waiting for the skillful and diligent student. *Review and Herald*, July 17, 1888.

The Bible a Guide

Let the student take the Bible as his guide, and stand firm for principle, and he may aspire to any height of attainment. *The Ministry of Healing*, p. 465.

CHAPTER 85

The Bible as an Educator

As an educator, the Holy Scriptures are without a rival. The Bible is the most ancient and the most comprehensive history that men possess. It came fresh from the Fountain of eternal truth; and throughout the ages a divine hand has preserved its purity. It lights up the far-distant past, where human research seeks in vain to penetrate. In God's Word only do we behold the power that laid the foundations of the earth, and that stretched out the heavens. Here only do we find an authentic account of the origin of nations. Here only is given a history of our race unsullied by human pride or prejudice.

The Voice of the Eternal

In the Word of God the mind finds subjects for the deepest thought, the loftiest aspirations. Here we may hold communion with patriarchs and prophets, and listen to the voice of the Eternal as He speaks with men. Here we behold the Majesty of heaven as He humbled Himself to become our substitute and surety, to cope single-handed with the powers of darkness, and to gain the victory in our behalf. A reverent contemplation of such themes as these cannot fail to soften, purify, and ennoble the heart, and at the same time to inspire the mind with new strength and vigor.

Those who regard it as brave and manly to treat the claims of God with indifference and contempt, are thereby betraying their own folly and ignorance. While they boast their freedom and independence, they are really in bondage to sin and Satan.

True Philosophy of Life

A clear conception of what God is, and what He requires us to be, will lead to wholesome humility. He who studies aright the sacred Word will learn that human intellect is not omnipotent. He will learn that without the help which none but God can give, human strength and wisdom are but weakness and ignorance.

He who is following the divine guidance has found the only true source of saving grace and real happiness, and has gained the power of imparting happiness to all around him. No man can really enjoy life without religion. Love to God purifies and ennobles every taste and desire, intensifies every affection, and brightens every worthy pleasure. It enables men to appreciate and enjoy all that is true, and good, and beautiful.

But that which above all other considerations should lead us to prize the Bible, is that in it is revealed to men the will of God. Here we learn the object of our creation, and the means by which that object may be attained. We learn how to improve wisely the present life, and how to secure the future life. No other book can satisfy the questionings of the mind or the cravings of the heart. By obtaining a knowledge of God's Word and giving heed thereto, men may rise from the lowest depths of degradation to become the sons of God, the associates of sinless angels. *Counsels to Teachers, Parents, and Students*, pp. 52-54.

CHAPTER 86

Reverence

It is your privilege, dear young friends, to glorify God upon the earth. In order to do this, you must direct your minds away from things that are superficial, frivolous, and unimportant, to those that are of eternal worth.

We are living in an age when all should especially give heed to the injunction of the Saviour, "Watch and pray, that ye enter not into temptation." One of your strong temptations is to irreverence. God is high and holy; and to the humble, believing soul, His house on earth, the place where His people meet for worship, is as the gate of heaven. The song of praise, the words spoken by Christ's ministers, are God's appointed agencies to prepare a people for the church above, for that loftier worship into which there can enter nothing that is impure, unholy. . . .

Conduct in the House of God

Reverence is greatly needed in the youth of this age. I am alarmed as I see children and youth of religious parents so heedless of the order and propriety that should be observed in the house of God. While God's servants are presenting the words of life to the people, some will be reading, others whispering and laughing. Their eyes are sinning by diverting the attention of those around them. This habit, if allowed to remain unchecked, will grow and influence others.

Children and youth should never feel that it is something to be proud of to be indifferent and careless in meetings where God is worshiped. God sees every irreverent thought or action, and it is registered in the books of heaven. He says, "I know thy works." Nothing is hid from His all-searching eye. If you have formed in any degree the habit of inattention and indifference in the house of God, exercise the powers you have to correct it, and show that you have self-respect. Practice reverence until it becomes a part of yourself.

Do not have so little reverence for the house and worship of God as to communicate with one another during the sermon. If those who commit this fault could see the angels of God looking upon them and marking their doings, they would be filled with shame and abhorrence of themselves. God wants attentive hearers. It was while men slept, that the enemy sowed tares.

Nothing that is sacred, nothing that pertains to the worship of God, should be treated with carelessness and indifference. When the word of life is spoken, you should remember that you are listening to the voice of God through His delegated servant. Do not lose these words through inattention; if heeded, they may keep your feet from straying into wrong paths.

Trifling Regarding Religious Things

I am sorry to see that many youth who profess religion do not have any knowledge of a change of heart. There is no transformation of character. They do not realize that it is a solemn thing to profess to be a Christian. Their life is entirely inconsistent with a religious frame of mind. If they were of that number who are indeed the sons and daughters of God, they would not be filled with nonsense and pleasantry and trifling; neither would the foolish remarks and conduct of others awaken the same in them. A mind that is intent upon having the prize, upon securing heaven, will reject with firm, determined purpose every attempt at wit and jest concerning religious things.

There is great danger in indifference upon this subject; no folly is so subtle as thoughtlessness and levity. On every hand we see youth of a frivolous character. All young people of this class should be avoided; for they are dangerous. If they profess to be Christians, they are the more to be dreaded. Their minds have been cast in an inferior mold; and it will be far easier for them to bring you down to their level than for you to bring them up to elevated and ennobling thoughts and a correct course of action. Let your companions be those who observe decorum in words and deportment.

In order to do your best in showing forth the praises of God, your associations must be such as to keep in your minds the sacred distinct from the common. If you would have broad views, noble thoughts and aspirations, choose associations that will strengthen right principles. Let every thought and the purpose of every action bend to the securing of the future life, with eternal happiness. *Youth's Instructor*, October 8, 1896.

CHAPTER 87

A Well-grounded Hope

How are you to know that you are accepted of God? Study His Word prayerfully. Lay it not aside for any other book. This book convinces of sin. It plainly reveals the way of salvation. It brings to view a bright and glorious reward. It reveals to you a complete Saviour, and teaches you that through His boundless mercy alone can you expect salvation.

Do not neglect secret prayer, for it is the soul of religion. With earnest, fervent prayer, plead for purity of soul. Plead as earnestly, as eagerly, as you would for your mortal life, were it at stake. Remain before God until unutterable longings are begotten within you for salvation, and the sweet evidence is obtained of pardoned sin.

The hope of eternal life is not to be received upon slight grounds. It is a subject to be settled between God and your own soul—settled for eternity. A supposed hope, and nothing more, will prove your ruin. Since you are to stand or fall by the Word of God, it is to that Word you must look for testimony in your case. There you can see what is required of you to become a Christian. Do not lay off your armor, or leave the battlefield until you have obtained the victory, and triumph in your Redeemer. *Testimonies for the Church*, Vol. 1, pp. 163, 164.

SECTION IX
Reading and Music

Young men and young women, read the literature that will give you true knowledge, and that will be a help to the entire family. Say firmly: "I will not spend precious moments in reading that which will be of no profit to me, and which only unfits me to be of service to others. I will devote my time and my thoughts to acquiring a fitness for God's service. I will close my eyes to frivolous and sinful things. My ears are the Lord's, and I will not listen to the subtle reasoning of the enemy. My voice shall not in any way be subject to a will that is not under the influence of the Spirit of God. My body is the temple of the Holy Spirit, and every power of my being shall be consecrated to worthy pursuits."
Testimonies for the Church, *Vol. 7, p. 64.*

CHAPTER 88

Choice of Reading

Education is but a preparation of the physical, intellectual, and spiritual powers for the best performance of all the duties of life. The powers of endurance, and the strength and activity of the brain, are lessened or increased by the way in which they are employed. The mind should be so disciplined that all its powers will be symmetrically developed.

Many youth are eager for books. They desire to read everything that they can obtain. Let them take heed what they read as well as what they hear. I have been instructed that they are in the greatest danger of being corrupted by improper reading. Satan has a thousand ways of unsettling the minds of youth. They cannot safely be off guard for a moment. They must set a watch upon their minds, that they may not be allured by the enemy's temptations.

Influence of Unwholesome Reading

Satan knows that to a great degree the mind is affected by that upon which it feeds. He is seeking to lead both the youth and those of mature age to read story-books, tales, and other literature. The readers of such literature become unfitted for the duties lying before them. They live an unreal life, and have no desire to search the Scriptures, to feed upon the heavenly manna. The mind that needs strengthening is enfeebled, and loses its power to study the great truths that relate to the mission and work of Christ—truths that would fortify the mind, awaken the imagination, and kindle a strong, earnest desire to overcome as Christ overcame.

Enemies to Spirituality

Could a large share of the books published be consumed, a plague would be stayed that is doing a fearful work upon mind and heart. Love stories, frivolous and exciting tales, and even that class of books called religious novels—books in which the author attaches to his story a moral lesson—are a curse to the readers. Religious sentiments may be woven all through a story-book, but, in most cases, Satan is but clothed in angel-robes, the more effectively to deceive and allure. None are so confirmed in right principles, none so secure from temptation, that they are safe in reading these stories.

The readers of fiction are indulging an evil that destroys spirituality, eclipsing the beauty of the sacred page. It creates an unhealthy excitement, fevers the imagination, unfits the mind for usefulness, weans the soul from prayer, and disqualifies it for any spiritual exercise.

God has endowed many of our youth with superior capabilities; but too often they have enervated their powers, confused and enfeebled their minds, so that for years they have made no growth in grace or in a knowledge of the reasons of our faith, because of their unwise choice of reading. Those who are looking for the Lord soon to come, looking for that wondrous change, when "this corruptible shall put on incorruption," should in this probationary time be standing upon a higher plane of action.

My dear young friends, question your own experience as to the influence of exciting stories. Can you, after such reading, open the Bible and read with interest the words of life? Do you not find the Book of God uninteresting? The charm of that love story is upon the mind, destroying its healthy tone, and making it impossible for you to fix the attention upon the important, solemn truths that concern your eternal welfare.

Resolutely discard all trashy reading. It will not strengthen your spirituality, but will introduce into the mind sentiments that pervert the imagination, causing you to think less of Jesus and to dwell less upon His precious lessons. Keep the mind free from everything that would lead it in a wrong direction. Do not encumber it with trashy stories, which impart no strength to the mental powers. The thoughts are of the same character as the food provided for the mind.

The Book of Books

The nature of one's religious experience is revealed by the character of the books one chooses to read in one's leisure moments. In order to have a healthy tone of mind and sound religious principles, the youth must live in communion with God through His Word. Pointing out the way of salvation through Christ, the Bible is our guide to a higher, better life. It contains the most interesting and the most instructive history and biography that were ever written. Those whose imagination has not become perverted by the reading of fiction will find the Bible the most interesting of books.

The Bible is the book of books. If you love the Word of God, searching it as you have opportunity, that you may come into possession of its rich treasures, and be thoroughly furnished unto all good works, then you may be assured that Jesus is drawing you to Himself. But to read the Scriptures in a casual way, without seeking to comprehend Christ's lesson that you may comply with His requirements, is not enough. There are treasures in the Word of God that can be discovered only by sinking the shaft deep into the mine of truth.

The carnal mind rejects the truth; but the soul that is converted undergoes a marvelous change. The book that before was unattractive because it revealed truths which testified against the sinner, now becomes the food of the soul, the joy and consolation of the life. The Sun of Righteousness illuminates the sacred pages, and the Holy Spirit speaks through them to the soul. . . .

Let all who have cultivated a love for light reading, now turn their attention to the sure word of prophecy. Take your Bibles, and begin to study with fresh interest the sacred records of the Old and New Testaments. The oftener and more diligently you study the Bible, the more beautiful will it appear, and the less relish you will have for light reading. Bind this precious volume to your hearts. It will be to you a friend and guide. *Youth's Instructor*, October 9, 1902.

CHAPTER 89

Example of the Ephesians

When the Ephesians were converted, they changed their habits and practices. Under the conviction of the Spirit of God, they acted with promptness, and laid bare all the mysteries of their witchcraft. They came and confessed, and showed their deeds, and their souls were filled with holy indignation because they had given such devotion to magic, and had so highly prized the books in which the rules of Satan's devising had laid down the methods whereby they might practice witchcraft. They were determined to turn from the service of the evil one, and they brought their costly volumes and publicly burned them. Thus they made manifest their sincerity in turning to God. . . .

The books the Ephesians committed to the flames on their conversion to the gospel, they formerly delighted in, and permitted them to rule their consciences and guide their minds. They might have sold them, but by so doing the evil would be perpetuated. They afterward abhorred the satanic mysteries, the magical arts, and regarded with aversion the knowledge they had obtained from them. I would ask the young who have been connected with the truth, Have you burned your magical books?

The Magic Books of Today

We do not charge you with the evil that had bound the Ephesians, or claim that you have practiced magic, and dealt in the arts of sorcery in the same way as they had. We do not say that you have followed the mysteries of necromancy, or held communion with evil spirits. But are you not in communion with the author of all evil, with the deviser of all these mysteries and hellish arts? Do you not listen to the suggestions of him who is the god of this world, the prince of the power of the air? Have you not submitted to his falsehoods, and yielded yourselves as his agents to work that which was in harmony with your life before conversion? Have you not given yourselves up to be Satan's agents and, in a broader sense, are you not holding intercourse with fallen angels, and learning lessons from them in the art of deceiving your own souls and the souls of others?

What about the magical books? What have you been reading? How have you been employing your time? Have you been seeking to study the sacred oracles in order that you may hear the voice of God speaking to you out of His Word? The world is deluged with books which sow the seeds of skepticism, infidelity, and atheism, and to a larger or less degree you have been learning your lessons from these books, and they are magical books. They put God out of the mind, and separate the soul from the true Shepherd.

Mind Unfitted for Solemn Thought

The volumes you have read have been devised by the agents of Satan to bewitch the mind with theories formed in the synagogue of Satan, to show you how you may serve the evil one with satanic dignity. How numerous are the books of infidel tendencies, which are calculated to unsettle the mind through specious doubts! Satan has breathed his poisonous breath upon them, and a deadly, spiritual malaria affects the soul that reads them.

What a mass of fictitious reading is there in the world, to fill the mind with fancies and follies, thus creating a disrelish for the words of truth and righteousness! The mind is thus unfitted for solemn thought, for patient, persevering investigation of the Scriptures, which is the guide book by which you are to be directed to the paradise of God.

Much is written in regard to gaining earthly treasure, as though the wealth of this world would buy us a passport into heaven. What volumes of history have been written, filled with the daring, presumptuous achievements of men whose lives do not throw one glimmer of light upon the pathway that leads to the better country!

Misleading Books

How many books are there concerning war and bloodshed, which mislead the youth! As they read, Satan stands at their side to inspire them with the spirit of the warrior of whom they read, and their blood becomes heated in their veins, and they are stirred up to do cruel actions. How numerous are immoral books, which lead to unholy desires, and fire the passions of the heart, and lead away from all that is pure and holy!

You have had your magical books, in which the very scenes and pictures were inspired by him who was once an exalted angel in the courts of heaven. . . .

Breaking the Spell of Satan's Sorcery

I would ask, Shall the magical books be burned up? In the synagogue of Satan there are places of attraction where licentiousness is fostered and indulged; but the witness is there, and an unseen visitant testifies to the deeds done in darkness. In the associations of the vain, the proud, the mirthful, Satan presides, and is the chief mover in scenes of gayety. He is there in disguise. Witchcraft is going on around us on every hand, and the world and the church are under the influence of one who will lead them to do things they never dreamed of doing. Should they be informed of the deeds they will perform, they would be as much astonished as was Hazael when the prophet told him of his future course. . . .

Every man, woman, and child that is not under the control of the Spirit of God is under the influence of Satan's sorcery, and by his words and example he will lead others away from the path of truth. When the transforming grace of Christ is upon the heart, a righteous indignation will take possession of the soul because the sinner has so long neglected the great salvation that God has provided for him. He will then surrender himself, body, soul, and spirit, to God and will withdraw from companionship with Satan, through the grace given him of God. He will, like the Ephesians, denounce sorcery, and will cut the last thread that binds him to Satan. He will leave the banner of the prince of darkness, and will come under the bloodstained banner of Prince Emmanuel. He will burn the magical books. *Youth's Instructor*, November 16, 1893.

CHAPTER 90

Proper Mental Food

What shall our children read? is a serious question, and demands a serious answer. I am troubled to see, in Christian families, periodicals and newspapers containing continued stories that leave no impress of good upon the mind. I have watched those whose taste for fiction has been thus cultivated. They have had the privilege of listening to the truths of God's Word, of becoming acquainted with the reasons of our faith; but they have grown to mature years destitute of true piety.

These dear youth need so much to put into their character building the very best material—the love and fear of God and a knowledge of Christ. But many have not an intelligent understanding of the truth as it is in Jesus. The mind is feasted upon sensational stories. They live in an unreal world, and are unfitted for the practical duties of life.

Results of Reading Fiction

I have observed children allowed to come up in this way. Whether at home or abroad, they are either restless or dreamy, and are unable to converse, save upon the most commonplace subjects. The nobler faculties, those adapted to higher pursuits, have been degraded to the contemplation of trivial or worse than trivial subjects, until their possessor has become satisfied with such topics, and scarcely has power to reach anything higher. Religious thought and conversation has become distasteful.

The mental food for which he has acquired a relish is contaminating in its effects, and leads to impure and sensual thoughts. I have felt sincere pity for these souls as I have considered how much they are losing by neglecting opportunities to gain a knowledge of Christ, in whom our hopes of eternal life are centered. How much precious time is wasted, in which they might be studying the Pattern of true goodness.

I am personally acquainted with some who have lost the healthy tone of the mind through wrong habits of reading. They go through life with a diseased imagination, magnifying every little grievance. Things which a sound, sensible mind would not notice, become to them unendurable trials, insurmountable obstacles. To them, life is in constant shadow.

Those who have indulged the habit of racing through exciting stories, are crippling their mental strength, and disqualifying themselves for vigorous thought and research. There are men and women now in the decline of life who have never recovered from the effects of intemperate reading.

The habit, formed in early years, has grown with their growth and strengthened with their strength; and their efforts to overcome it, though determined, have been only partially successful. Many have never recovered their original vigor of mind. All attempts to become practical Christians end with the desire. They cannot be truly Christlike, and continue to feed the mind upon this class of literature.

Nor is the physical effect less disastrous. The nervous

system is unnecessarily taxed by this passion for reading. In some cases youth, and even those of mature age, have been afflicted with paralysis from no other cause than excess in reading. The mind was kept under constant excitement until the delicate machinery of the brain became so weakened that it could not act, and paralysis was the result.

Mental Inebriates

When an appetite for exciting, sensational stories is cultivated, the moral taste becomes perverted, and the mind is unsatisfied unless constantly fed upon this trashy, unwholesome food. I have seen young ladies, professed followers of Christ, who were really unhappy unless they had on hand some new novel or story-paper. The mind craved stimulation as the drunkard craves intoxicating drink. These youth manifested no spirit of devotion; no heavenly light was shed upon their associates to lead them to the fount of knowledge. They had no deep, religious experience. If this class of reading had not been constantly before them, there might have been some hope of their reforming; but they craved it, and would have it.

I am pained to see young men and women thus ruining their usefulness in this life, and failing to obtain an experience that will prepare them for an eternal life in heavenly society. We can find no more fit name for them than "mental inebriates."

Intemperate habits of reading exert a pernicious influence upon the brain as surely as does intemperance in eating and drinking.

The Remedy

The best way to prevent the growth of evil is to preoccupy the soil. The greatest care and watchfulness is needed in cultivating the mind and sowing therein the precious seeds of Bible truth. The Lord, in His great mercy, has revealed to us in the Scriptures the rules of holy living. . . .

He has inspired holy men to record, for our benefit, instruction concerning the dangers that beset the path, and how to escape them. Those who obey His injunction to search the Scriptures will not be ignorant of these things. Amid the perils of the last days, every member of the church should understand the reasons of his hope and faith—reasons which are not difficult of comprehension. There is enough to occupy the mind, if we would grow in grace and in the knowledge of our Lord Jesus Christ. *Christian Temperance and Bible Hygiene*, pp. 123-126. (1890.)

First Steps in Sin

A long preparatory process, unknown to the world, goes on in the heart before the Christian commits open sin. The mind does not come down at once from purity and holiness to depravity, corruption, and crime. It takes time to degrade those formed in the image of God to the brutal or the satanic. By beholding, we become changed. By the indulgence of impure thoughts, man can so educate his mind that sin which he once loathed will become pleasant to Him. *Patriarchs and Prophets*, p. 459.

CHAPTER 91

The Bible the Most Interesting Book

Both old and young neglect the Bible. They do not make it their study, the rule of their life. Especially are the young guilty of this neglect. Most of them find time to read other books, but the book that points out the way to eternal life is not daily studied. Idle stories are attentively read, while the Bible is neglected. This book is our guide to a higher, holier life. The youth would pronounce it the most interesting book they ever read had not their imagination been perverted by the reading of fictitious stories.

Youthful minds fail to reach their noblest development when they neglect the highest source of wisdom—the Word of God. That we are in God's world, in the presence of the Creator; that we are made in His likeness; that He watches over us and loves us and cares for us—these are wonderful themes for thought, and lead the mind into broad, exalted fields of meditation. He who opens mind and heart to the contemplation of such themes as these will never be satisfied with trivial, sensational subjects.

The importance of seeking a through knowledge of the Scriptures can hardly be estimated. "Given by inspiration of God," able to make us "wise unto salvation," rendering the man of God "perfect, throughly furnished unto all good works" (2 Timothy 3:15-17), the Bible has the highest claim to our reverent attention. We should not be satisfied with a superficial knowledge, but should seek to learn the full meaning of the words of truth, to drink deep of the spirit of the Holy Oracles. *Counsels to Teachers, Parents, and Students*, pp. 138, 139.

The Portrayal of Sin

Books on sensational topics, published and circulated as a money-making scheme, might better never be read by the youth. There is a satanic fascination in such books. The heart-sickening recital of crimes and atrocities has a bewitching power upon many, exciting them to see what they can do to bring themselves into notice, even by the wickedest deeds. The enormities, the cruelties, the licentious practices, portrayed in some of the strictly historical writings have acted as leaven on many minds, leading to the commission of similar acts.

Books that delineate the satanic practices of human beings are giving publicity to evil. These horrible particulars need not be lived over, and no one who believes the truth for this time should act a part in perpetuating the memory of them. When the intellect is fed and stimulated by this depraved food, the thoughts become impure and sensual. *Counsels to Teachers, Parents, and Students*, pp. 133, 134.

CHAPTER 92

Guard Well the Avenues of the Soul

"Keep thy heart with all diligence," is the counsel of the wise man; "for out of it are the issues of life." As man "thinketh in his heart, so is he." The heart must be renewed by divine grace, or it will be in vain to seek for purity of life. He who attempts to build up a noble, virtuous character independent of the grace of Christ, is building his house upon the shifting sand. In the fierce storms of temptation it will surely be overthrown. David's prayer should be the petition of every soul: "Create in me a clean heart, O God; and renew a right spirit within me." And having become partakers of the heavenly gift, we are to go on unto perfection, being "kept by the power of God, through faith."

Yet we have a work to do to resist temptation. Those who would not fall a prey to Satan's devices must guard well the avenues of the soul; they must avoid reading, seeing, or hearing that which will suggest impure thoughts. The mind should not be left to wander at random upon every subject that the adversary of souls may suggest. "Gird up the loins of your mind," says the apostle Peter, "be sober, . . . not fashioning yourselves according to the former lusts in your ignorance: but as He which hath called you is holy, so be ye holy in all manner of living." Says Paul, "Whatsoever things are true, whatsoever things are honest, whatsoever things are just, whatsoever things are pure, whatsoever things are lovely, whatsoever things are of good report; if there be any virtue, and if there be any praise, think on these things." This will require earnest prayer and unceasing watchfulness. We must be aided by the abiding influence of the Holy Spirit, which will attract the mind upward, and habituate it to dwell on pure and holy things. And we must give diligent study to the Word of God. "Wherewithal shall a young man cleanse his way? By taking heed thereto according to Thy word." "Thy word," says the Psalmist, "have I hid in mine heart, that I might not sin against Thee." *Patriarchs and Prophets*, p. 460.

The Chaff and the Wheat

Dear youth, cease to read the magazines containing stories. Put away every novel. . . . We would do well to clear our houses of all the story magazines and the publications containing ridiculous pictures—representations originated by satanic agencies. The youth cannot afford to poison their minds with such things. "What is the chaff to the wheat?" Let every one who claims to be a follower of Christ read only that which is true and of eternal value.

We must prepare ourselves for most solemn duties. A world is to be saved. . . . In view of the great work to be done, how can any one afford to waste precious time and God-given means in doing those things that are not for his best good or for the glory of God? *Youth's Instructor*, August 14, 1906.

CHAPTER 93

Building Christian Character*

There are books that are of vital importance that are not looked at by our young people. They are neglected because they are not so interesting to them as some lighter reading.

We should advise the young to take hold of such reading matter as recommends itself for the upholding of Christian character. The most essential points of our faith should be stamped upon the memory of the young. They have had a glimpse of these truths, but not such an acquaintance as would lead them to look upon their study with favor. Our youth should read that which will have a healthful, sanctifying effect upon the mind. This they need in order to be able to discern what is true religion. There is much good reading that is not sanctifying.

Now is our time and opportunity to labor for the young people. Tell them that we are now in a perilous crisis, and we want to know how to discern true godliness. Our young people need to be helped, uplifted, and encouraged, but in the right manner; not, perhaps, as they would desire it, but in a way that will help them to have sanctified minds. They need good, sanctifying religion more than anything else.

I do not expect to live long. My work is nearly done. Tell our young people that I want my words to encourage them in that

*This was Sister White's last message for our young people, during her last illness.

manner of life that will be most attractive to the heavenly intelligences, and that their influence upon others may be most ennobling.

Selected Course of Reading Recommended

In the night season I was selecting and laying aside books that are of no advantage to the young. We should select for them books that will encourage them to sincerity of life, and lead them to the opening of the Word. This has been presented to me in the past, and I thought I would get it before you and make it secure. We cannot afford to give to young people valueless reading. Books that are a blessing to mind and soul are needed. These things are too lightly regarded; therefore our people should become acquainted with what I am saying.

I do not think I shall have more Testimonies for our people. Our men of solid minds know what is good for the uplifting and upbuilding of the work. But with the love of God in their hearts, they need to go deeper and deeper into the study of the things of God. I am very anxious that our young people shall have the proper class of reading; then the old people will get it also. We must keep our eyes on the religious attraction of the truth. We are to keep mind and brain open to the truths of God's Word. Satan comes when men are unaware. We are not to be satisfied because the message of warning has been once presented. We must present it again and again.

We could begin a course of reading so intensely interesting that it would attract and influence many minds. If I am spared for further labor, I should gladly help to prepare books for the young.

There is a work to be done for the young by which their minds will be impressed and molded by the sanctifying truth of God. It is my sincere wish for our young people that they find the true meaning of justification by faith, and the perfection of character that will prepare them for eternal life. I do not expect to live long, and I leave this message for the young, that the aim which they make shall not miscarry.

I exhort my brethren to encourage the young ever to keep the preciousness and grace of God highly exalted. Work and pray constantly for a sense of the preciousness of true religion. Bring in the blessedness and the attractiveness of holiness and the grace of God. I have felt a burden regarding this because I know it is neglected.

I have no assurance that my life will last long, but I feel that I am accepted of the Lord. He knows how much I have suffered as I have witnessed the low standards of living adopted by so-called Christians. I have felt that it was imperative that the truth should be seen in my life, and that my testimony should go to the people. I want that you should do all you can to have my writings placed in the hands of the people in foreign lands.

Tell the young that they have had many spiritual advantages. God wants them to make earnest efforts to get the truth before the people. I am impressed that it is my special duty to say these things. *Fundamentals of Christian Education*, pp. 547-549.

CHAPTER 94

The Effect of Fiction

Many of the youth say, "I have no time to study my lesson." But what are they doing? Some are crowding in every moment to earn a few cents more, when this time pressed into work, if given to the study of the Bible would, if they practiced its lessons, save them more than the amount gained by overwork. It would save much that is expended in needless ornaments, and preserve vigor of mind to understand the mystery of godliness. "The fear of the Lord is the beginning of wisdom."

But these very youth who profess to be Christians gratify the desires of the carnal heart in following their own inclinations; and God-given, probationary time, granted them to become acquainted with the precious truths of the Bible, is devoted to the reading of fictitious tales. This habit once formed is difficult to overcome; but it can be done, it must be done by all who are candidates for the heavenly world.

That mind is ruined which is allowed to be absorbed in story-reading. The imagination becomes diseased, sentimentalism takes possession of the mind, and there is a vague unrest, a strange appetite for unwholesome mental food, which is constantly unbalancing the mind. Thousands are today in the insane asylum whose minds became unbalanced by novel reading, which results in air-castle building and love-sick sentimentalism. *Signs of the Times*, February 10, 1881.

CHAPTER 95

The Benefits of Music

The melody of praise is the atmosphere of heaven; and when heaven comes in touch with the earth there is music and song—"thanksgiving, and the voice of melody."

Above the new-created earth, as it lay, fair and unblemished, under the smile of God, "the morning stars sang together, and all the sons of God shouted for joy." So human hearts, in sympathy with heaven, have responded to God's goodness in notes of praise. Many of the events of human history have been linked with song. . . .

Music a Precious Gift

The history of the songs of the Bible is full of suggestion as to the uses and benefits of music and song. Music is often perverted to serve purposes of evil, and it thus becomes one of the most alluring agencies of temptation. But, rightly employed, it is a precious gift of God, designed to uplift the thoughts to high and noble themes, to inspire and elevate the soul.

As the children of Israel, journeying through the wilderness, cheered their way by the music of sacred song, so God bids His children today gladden their pilgrim life. There are few means more effective for fixing His words in the memory than repeating them in song. And such song has wonderful power. It has power to subdue rude and uncultivated natures; power to quicken thought and to awaken sympathy, to promote harmony of action, and to banish the gloom and foreboding that destroy courage and weaken effort.

It is one of the most effective means of impressing the heart with spiritual truth. How often to the soul hard-pressed and ready to despair, memory recalls some word of God's—the long-forgotten burden of a childhood song—and temptations lose their power, life takes on new meaning and new purpose, and courage and gladness are imparted to other souls!

The value of song as a means of education should never be lost sight of. Let there be singing in the home, of songs that are sweet and pure, and there will be fewer words of censure, and more of cheerfulness and hope and joy. Let there be singing in the school, and the pupils will be drawn closer to God, to their teachers, and to one another.

As a part of religious service, singing is as much an act of worship as is prayer. Indeed, many a song is prayer. If the child is taught to realize this, he will think more of the meaning of the words he sings, and will be more susceptible to their power.

As our Redeemer leads us to the threshold of the Infinite, flushed with the glory of God, we may catch the themes of praise and thanksgiving from the heavenly choir round about the throne; and as the echo of the angels' song is awakened in our earthly homes, hearts will be drawn closer to the heavenly singers. Heaven's communion begins on earth. We learn here the keynote of its praise. *Education*, pp. 161-168.

CHAPTER 96

Uses of Music

Music was made to serve a holy purpose, to lift the thoughts to that which is pure, noble, and elevating, and to awaken in the soul devotion and gratitude to God. What a contrast between the ancient custom and the uses to which music is now too often devoted! How many employ this gift to exalt self, instead of using it to glorify God! A love for music leads the unwary to unite with world lovers in pleasure gatherings where God has forbidden His children to go. Thus that which is a great blessing, when rightly used, becomes one of the most successful agencies by which Satan allures the mind from duty and from the contemplation of eternal things.

Music forms a part of God's worship in the courts above, and we should endeavor, in our songs of praise, to approach as nearly as possible to the harmony of the heavenly choirs. The proper training of the voice is an important feature in education, and should not be neglected. *Patriarchs and Prophets*, p. 594.

A Talent of Influence

There are those who have a special gift of song, and there are times when a special message is borne by one singing alone or by several uniting in song. But the singing is seldom to be done by a few. The ability to sing is a talent of influence, which God desires all to cultivate and use to His name's glory. *Testimonies for the Church*, Vol. 7, pp. 115, 116.

In Tune with Heavenly Musicians

When human beings sing with the spirit and the understanding, heavenly musicians take up the strain and join in the song of thanksgiving. He who has bestowed upon us all the gifts that enable us to be workers together with God, expects His servants to cultivate their voices, so that they can speak and sing in a way that all can understand. It is not loud singing that is needed, but clear intonation, correct pronunciation, and distinct utterance. Let all take time to cultivate the voice, so that God's praise can be sung in clear, soft tones, not with harshness and shrillness that offend the ear. The ability to sing is the gift of God; let it be used to His glory.

In the meetings held, let a number be chosen to take part in the song service. And let the singing be accompanied with musical instruments skilfully handled. We are not to oppose the use of instrumental music in our work. This part of the service is to be carefully conducted; for it is the praise of God in song.

The singing is not always to be done by a few. As often as possible, let the entire congregation join. *Testimonies for the Church*, Vol. 9, pp. 143, 144.

God Glorified by Songs

God is glorified by songs of praise from a pure heart filled with love and devotion to Him. *Testimonies for the Church*, Vol 1, p. 509.

CHAPTER 97

A Wrong Use of Music

Angels are hovering around yonder dwelling. The young are there assembled; there is the sound of vocal and instrumental music. Christians are gathered there, but what is that you hear? It is a song, a frivolous ditty, fit for the dance hall. Behold, the pure angels gather their light closer around them, and darkness envelops those in that dwelling. The angels are moving from the scene. Sadness is upon their countenances. Behold, they are weeping. This I saw repeated a number of times all through the ranks of Sabbath keepers, and especially in _____. Music has occupied the hours which should have been devoted to prayer. Music is the idol which many professed Sabbath-keeping Christians worship. Satan has no objection to music, if he can make that a channel through which to gain access to the minds of the youth. Anything will suit his purpose that will divert the mind from God, and engage the time which should be devoted to His service. He works through the means which will exert the strongest influence to hold the largest numbers in a pleasing infatuation, while they are paralyzed by his power. When turned to good account, music is a blessing, but it is often made one of Satan's most attractive agencies to ensnare souls. When abused, it leads the unconsecrated to pride, vanity, and folly. When allowed to take the place of devotion and prayer, it is a terrible curse. Young persons assemble to sing and, although professed

Christians, frequently dishonor God and their faith by their frivolous conversation and their choice of music. Sacred music is not congenial to their taste. I was directed to the plain teachings of God's Word, which had been passed by unnoticed. In the judgment all these words of inspiration will condemn those who have not heeded them. *Testimonies for the Church*, Vol. 1, p. 506.

Music a Power for Good

Music can be made a great power for good; yet we do not make the most of this branch of worship. The singing is generally done from impulse or to meet special cases, and at other times those who sing are left to blunder along, and the music loses its proper effect upon the minds of those present. Music should have beauty, pathos, and power. Let the voices be lifted in songs of praise and devotion. Call to your aid, if practicable, instrumental music, and let the glorious harmony ascend to God, an acceptable offering. *Testimonies for the Church*, Vol. 4, p. 71.

SECTION X
Stewardship

However small your talent, God has a place for it. That one talent, wisely used, will accomplish its appointed work. By faithfulness in little duties, we are to work on the plan of addition, and God will work for us on the plan of multiplication. These littles will become the most precious influences in His work. Christ's Object Lessons, *p. 360.*

CHAPTER 98

Lessons in Economy

Much might be said to the young people regarding their privilege to help the cause of God by learning lessons of economy and self-denial. Many think that they must indulge in this pleasure and that, and in order to do this they accustom themselves to live up to the full extent of their income. God wants us to do better in this respect.

We sin against ourselves when we are satisfied with enough to eat and drink and wear. God has something higher than this before us. When we are willing to put away our selfish desires, and give the powers of heart and mind to the work of the cause of God, heavenly agencies will cooperate with us, making us a blessing to humanity.

Saving for Missions

Even though he may be poor, the youth who is industrious and economical can save a little for the cause of God. When I was only twelve years old, I knew what it was to economize. With my sister I learned a trade, and although we would earn only twenty-five cents a day, from this sum we were able to save a little to give to missions. We saved little by little until we had thirty dollars. Then when the message of the Lord's soon coming came to us, with a call for men and means, we felt it a privilege to hand over the thirty dollars to father, asking him to invest it in tracts and pamphlets to send the message to those who were in darkness.

It is the duty of all who touch the work of God to learn economy in the use of time and money. Those who indulge in idleness reveal that they attach little importance to the glorious truths committed to us. They need to be educated in habits of industry, and to learn to work with an eye single to the glory of God.

Self-denial

Those who have not good judgment in the use of time and money, should advise with those who have had experience. With the money that we had earned at our trade, my sister and I provided ourselves with clothes. We would hand our money to mother, saying, "Buy, so that after we have paid for our clothing, there will be something left to give for missionary work." And she would do this, thus encouraging in us a missionary spirit.

The giving that is the fruit of self-denial is a wonderful help to the giver. It imparts an education that enables us more fully to comprehend the work of Him who went about doing good, relieving the suffering, and supplying the needs of the destitute. The Saviour lived not to please Himself. In His life there was no trace of selfishness. Though in a world that He himself had created, He claimed no part of it as His home. "Foxes have holes, and the birds of the air have nests," He said; "but the Son of man hath not where to lay His head."

Proper Use of Talents

If we make the best use of our talents, the Spirit of God will continually lead us to greater efficiency. To the man who had faithfully traded with his talents the Lord said, "Well done, good and faithful servant; thou hast been faithful over a few things, I will make thee ruler over many things: enter thou into the joy of thy Lord." The one-talented man was also expected to do his best. Had he traded with his lord's goods, the Lord would have multiplied the talent.

To every man God has given his work, "according to his several ability." God has the measure of our ability, and knows just what to lay upon us. Of the one who is found faithful, the command is given, Intrust him with greater responsibility. If he proves faithful to that trust, the word is given again, Trust him with still more. Thus through the grace of Christ he grows to the full measure of a man in Christ Jesus.

Have you only one talent? Put it out to the exchangers, by wise investment increasing it to two. Do with your might what your hands find to do. Use your talent so wisely that it will fulfil its appointed mission. It will be worth everything to you to hear the words spoken to you at last. "Well done." But only to those who have done well will the "Well done" be spoken.

No Time to Lose

Young men and women, you have no time to lose. Seek earnestly to bring solid timbers into your character building. We beseech you for Christ's sake to be faithful. Seek to redeem the time. Consecrate yourselves every day to the service of God, and you will find that you do not need many holidays to spend in idleness, nor much money to spend in self-gratification. Heaven is watching for those who are seeking to improve and to become molded to the likeness of Christ. When the human agent submits to Christ, the Holy Spirit will accomplish a great work for him.

Every true, self-sacrificing worker for God is willing to spend and be spent for the sake of others. Christ says, "He that loveth his life shall lose it; and he that hateth his life in this world shall keep it unto life eternal." By earnest, thoughtful efforts to help where help is needed, the true Christian shows his love for God and for his fellow beings. He may lose his life in service; but when Christ comes to gather His jewels to Himself, he will find it again. *Youth's Instructor*, September 10, 1907.

The Reward of Sacrifice

The means used to bless others will bring returns. Riches rightly employed will accomplish great good. Souls will be won to Christ. He who follows Christ's plan of life will see in the courts of God those for whom he has labored and sacrificed on earth. Gratefully will the ransomed ones remember those who have been instrumental in their salvation. Precious will heaven be to those who have been faithful in the work of saving souls. *Christ's Object Lessons*. p. 373.

CHAPTER 99

Spirit of Sacrifice

The spirit of covetousness, of seeking for the highest position and the highest wage, is rife in the world. The old-time spirit of self-denial and self-sacrifice is too seldom met with. But this is the only spirit that can actuate a true follower of Jesus. Our divine Master has given us an example of how we are to work. And to those whom He bade, "Follow Me, and I will make you fishers of men," He offered no stated sum as a reward for their services. They were to share with Him His self-denial and sacrifice.

Those who claim to be followers of the Master Worker, and who engage in His service as co-laborers with God, are to bring into their work the exactitude and skill, the tact and wisdom, that the God of perfection required in the building of the earthly tabernacle. And now, as in that time and as in the days of Christ's earthly ministry, devotion to God and a spirit of sacrifice should be regarded as the first requisites of acceptable service. God designs that not one thread of selfishness shall be woven into His work. *Review and Herald*, January 4, 1906.

Signs of Grace in the Heart

Humility, self-denial, benevolence, and the payment of a faithful tithe, these show that the grace of God is working in the heart. *Counsels on Health*, p. 590.

CHAPTER 100

The Tithe

The great work which Jesus announced that He came to do was intrusted to His followers upon the earth. Christ, as our head, leads out in the great work of salvation, and bids us follow His example. He has given us a world-wide message. This truth must be extended to all nations, tongues, and people. Satan's power was to be contested, and he was to be overcome by Christ and also by His followers. An extensive war was to be maintained against the powers of darkness. And in order to do this work successfully, means were required. God does not propose to send means direct from heaven, but He gives into the hands of His followers talents of means to use for the very purpose of sustaining this warfare.

He has given His people a plan for raising sums sufficient to make the enterprise self-sustaining. God's plan in the tithing system is beautiful in its simplicity and equality. All may take hold of it in faith and courage, for it is divine in its origin. In it are combined simplicity and utility, and it does not require depth of learning to understand and execute it. All may feel that they can act a part in carrying forward the precious work of salvation. Every man, woman and youth may become a treasurer for the Lord, and may be an agent to meet the demands upon the treasury. Says the apostle, "Let every one of you lay by him in store, as God hath prospered him."

Great objects are accomplished by this system. If one and all would accept it, each would be made a vigilant and faithful treasurer for God; and there would be no want of means with which to carry forward the great work of sounding the last message of warning to the world. The treasury will be full if all adopt this system, and the contributors will not be left the poorer. Through every investment made, they will become more wedded to the cause of present truth. They will be "laying up in store for themselves a good foundation against the time to come, that they may lay hold on eternal life." *Testimonies for the Church*, Vol. 3, pp. 388, 389.

Recognition of God's Ownership

The consecration to God of a tithe of all increase, whether of the orchard and harvest-field, the flocks and herds, or the labor of brain or hand; the devotion of a second tithe for the relief of the poor and other benevolent uses, tended to keep fresh before the people the truth of God's ownership of all, and of their opportunity to be channels of His blessings. It was a training adapted to kill out all narrowing selfishness, and to cultivate breadth and nobility of character. *Education*, p. 44.

Belongs to God

"The tithe . . . is the Lord's." Here the same form of expression is employed as in the law of the Sabbath. "The seventh day is the Sabbath of the Lord thy God." God reserved to Himself a specified portion of man's time and of his means, and no man could, without guilt, appropriate either for his own interests. *Patriarchs and Prophets*, pp. 525, 526.

CHAPTER 101

"Honor the Lord With Thy Substance"

"How much owest thou unto my Lord?" Shall we receive every blessing from the hand of God, and yet make no returns to Him—not even in giving Him our tithe, the portion which He has reserved unto Himself? It has become customary to turn everything out of the true line of self-sacrifice into the path of self-pleasing. But shall we continually receive His favors with indifference, and make no response to His love?

Will you not, dear youth, become missionaries for God? Will you, as you have never done before, learn the precious lesson of making gifts to the Lord by putting into the treasury of that which He has freely given you to enjoy? Whatever you have received, let a portion be returned to the Giver as a gratitude offering. A part should also be put into the treasury for the missionary work to be done both at home and abroad.

Treasures in Heaven

The cause of God should lie very near our hearts. The light of truth which has been a blessing to one family will, if communicated by parents and children, prove as great a blessing to other families also. But when God's bounties, so richly and abundantly given, are withheld from Him, and selfishly bestowed upon ourselves, God's curse, in the place of His blessing, will surely be experienced; for this the Lord has declared.

God's claim is to take the precedence of any other claim, and must be discharged first. Then the poor and the needy are to be cared for. These must not be neglected, at whatever cost or sacrifice to ourselves.

"That there may be meat in Mine house." It is our duty to be temperate in all things, in eating, in drinking, and in dressing. Our buildings and the furnishing of our homes should be carefully considered with the heart's desire to render to God His own, not only in tithes, but as far as possible in gifts and offerings also. Very many might be laying up for themselves treasures in heaven, by keeping the Lord's storehouse supplied with the portion He claims as His own, and with gifts and offerings.

Those who are honestly inquiring what God requires of them in regard to the property they claim as their own should search the Old Testament Scriptures, and see what Christ, the invisible leader of Israel in their long wilderness journey, directed His people to do in this respect. We should individually be willing to be put to any inconvenience, to be brought into any straits, rather than rob God of the portion that should come into His house. Those who are Bible readers and Bible believers will have an intelligent knowledge of "What saith the Lord" in this matter.

Without Excuse

In that day when every man shall be judged according to the deeds done in the body, every excuse that selfishness may now make for withholding the tithe, the gifts and offerings, from the Lord will melt away as the dew before the sun. If it were not forever too late, how glad would many be to go back and rebuild their characters! But it will be too late then to change the record of those who, weekly, monthly, and yearly, have robbed God. Their destiny will be fixed, unalterably fixed. . . .

Selfishness is a deadly evil. Self-love and careless indifference to the specific terms of agreement between God and man, the refusal to act as his faithful stewards, have brought upon them His curse, just as He declared would be the case. These souls have separated themselves from God; by precept and example they have led others to disregard God's plain commandments, and He could not bestow His blessing upon them.

The Tithe

The Lord has specified: The tenth of all your possessions is Mine; your gifts and offerings are to be brought into the treasury, to be used to advance My cause, to send the living preacher to open the Scriptures to those who sit in darkness.

Then will any one run the risk of withholding from God His own, doing as did the unfaithful servant who hid His Lord's money in the earth? Shall we, as did this man, seek to justify our unfaithfulness by complaining of God, saying, "Lord, I knew Thee that Thou art an hard man, reaping where Thou hast not sown, and gathering where Thou hast not strawed: and I was afraid, and went and hid Thy talent in the earth: lo, there Thou hast that is Thine"? Shall we not rather present our gratitude offerings to God? *Youth's Instructor*, August 26, 1897.

CHAPTER 102

Individual Responsibility

Our heavenly Father requires no more nor less than He has given us ability to do. He lays upon His servants no burdens that they are not able to bear. "He knoweth our frame; He remembereth that we are dust." All that He claims from us we through divine grace can render.

"Unto whomsoever much is given, of him shall be much required." We shall individually be held responsible for doing one jot less than we have ability to do. The Lord measures with exactness every possibility for service. The unused capabilities are as much brought into account as are those that are improved. For all that we might become through the right use of our talents God holds us responsible. We shall be judged according to what we ought to have done, but did not accomplish because we did not use our powers to glorify God. Even if we do not lose our souls, we shall realize in eternity the result of our unused talents. For all the knowledge and ability that we might have gained and did not, there will be an eternal loss.

But when we give ourselves wholly to God, and in our work follow His directions. He makes Himself responsible for its accomplishment. He would not have us conjecture as to the success of our honest endeavors. Not once should we even think of failure. We are to cooperate with One who knows no failure.

We should not talk of our own weakness and inability. This is a manifest distrust of God, a denial of His Word. When we murmur because of our burdens, or refuse the responsibilities He calls upon us to bear, we are virtually saying that He is a hard master, that He requires what He has not given us power to do. *Christ's Object Lessons*, pp. 362, 363.

Value of Money

Our money has not been given us that we might honor and glorify ourselves. As faithful stewards we are to use it for the honor and glory of God. Some think that only a portion of their means is the Lord's. When they have set apart a portion for religious and charitable purposes, they regard the remainder as their own, to be used as they see fit. But in this they mistake. All we possess is the Lord's, and we are accountable to Him for the use we make of it. In the use of every penny it will be seen whether we love God supremely and our neighbor as ourselves.

Money has great value, because it can do great good. In the hands of God's children it is food for the hungry, drink for the thirsty, and clothing for the naked. It is a defense for the oppressed, and a means of help to the sick. But money is of no more value than sand, only as it is put to use in providing for the necessities of life, in blessing others, and advancing the cause of Christ. *Christ's Object Lessons*, p. 351.

CHAPTER 103

Holiday Presents

The holidays are approaching. In view of this fact, it will be well to consider how much money is expended yearly in making presents to those who have no need of them. The habits of custom are so strong that to withhold gifts from our friends on these occasions would seem to us almost a neglect of them. But let us remember that our kind heavenly Benefactor has claims upon us far superior to those of any earthly friends. Shall we not, during the coming holidays, present our offerings to God? Even the children may participate in this work. Clothing and other useful articles may be given to the worthy poor, and thus a work may be done for the Master.

Evils of Self-indulgence

Let us remember that Christmas is celebrated in commemoration of the birth of the world's Redeemer. This day is generally spent in feasting and gluttony. Large sums of money are spent in needless self-indulgence. The appetite and sensual pleasures are indulged at the expense of physical, mental, and moral power. Yet this has become a habit. Pride, fashion, and gratification of the palate have swallowed up immense sums of money that have really benefited no one, but have encouraged a prodigality of means which is displeasing to God. These days are spent in glorifying self rather than God. Health has been sacrificed, money worse than thrown away, many have lost their lives by overeating or through demoralizing dissipation, and souls have been lost by this means.

God would be glorified by His children should they enjoy a plain, simple diet, and use the means intrusted to them in bringing to His treasury offerings, small and great, to be used in sending the light of truth to souls that are in the darkness of error. The hearts of the widow and fatherless may be made to rejoice because of gifts which will add to their comfort and satisfy their hunger.

Gifts to God

Let all who profess to believe the present truth calculate how much they spend yearly, and especially upon the recurrence of the annual holidays, for the gratification of selfish and unholy desires, how much in the indulgence of appetite, and how much to compete with others in unchristian display. Sum up the means thus spent all needlessly, and then estimate how much might be saved as consecrated gifts to God's cause without injury to soul or body.

Mites and more liberal gifts may be brought in, according to the ability of the giver, to aid in lifting debts from churches which have been dedicated to God. Then there are missionaries to be sent into new fields, and others to be supported in their respective fields of labor. These missionaries have to practice the strictest economy, even denying themselves the very things you enjoy daily, and which you consider the necessaries of life. They enjoy few luxuries. *Review and Herald*, November 21, 1878.

CHAPTER 104

Economy in Dress

God's people should practice strict economy in their outlay of means, that they may have something to bring to Him, saying, "Of Thine own have we given Thee." Thus they are to offer God thanksgiving for the blessings received from Him. Thus, too, they are to lay up for themselves treasure beside the throne of God.

Worldlings spend upon dress large sums of money that ought to be used to feed and clothe those suffering from hunger and cold. Many for whom Christ gave His life have barely sufficient of the cheapest, most common clothing, while others spend thousands of dollars in the efforts to satisfy the never-ending demands of fashion.

The Lord has charged His people to come out from the world, and be separate. Gay or expensive clothing is not becoming to those who believe that we are living in the last days of probation. "I will therefore," the apostle Paul writes, "that men pray everywhere, lifting up holy hands, without wrath and doubting. In like manner also, that women adorn themselves in modest apparel, with shamefacedness and sobriety; not with broided hair, or gold, or pearls, or costly array; but (which becometh women professing godliness) with good works."

Even among those who profess to be children of God, there are those who spend more than is necessary upon dress. We should dress neatly and tastefully, but, my sisters, when you are buying and making your own and your children's clothing, think of the work in the Lord's vineyard that is still waiting to be done. It is right to buy good material, and have it carefully made. This is economy. But rich trimmings are not needed, and to indulge in them is to spend for self-gratification money that should be put into God's cause.

It is not your dress that makes you of value in the Lord's sight. It is the inward adorning, the graces of the Spirit, the kind word, the thoughtful consideration for others, that God values. Do without the unnecessary trimmings, and lay aside for the advancement of the cause of God the means thus saved.

Self-denial Pleasing to God

Learn the lesson of self-denial, and teach it to your children. All that can be saved by self-denial is needed now in the work to be done. The suffering must be relieved, the naked clothed, the hungry fed; the truth for this time must be told to those who know it not. . . .

We are Christ's witnesses, and we are not to allow worldly interests so to absorb our time and attention that we pay no heed to the things that God has said must come first. There are higher interests at stake. "Seek ye first the kingdom of God and His righteousness." Christ gave His all to the work that He came to do, and His word to us is, "If any man will come after Me, let him deny himself, and take up his cross, and follow Me." "So shall ye be My disciples." Willingly and cheerfully Christ gave Himself to the carrying out of the will of God. He became obedient unto death, even the death of the cross. Shall we feel it a hardship to deny ourselves? Shall we draw back from being partakers of His sufferings? His death ought to stir every fiber of the being, making us willing to consecrate to His work all that we have and are. As we think of what He has done for us, our hearts should be filled with love.

When those who know the truth practice the self-denial enjoined in God's Word, the message will go with power. The Lord will hear our prayers for the conversion of souls. God's people will let their light shine forth, and unbelievers, seeing their good works, will glorify our heavenly Father. *Review and Herald*, December 1, 1910.

The Love of Display

The love of display produces extravagance, and in many young people kills the aspiration for a nobler life. Instead of seeking an education, they early engage in some occupation to earn money for indulging the passion for dress. And through this passion many a young girl is beguiled to ruin. *Education*, p. 247.

Puritan Plainness

Puritan plainness and simplicity should mark the dwellings and apparel of all who believe the solemn truths for this time. All means needlessly expended in dress or in the adorning of our houses is a waste of our Lord's money. It is defrauding the cause of God for the gratification of pride. *Testimonies for the Church*, Vol. 1, p. 189.

CHAPTER 105

Self-gratification

As I visit the homes of our people and our schools, I see that all the available space on tables, what-nots, and mantelpieces is filled up with photographs. On the right hand and on the left are seen the pictures of human faces. God desires this order of things to be changed. Were Christ on earth, He would say, "Take these things hence." I have been instructed that these pictures are as so many idols, taking up the time and thought which should be sacredly devoted to God.

These photographs cost money. Is it consistent for us, knowing the work that is to be done at this time, to spend God's money in producing pictures of our own faces and the faces of our friends? Should not every dollar that we can spare be used in the upbuilding of the cause of God? These pictures take money that should be sacredly devoted to God's service; and they divert the mind from the truths of God's Word.

A Species of Idolatry

This making and exchanging photographs is a species of idolatry. Satan is doing all he can to eclipse heaven from our view. Let us not help him by making picture-idols. We need to reach a higher standard than these human faces suggest. The Lord says, "Thou shalt have no other gods before Me." Those who claim to believe in Christ need to realize that they are to reflect His image.

It is His likeness that is to be kept before the mind. The words that are spoken are to be freighted with heavenly inspiration. . . .

First Things First

Those who have taken part in the solemn rite of baptism have pledged themselves to seek for those things which are above, where Christ sitteth on the right hand of God; pledged themselves to labor earnestly for the salvation of sinners. God asks those who take His name, How are you using the powers that have been redeemed by the death of My Son? Are you doing all in your power to rise to a greater height in spiritual understanding? Are you adjusting your interests and actions in harmony with the momentous claims of eternity?

Let there be a reformation among the people of God. "Whether therefore ye eat, or drink, or whatsoever ye do, do all to the glory of God." Those upon whom the Lord has placed the burden of His work are struggling to proclaim the message, that souls perishing in ignorance may be warned. Can you not, by self-denial, do something to help them in their work? Arouse, and show by your unselfish zeal and earnestness that you are converted.

Every dollar is required in the work of saving souls. The money invested by the professed people of God in getting pictures made of human faces would support several missionaries in the field. Many small streams, when put together, swell into a large river. We embezzle our Lord's goods when we use for selfish pleasure the means which should be used to proclaim the last message of warning. If you spend the Lord's money for self-gratification, how can you expect Him to continue to bestow His goods on you? How does the Master regard those who selfishly invest His money in photographs? That very money could have been used to purchase reading matter to send to those in the darkness of ignorance.

The truth that God has given us must be heralded to the world. We have been given the privilege of doing this work. We are to sow the seed of truth beside all waters. The Lord calls upon us to practice self-denial and self-sacrifice. The gospel demands entire consecration. The necessities of the cause demand all that we can give. Our indulgence in photographs has been a selfish gratification on our part, which bears silent witness against us. By this indulgence a large amount of wood, hay, and stubble has been brought to the foundation, to be consumed by the fires of the last day.

Duty of Self-denial

After going from home to home, and seeing the many photographs, I was instructed to warn our people against this evil.

This much we can do for God. We can put these picture-idols out of sight. They have no power for good, but interpose between God and the soul. They can do nothing to help in sowing the seeds of truth. Christ calls upon those who claim to be following Him to put on the whole armor of God.

Our educational institutions need to feel the reforming power of the Spirit of God. "If the salt have lost his savor, wherewith shall it be salted? It is thenceforth good for nothing, but to be cast out, and to be trodden under foot of men." Those who are engaged as teachers in our schools and sanitariums should reach a high standard of consecration. And the students in these institutions, who are fitting themselves to go forth as missionaries, should learn to practice self-denial.

We are God's stewards, and "it is required in stewards, that a man be found faithful." The money that God has intrusted to us is to be carefully husbanded. We are to increase in efficiency by putting to the best use the talents given us, that at God's coming we may return to Him His own with usury. *Review and Herald*, June 13, 1907.

Repeated Taking of Pictures

The youth have their hearts filled with the love of self. This is manifested in their desire to see their faces daguerreotyped by the artist; and they are not satisfied with being once represented, but sit again and again for their picture, each time hoping that the last will excel all their previous efforts, and appear really more beautiful than the original. Their Lord's money is squandered in this way, and what is gained? *Testimonies for the Church*, Vol. 1, p. 500.

CHAPTER 106

Economy and Benevolence

Many despise economy, confounding it with stinginess and narrowness. But economy is consistent with the broadest liberality. Indeed, without economy there can be no true liberality. We are to save that we may give.

No one can practice real benevolence without self-denial. Only by a life of simplicity, self-denial, and close economy is it possible for us to accomplish the work appointed us as Christ's representatives. Pride and worldly ambition must be put out of our hearts. In all our work, the principle of unselfishness revealed in Christ's life is to be carried out. Upon the walls of our homes, the pictures, the furnishings, we are to read, "Bring the poor that are cast out to thy house." On our wardrobes were are to see written, as with the finger of God, "Clothe the naked." In the dining-room, on the table laden with abundant food, we should see traced, "Is it not to deal thy bread to the hungry?"

Open Doors of Usefulness

A thousand doors of usefulness are open before us. Often we lament the scanty resources available, but were Christians thoroughly in earnest, they could multiply the resources a thousandfold. It is selfishness, self-indulgence, that bars the way to our usefulness.

How much means is expended for things that are mere idols, things that engross thought and time and strength which should be put to a higher use! How much money is wasted on expensive houses and furniture, on selfish pleasures, luxurious and unwholesome food, hurtful indulgences! How much is squandered on gifts that benefit no one! For things that are needless, often harmful, professed Christians are today spending more, many times more, than they spend in seeking to rescue souls from the tempter.

Many who profess to be Christians spend so much on dress that they have nothing to spare for the needs of others. Costly ornaments and expensive clothing they think they must have, regardless of the needs of those who can with difficulty provide themselves with even the plainest clothing.

Saving the Fragments

My sisters, if you would bring your manner of dressing into conformity with the rules given in the Bible, you would have an abundance with which to help your poorer sisters. You would have not only means, but time. Often this is most needed. There are many whom you might help with your suggestions, your tact and skill. Show them how to dress simply and yet tastefully. Many a woman remains away from the house of God because her shabby, ill-fitting garments are in such striking contrast to the dress of others. Many a sensitive spirit cherishes a sense of bitter humiliation and injustice because of this contrast. And because of it many are led to doubt the reality of religion and to harden their hearts against the gospel.

Christ bids us, "Gather up the fragments that remain, that

nothing be lost." While thousands are every day perishing from famine, bloodshed, fire, and plague, it becomes every lover of his kind to see that nothing is wasted, that nothing is needlessly expended, whereby he might benefit a human being.

It is wrong to waste our time, wrong to waste our thoughts. We lose every moment that we devote to self-seeking. If every moment were valued and rightly employed, we should have time for everything that we need to do for ourselves or for the world. In the expenditure of money, in the use of time, strength, opportunities, let every Christian look to God for guidance. "If any of you lack wisdom, let him ask of God, that giveth to all men liberally, and upbraideth not; and it shall be given him." *The Ministry of Healing*, pp. 206-208.

Guide to Economy

It is not necessary to specify here how economy may be practiced in every particular. Those whose hearts are fully surrendered to God, and who take His Word as their guide, will know how to conduct themselves in all the duties of life. They will learn of Jesus, who is meek and lowly of heart; and in cultivating the meekness of Christ they will close the door against innumerable temptations. *Fundamentals of Christian Education*, p. 152.

SECTION XI
The Home Life

The restoration and uplifting of humanity begins in the home. The work of parents underlies every other. Society is composed of families, and is what the heads of families make it. Out of the heart are "the issues of life": and the heart of the community, of the church, and of the nation, is the household. The well-being of society, the success of the church, the prosperity of the nation, depend upon home influences. The Ministry of Healing, *p. 349.*

CHAPTER 107

A Christian Household

Like the patriarchs of old, those who profess to love God should erect an altar to the Lord wherever they pitch their tent. If ever there was a time when every house should be a house of prayer, it is now. Fathers and mothers should often lift up their hearts to God in humble supplication for themselves and their children. Let the father, as priest of the household, lay upon the altar of God the morning and evening sacrifice, while the wife and children unite in prayer and praise. In such a household, Jesus will love to tarry.

From every Christian home a holy light should shine forth. Love should be revealed in action. It should flow out in all home intercourse, showing itself in thoughtful kindness, in gentle, unselfish courtesy. There are homes where this principle is carried out—homes where God is worshiped, and truest love reigns. From these homes, morning and evening prayer ascends to God as sweet incense, and His mercies and blessings descend upon the suppliants like the morning dew.

A well-ordered Christian household is a powerful argument in favor of the reality of the Christian religion—an argument that the infidel cannot gainsay. All can see that there is an influence at work in the family that affects the children, and that the God of Abraham is with them. *Patriarchs and Prophets*, p. 144.

CHAPTER 108

Faithfulness in Home Duties

The highest duty that devolves upon youth is in their own homes, blessing father and mother, brothers and sisters, by affection and true interest. Here they can show self-denial and self-forgetfulness in caring and doing for others. Never will woman be degraded by this work. It is the most sacred, elevated office that she can fill. What an influence a sister may have over brothers! If she is right, she may determine the character of her brothers. Her prayers, her gentleness, and her affection may do much in a household.

My sister, these noble qualities can never be communicated to other minds unless they first exist in your own. That contentment of mind, that affection, gentleness, and sunniness of temper which will reach every heart, will reflect upon you what your heart gives forth to others. If Christ does not reign in the heart, there will be discontent and moral deformity. Selfishness will require of others that which we are unwilling to give them. . . .

It is not a great work and great battles alone which try the soul and demand courage. Everyday life brings its perplexities, trials, and discouragements. It is the humble work which frequently draws upon the patience and the fortitude. Self-reliance and resolution will be necessary to meet and conquer all difficulties. Secure the Lord to stand with you, in every place to be your consolation and comfort. *Testimonies for the Church*, Vol. 3, pp. 80, 81.

CHAPTER 109

Home Religion

Home religion is greatly needed, and our words in the home should be of a right character, or our testimonies in the church will amount to nothing. Unless you manifest meekness, kindness, and courtesy in your home, your religion will be in vain. If there were more genuine home religion, there would be more power in the church.

Unkind Speech in the Home

What harm is wrought in the family circle by the utterance of impatient words; for the impatient utterance of one leads another to retort in the same spirit and manner. Then come words of retaliation, words of self-justification, and it is by such words that a heavy, galling yoke is manufactured for your neck; for all these bitter words will come back in a baleful harvest to your soul.

Those who indulge in such language will experience shame, loss of self-respect, loss of self-confidence, and will have bitter remorse and regret that they allowed themselves to lose self-control and speak in this way. How much better would it be if words of this character were never spoken. How much better to have the oil of grace in the heart, to be able to pass by all provocation, and bear all things with Christlike meekness and forbearance.

If you fulfill the conditions of God's promises, the promises will be fulfilled to you. If your mind is stayed upon God, you will not go from a state of ecstasy to the valley of despondency when trial and temptation come upon you. You will not talk doubt and gloom to others.

Satan cannot read our thoughts, but he can see our actions, hear our words; and from his long knowledge of the human family, he can shape his temptations to take advantage of our weak points of character. And how often do we let him into the secret of how he may obtain the victory over us. Oh, that we might control our words and actions! How strong we would become if our words were of such an order that we would not be ashamed to meet the record of them in the day of judgment. How different will they appear in the day of God from what they seem when we utter them. *Review and Herald*, February 27, 1913.

The Home an Object Lesson

The mission of the home extends beyond its own members. The Christian home is to be an object lesson, illustrating the excellence of the true principles of life. Such an illustration will be a power for good in the world. Far more powerful than any sermon that can be preached is the influence of a true home upon human hearts and lives. As the youth go out from such a home, the lessons they have learned are imparted. Nobler principles of life are introduced into other households, and an uplifting influence works in the community. *The Ministry of Healing*, p. 352.

CHAPTER 110

The Home a Training School

The youth will not become weak-minded or inefficient by consecrating themselves to the service of God. The fear of the Lord is the beginning of wisdom. The youngest child that loves and fears God is greater in His sight than the most talented and learned man who neglects the great salvation. The youth who consecrate their hearts and lives to God have, in so doing, placed themselves in connection with the Fountain of all wisdom and excellence.

Everyday Duties

If children were taught to regard the humble round of everyday duties as the course marked out for them by the Lord, as a school in which they were to be trained to render faithful and efficient service, how much more pleasant and honorable would their work appear. To perform every duty as unto the Lord, throws a charm around the humblest employment, and links the workers on earth with the holy beings who do God's will in heaven.

And in our appointed place we should discharge our duties with as much faithfulness as do the angels in their higher sphere. Those who feel that they are God's servants will be men who can be trusted anywhere. Citizens of heaven will make the best citizens of earth. A correct view of our duty to God leads to clear perceptions of our duty to our fellow men.

The Mother's Reward

When the judgment shall sit, and the books shall be opened; when the "well done" of the great Judge is pronounced, and the crown of immortal glory is placed upon the brow of the victor, many will raise their crowns in sight of the assembled universe and, pointing to their mother, say, "She made me all I am through the grace of God. Her instruction, her prayers, have been blessed to my eternal salvation." . . .

Young men should be trained to stand firm for the right amid the prevailing iniquity, to do all in their power to arrest the progress of vice, and to promote virtue, purity, and true manliness. The impressions made upon the mind and character in early life are deep and abiding. Injudicious training or evil associations will often exert upon the young mind an influence for evil that all after-effort is powerless to efface. *Signs of the Times*, November 3, 1881.

Possibilities of Home Training

It is by the youth and children of today that the future of society is to be determined, and what these youth and children shall be depends upon the home. To the lack of right home training may be traced the larger share of the disease and misery and crime that curse humanity. If the home life were pure and true, if the children who went forth from its care were prepared to meet life's responsibilities and dangers, what a change would be seen in the world! *The Ministry of Healing*, p. 351.

CHAPTER 111

Respect and Love for Parents

Those who would truly follow Christ must let Him abide in the heart, and enthrone Him there as supreme. They must represent His spirit and character in their home life, and show courtesy and kindness to those with whom they come in contact.

There are many children who profess to know the truth, who do not render to their parents the honor and affection that are due to them, who manifest but little love to father and mother, and fail to honor them in deferring to their wishes, or in seeking to relieve them of anxiety. Many who profess to be Christians do not know what it means to "honor thy father and thy mother," and consequently will know just as little what it means, "that thy days may be long upon the land which the Lord thy God giveth thee."

Our youth profess to be among those who keep the commandments of God, and yet many of them neglect and break the fifth commandment; and the rich blessing promised to those who observe this precept, and honor father and mother, cannot be fulfilled to them. Unless they repent of their sin, and reform their practices and character through the grace of Christ, they will never enter into the new earth, upon which they may live eternally. Those who do not respect and love their parents will not respect and honor God. Those who fail to bear the test, who fail to honor their God-fearing parents, fail to obey God, and therefore cannot expect to come into the land of promise.

A Destiny in Obedience

The youth are now deciding their own eternal destiny, and I would appeal to you to consider the commandment to which God has annexed such a promise, "that thy days may be long upon the land which the Lord thy God giveth thee." Children, do you desire eternal life? Then respect and honor your parents. . . .

If you have sinned in not rendering love and obedience to them, begin now to redeem the past. You cannot afford to take any other course; for it means to you the loss of eternal life. The Heart-searcher knows what is your attitude toward your parents; for He is weighing moral character in the golden scales of the heavenly sanctuary. O, confess your neglect of your parents, confess your indifference toward them, and your contempt of God's holy commandment. . . .

The hearts of your parents have been drawn out in tender sympathy toward you, and can you return their love with cold ingratitude? They love your souls, they want you to be saved; but have you not often despised their counsel and done your own will, your own way? Have you not followed your own independent judgment, when you knew that such a stubborn course would not meet the approval of God? Many fathers and mothers have gone down broken-hearted to the grave because of the ingratitude, the lack of respect, shown them by their children. *Youth's Instructor*, June 22, 1893.

CHAPTER 112

A Blessing in the Home

The Lord says to the young, "My son, give Me thine heart." The Saviour of the world loves to have children and youth give their hearts to Him. There may be a large army of children who shall be found faithful to God, because they walk in the light, as Christ is in the light. They will love the Lord Jesus, and it will be their delight to please Him. They will not be impatient if reproved; but will make glad the heart of father and mother by their kindness, their patience, their willingness to do all they can in helping to bear the burdens of daily life. Through childhood and youth, they will be found faithful disciples of our Lord.

Children and youth, in your earliest years you may be a blessing in the home. What a grief it is to see children of God-fearing parents unruly and disobedient, unthankful and self-willed, full of determination to have their own way, regardless of the inconvenience or sorrow it causes their parents. Satan takes delight in ruling the hearts of children, and if he is permitted he will inspire them with his own hateful spirit.

Obedience to Parents

Parents may do everything in their power to give their children every privilege and instruction, in order that they may give their hearts to God; yet the children may refuse to walk in the light and, by their evil course, cast unfavorable reflections upon their parents who love them, and whose hearts yearn after their salvation.

It is Satan who tempts children to follow in a course of sin and disobedience; and then if he is permitted he will take the life of the children while they are yet in their sins, in order to cut them off from all hope of salvation, and to pierce, as with a sword, the hearts of the God-fearing fathers and mothers, who will be bowed down with a sorrow that never can be lifted, because of their children's final impenitence and rebellion against God. . . .

Children and youth, I entreat you, for Christ's sake, to walk in the light. Submit your will to the will of God. When "sinners entice thee, consent thou not." Keep the way of the Lord, for you will have no peace in transgression. By an evil course you bring discredit upon your parents and dishonor upon the religion of Christ. Remember that your life is recorded in the books of Heaven, to be opened before the assembled universe. Think what shame, what remorse, would be yours, should it be your unhappy lot to lose eternal life! "Turn you at My reproof: behold, I will pour out My Spirit unto you, I will make known my words unto you. . . . Then shall they call upon Me. . . . Whoso hearkeneth unto Me shall dwell safely, and shall be quiet from fear of evil." Heed the instruction of Christ, "Walk while ye have the light, lest darkness come upon you." *Youth's Instructor*, August 10, 1893.

CHAPTER 113

Building Character at Home

Satan tempts children to be reserved with their parents, and to choose as their confidants their young and inexperienced companions, such as cannot help them, but will give them bad advice. . . .

Children would be saved from many evils if they would be more familiar with their parents. Parents should encourage in their children a disposition to be open and frank with them, to come to them with their difficulties and, when they are perplexed as to what course is right, to lay the matter just as they view it before the parents, and ask their advice. Who are so well calculated to see and point out their dangers as godly parents? Who can understand the peculiar temperaments of their own children as well as they? The mother who has watched every turn of mind from infancy, and is thus acquainted with the natural disposition, is best prepared to counsel her children. Who can tell as well what traits of character to check and restrain as the mother, aided by the father?

Making Parents Happy

Children who are Christians will prefer the love and approbation of their God-fearing parents above every earthly blessing. They will love and honor their parents. It should be one of the principal studies of their lives how to make their parents happy.

In this rebellious age, children who have not received right instruction and discipline have but little sense of their obligations to their parents. It is often the case that the more their parents do for them the more ungrateful they are, and the less they respect them.

Children who have been petted and waited upon always expect it; and if their expectations are not met they are disappointed and discouraged. This same disposition will be seen through their whole lives; they will be helpless, leaning upon others for aid, expecting others to favor them and yield to them. And if they are opposed, even after they have grown to manhood and womanhood, they think themselves abused; and thus they worry their way through the world, hardly able to bear their own weight, often murmuring and fretting because everything does not suit them. . . .

Children should feel that they are indebted to their parents, who have watched over them in infancy and nursed them in sickness. They should realize that their parents have suffered much anxiety on their account. Especially have conscientious, godly parents felt the deepest interest that their children should take a right course. As they have seen faults in their children, how heavy have been their hearts. If the children who caused those hearts to ache could see the effect of their course, they would certainly relent. If they could see their mother's tears, and hear her prayers to God in their behalf, if they could listen to her suppressed and broken sighs, their hearts would feel, and they would speedily confess their wrongs and ask to be forgiven. . . .

Strength for the Conflict

We are living in an unfortunate age for children. A heavy current is setting downward to perdition, and more than childhood's experience and strength is needed to press against this current, and not be borne down by it. The youth generally seem to be Satan's captives, and he and his angels are leading them to certain destruction. Satan and his hosts are warring against the government of God, and all who have a desire to yield their hearts to Him and obey His requirements Satan will try to perplex and overcome with his temptations that they may become discouraged and give up the warfare. . . .

By earnest prayer and living faith, great victories will be gained. Some parents have not realized the responsibilities resting upon them, and have neglected the religious education of their children. In the morning the Christian's first thoughts should be upon God. Worldly labor and self-interest should be secondary. Children should be taught to respect and reverence the hour of prayer. Before leaving the house for labor, all the family should be called together, and the father, or the mother in the father's absence, should plead fervently with God to keep them through the day. . . .

Impatience at Restraint

Sabbath-keeping children may become impatient of restraint, and think their parents too strict; hard feelings may even arise in their hearts, and discontented, unhappy thoughts may be cherished by them against those who are working for their present and their future and eternal good. But if life shall be spared a few years, they will bless their parents for that strict care and faithful watchfulness over them in their years of inexperience. . . .

Individual Responsibility

Children, God has seen fit to intrust you to the care of your parents, for them to instruct and discipline, and thus act their part in forming your character for heaven. And yet it rests with you to say whether you will develop a good Christian character by making the best of the advantages you have had from godly, faithful, praying parents. Notwithstanding all the anxiety and faithfulness of parents in behalf of their children, they alone cannot save them. There is a work for the children to do. Every child has an individual case to attend to.

Believing parents, you have a responsible work before you, to guide the footsteps of your children, even in their religious experience. When they truly love God, they will bless and reverence you for the care which you have manifested for them, and for your faithfulness in restraining their desires and subduing their wills. *Testimonies for the Church*, Vol. 1, pp. 391-403.

Clothed with Christ's Righteousness

When we are clothed with the righteousness of Christ, we shall have no relish for sin; for Christ will be working with us. We may make mistakes, but we will hate the sin that caused the sufferings of the Son of God. *Review and Herald*, March 18, 1890.

CHAPTER 114

Youth to Bear Responsibilities*

These young men have duties at home which they overlook. They have not learned to take up the duties, and bear the home responsibilities, which it is their duty to bear. They have a faithful, practical mother, who has borne many burdens which her children should not have suffered her to bear. In this they have failed to honor their mother. They have not shared the burdens of their father as was their duty, and have neglected to honor him as they should. They follow inclination rather than duty.

They have pursued a selfish course in their lives, in shunning burdens and toil, and have failed to obtain a valuable experience which they cannot afford to be deprived of if they would make life a success. They have not felt the importance of being faithful in little things, nor have they felt under obligation to their parents to be true, thorough, and faithful in the humble, lowly duties of life which lie directly in their pathway. They look above the common branches of knowledge, so very necessary for practical life.

Making Home Happy

If these young men would be a blessing anywhere, it should be at home. If they yield to inclination, instead of being guided by the cautious decision of sober reason, sound judgment, and enlightened conscience, they cannot be a blessing to society or

*Addressed to two young men.

to their father's family, and their prospects in this world and in the better world may be endangered.

Many youth receive the impression that their early life is not designed for care-taking, but to be frittered away in idle sport, in jesting, in joking, and in foolish indulgences. While engaged in folly and indulgences of the senses, some think of nothing but the momentary gratification connected with it. Their desire for amusement, their love for society and for chatting and laughing, increases by indulgence, and they lose all relish for the sober realities of life, and home duties seem uninteresting. There is not enough change to meet their minds, and they become restless, peevish, and irritable. These young men should feel it a duty to make home happy and cheerful. . . .

A change from physical labor that has taxed the strength severely may be very necessary for a time, that they may again engage in labor, putting forth exertion with greater success. But entire rest may not be necessary, or even be attended with the best results so far as their physical strength is concerned.

They need not, even when weary with one kind of labor, trifle away their precious moments. They may then seek to do something not so exhausting, but which will be a blessing to their mother and sisters. In lightening their cares by taking upon themselves the roughest burdens they have to bear, they can find that amusement which springs from principle, and which will yield them true happiness, and their time will not be spent in trifling or in selfish indulgence. *Testimonies for the Church*, Vol. 3, pp. 221-223.

CHAPTER 115

The Hour of Worship

In arousing and strengthening a love for Bible study, much depends on the use of the hour of worship. The hours of morning and evening worship should be the sweetest and most helpful of the day. Let it be understood that into these hours no troubled, unkind thoughts are to intrude; that parents and children assemble to meet with Jesus, and to invite into the home the presence of holy angels. Let the services be brief and full of life, adapted to the occasion, and varied from time to time. Let all join in the Bible reading, and learn and often repeat God's law. It will add to the interest of the children if they are sometimes permitted to select the reading. Question them upon it, and let them ask questions. Mention anything that will serve to illustrate its meaning. When the service is not thus made too lengthy, let the little ones take part in prayer, and let them join in song, if it be but a single verse.

To make such a service what it should be, thought should be given to preparation. And parents should take time daily for Bible study with their children. No doubt it will require effort and planning and some sacrifice to accomplish this; but the effort will be richly repaid. *Education*, p. 186.

CHAPTER 116

Religious Hospitality

We would be much happier and more useful if our home life and social intercourse were governed by the meekness and simplicity of Christ. Instead of toiling for display, to excite the admiration or the envy of visitors, we should endeavor to make all around us happy by our cheerfulness, sympathy, and love. Let visitors see that we are striving to conform to the will of Christ. Let them see in us, even though our lot is humble, a spirit of content and gratitude. The very atmosphere of a truly Christian home is that of peace and restfulness. Such an example will not be without effect. . . .

In our efforts for the comfort and happiness of guests, let us not overlook our obligations to God. The hour of prayer should not be neglected for any consideration. Do not talk and amuse yourselves till all are too weary to enjoy the season of devotion. To do this is to present to God a lame offering. At an early hour of the evening, when we can pray unhurriedly and understandingly, we should present our supplications, and raise our voices in happy, grateful praise.

Let all who visit Christians see that the hour of prayer is the most precious, the most sacred, and the happiest hour of the day. These seasons of devotion exert a refining, elevating influence upon all who participate in them. They bring a peace and rest grateful to the spirit. *Review and Herald*, November 29, 1887.

SECTION XII
Dress and Adornment

A person's character is judged by his style of dress. A refined taste, a cultivated mind, will be revealed in the choice of simple and appropriate attire. Chaste simplicity in dress, when united with modesty of demeanor, will go far toward surrounding a young woman with that atmosphere of sacred reserve which will be to her a shield from a thousand perils. Education, *p. 248.*

CHAPTER 117

Elements in Character Building

It is important that children and youth should be trained to guard their words and deeds; for their course of action causes sunshine or shadow, not only in their own home, but also with all with whom they come in contact. But before the youth can be careful and thoughtful and refrain from every appearance of evil, they must have that wisdom which comes from above, and the strength which Jesus alone can impart. . . .

True Adornment

Many deceive themselves in thinking that good looks and a gay attire will gain for them consideration in the world. But the charms that consist only in the outward apparel are shallow and changeable; no dependence can be placed upon them. The adorning which Christ enjoins upon His followers will never fade. He says: "Whose adorning let it not be that outward adorning of plaiting the hair, and of wearing of gold, or of putting on of apparel; but let it be the hidden man of the heart, in that which is not corruptible, even the ornament of a meek and quiet spirit, which is in the sight of God of great price."

If half the time spent by the youth in making themselves attractive in outward appearances were given to soul-culture, to the inward adorning, what a difference would be seen in their deportment, words, and actions. Those who are truly seeking to follow Christ will have conscientious scruples in regard to the dress they wear; they will strive to meet the requirements of this injunction so plainly given by the Lord. The money now expended in extravagances in dress will be used for the advancement of the cause of God and in storing their minds with useful knowledge, thus qualifying themselves for positions of trust. They will seek to meet the expectations of Jesus, who has bought them at an infinite price.

Dear children and youth, Jesus has done all in His power to give you a home in the mansions that are prepared for them that love and serve Him here. He left His heavenly home, and came to a world marred by sin—came to a people who did not appreciate Him, who did not love His purity and holiness, who slighted His teachings, and finally put Him to a most cruel death. "God so loved the world, that He gave His only-begotten Son, that whosoever believeth in Him should not perish, but have everlasting life."

Outward Appearance

God wants something in return for this great sacrifice He has made in your behalf. He wants you to be Christians, not in name alone, but also in dress and conversation. He would have you be content to dress in modest apparel, not in ruffles and feathers and unnecessary trimmings. He wants you to make your manners attractive, such as Heaven can approve. Will you disappoint his expectations, dear youth?

The outside appearance is frequently an index to the mind,

and we should be careful what signs we hang out for the world to judge of our faith. We want you to follow Jesus as dear children, obedient to His expressed will in all things. We want you to please your Redeemer by seeking earnestly that inward adorning. Thus day by day, with the help of Jesus, you may overcome self. Pride and love of display will be discarded from your hearts and lives. Meekness and love of simplicity will be encouraged. Thus the youth may become an army of faithful soldiers for Christ.

We are living in perilous times, when those who profess to love and obey God deny Him in their daily lives. "For men shall be lovers of their own selves, covetous, boasters, proud, blasphemers, disobedient to parents, unthankful, unholy, without natural affection, trucebreakers, false accusers, incontinent, fierce, despisers of those that are good, traitors, heady, high-minded, lovers of pleasures more than lovers of God; having a form of godliness, but denying the power thereof." God does not want you to be found among this class, dear youth. In His Word you may learn how to shun these evils, and in the end be overcomers. . . .

"And they overcame him by the blood of the Lamb, and by the word of their testimony." "Then they that feared the Lord spake often one to another: and the Lord hearkened, and heard it, and a book of remembrance was written before Him for them that feared the Lord, and that thought upon His name."

Witnessing

It is not enough for you to avoid the appearance of evil; you must go farther than this; you must "learn to do well." You must represent Christ to the world. It must be your daily study how you can learn to work the works of God. His followers are to be living epistles, "known and read of all men."

You can never secure a good character by merely wishing for it. It can be gained only by labor. Your desires in this direction must be expressed in earnest, honest endeavor and patient toil. By taking advance steps each day up the ladder of progress, you will find at last at the top—a conqueror, yes, more than a conqueror, through Him who has loved you. *Youth's Instructor*, November 5, 1896.

Religion Judged by Dress

Dear youth, a disposition in you to dress according to the fashion, and to wear lace, and gold, and artificials for display, will not recommend to others your religion or the truth that you profess. People of discernment will look upon your attempts to beautify the external as proof of weak minds and proud hearts. Simple, plain, unpretending dress will be a recommendation to my youthful sisters. In no better way can you let your light shine to others than in your simplicity of dress and deportment. You may show to all that, in comparison with eternal things, you place a proper estimate upon the things of this life. *Testimonies for the Church*, Vol. 3, p. 376.

CHAPTER 118

Dress and Character

The followers of Christ are represented by Him as the salt of the earth and the light of the world. Without the saving influence of Christians, the world would perish in its own corruption. Look upon the class of professed Christians described, who are careless in their dress and person; loose in their business transactions, as their dress represents; coarse, uncourteous, and rough in their manners; low in their conversation; at the same time regarding these miserable traits as marks of true humility and Christian life. Think you that if our Saviour were upon earth He would point to them as being the salt of the earth and the light of the world?—No, never!

Christians are elevated in their conversation; and although they believe it to be sin to condescend to foolish flattery, they are courteous, kind and benevolent. Their words are those of sincerity and truth. They are faithful in their deal with their brethren and with the world. In their dress they avoid superfluity and display; but their clothing will be neat, not gaudy, modest, and arranged upon the person with order and taste. Especial care will be taken to dress in a manner that will show a sacred regard for the holy Sabbath and the worship of God.

The line of demarkation between such a class and the world will be too plain to be mistaken. The influence of believers would be tenfold greater if men and women who accept the truth, who have been formerly careless and slack in their habits, would be so elevated and sanctified through the truth as to observe habits of neatness, order, and good taste in their dress. Our God is a God of order, and He is not in any degree pleased with distraction, with filthiness, or with sin.

Relation to Fashions

Christians should not take pains to make themselves gazing-stocks by dressing differently from the world. But if, in accordance with their faith and duty in respect to their dressing modestly and healthfully, they find themselves out of fashion, they should not change their dress in order to be like the world. But they should manifest a noble independence and moral courage to be right, if all the world differs from them. If the world introduces a modest, convenient, and healthful mode of dress, which is in accordance with the Bible, it will not change our relation to God or to the world to adopt such a style of dress. Christians should follow Christ, and conform their dress to God's Word. They should shun extremes. They should humbly pursue a straight-forward course, irrespective of applause or of censure, and should cling to the right because of its own merits. *Review and Herald*, January 30, 1900.

CHAPTER 119

Proper Dress

The Bible teaches modesty in dress. "In like manner also, that women adorn themselves in modest apparel." 1 Timothy 2:9. This forbids display in dress, gaudy colors, profuse ornamentation. Any device designed to attract attention to the wearer or to excite admiration is excluded from the modest apparel which God's Word enjoins.

Economy in Dress

Our dress is to be inexpensive—not with "gold, or pearls, or costly array." Money is a trust from God. It is not ours to expend for the gratification of pride or ambition. In the hands of God's children it is food for the hungry and clothing for the naked. It is a defense to the oppressed, a means of health to the sick, or preaching the gospel to the poor. You could bring happiness to many hearts by using wisely the money that is now spent for show. Consider the life of Christ. Study His character, and be partakers with Him in His self-denial.

In the professed Christian world enough is expended for jewels and needlessly expensive dress to feed all the hungry and to clothe the naked. Fashion and display absorb the means that might comfort the poor and the suffering. They rob the world of the gospel of the Saviour's love. . . .

Quality and Taste

But our clothing, while modest and simple, should be of good quality, of becoming colors, and suited for service. It should be chosen for durability rather than display. It should provide warmth and proper protection. The wise woman described in the Proverbs "is not afraid of the snow for her household: for all her household are clothed with double garments." Proverbs 31:21, margin.

Health and Cleanliness

Our dress should be cleanly. Uncleanliness in dress is unhealthful, and thus defiling to the body and to the soul. "Ye are the temple of God. . . If any man defile the temple of God, him shall God destroy." 1 Corinthians 3:16, 17.

In all respects the dress should be healthful. "Above all things," God desires us to "be in health" (3 John 2)—health of body and of soul. And we are to be workers together with Him for the health of both soul and body. Both are promoted by healthful dress.

Grace and Natural Beauty

It should have the grace, the beauty, the appropriateness of natural simplicity.

Christ has warned us against the pride of life, but not against its grace and natural beauty. He pointed to the flowers of the field, to the lily unfolding in its purity, and said, "Even Solomon in all his glory was not arrayed like one of these." Matthew 6:29. Thus by the things of nature Christ illustrates the beauty that Heaven values, the modest grace, the simplicity, the purity, the appropriateness, that would make our attire pleasing to Him. *Counsels to Teachers, Parents, and Students*, pp. 302, 303.

CHAPTER 120

Influence of Dress

We do not discourage neatness in dress. Correct taste is not to be despised nor condemned. Our faith, if carried out, will lead us to be so plain in dress, and zealous of good works, that we shall be marked as peculiar. But when we lose taste for order and neatness in dress, we virtually leave the truth; for the truth never degrades, but elevates. When believers are neglectful of their dress, and are coarse and rough in their manners, their influence hurts the truth. "We are," said the inspired apostle, "made a spectacle unto the world, and to angels, and to men." All heaven is marking the daily influence that the professed followers of Christ exert upon the world. . . .

Simplicity of dress will make a sensible woman appear to the best advantage. We judge of a person's character by the style of dress worn. A modest, godly woman will dress modestly. A refined taste, a cultivated mind, will be revealed in the choice of a simple, appropriate attire. The young women who break away from the slavery of fashion will be ornaments to society. The one who is simple and unpretending in her dress and in her manners shows that she understands that a true woman is characterized by moral worth. How charming, how interesting, is simplicity in dress, which in comeliness can be compared with the flowers of the field. *Review and Herald*, November 17, 1904.

CHAPTER 121

Simplicity in Dress

"Whose adorning, let it not be that outward adorning of plaiting the hair, and of wearing of gold, or of putting on of apparel, but let it be the hidden man of the heart, in that which is not corruptible, even the ornament of a meek and quiet spirit, which is in the sight of God of great price."

Human reasoning has ever sought to evade or set aside the simple, direct instructions of the Word of God. In every age, a majority of the professed followers of Christ have disregarded those precepts which enjoin self-denial and humility, which require modesty and simplicity of conversation, deportment, and apparel. The result has ever been the same—departure from the teachings of the gospel leads to the adoption of the fashions, customs, and principles of the world. Vital godliness gives place to a dead formalism. The presence and power of God, withdrawn from those world-loving circles, are found with a class of humbler worshipers, who are willing to obey the teachings of the Sacred Word. Through successive generations, this course has been pursued. One after another, different denominations have risen and, yielding their simplicity, have lost, in a great measure, their early power.

A Snare to God's People

As we see the love of fashion and display among those who profess to believe present truth, we sadly ask, Will the people of God learn nothing from the history of the past? There are few who understand their own hearts. The vain and trifling lovers of fashion may claim to be followers of Christ; but their dress and conversation show what occupies the mind and engages the affections. Their lives betray their friendship for the world, and it claims them as its own.

How can one that has ever tasted the love of Christ be satisfied with the frivolities of fashion? My heart is pained to see those who profess to be followers of the meek and lowly Saviour, so eagerly seeking to conform to the world's standard of dress. Notwithstanding their profession of godliness, they can hardly be distinguished from the unbeliever. They do not enjoy a religious life. Their time and means are devoted to the one object of dressing for display.

Pride and extravagance in dress is a sin to which woman is especially prone. Hence the injunction of the apostle relates directly to her: "In like manner, also, that women adorn themselves in modest apparel, with shamefacedness and sobriety; not with broided hair, or gold, or pearls, or costly array; but (which becometh women professing godliness) with good works."

Reformation Needed

We see steadily gaining ground in the church an evil which the Word of God condemns. What is the duty of those in authority in regard to this matter? Will the influence of the church be what it should be, while many of its members obey the dictates of fashion, rather than the clearly expressed will of

God? How can we expect the presence and aid of the Holy Spirit while we suffer these things to exist among us? Can we remain silent while the teachings of Christ are set aside by His professed followers? These things bring grief and perplexity to those who have the oversight of the church of God. Will not my Christian sisters themselves reflect candidly and prayerfully upon this subject? Will they not seek to be guided by the Word of God? The extra time spent in the making up of apparel according to the fashions of the world should be devoted to close searching of heart and the study of the Scriptures. The hours that are worse than wasted in preparing unnecessary adornings, might be made more valuable than gold if spent in seeking to acquire right principles and solid attainments. My heart aches as I see young ladies professing to be followers of Christ who are practically ignorant of His character and His will. These youth have been satisfied to feed on husks. The glittering tinsel of the world appears more valuable to them than the eternal riches. The mental powers, that might be developed by thought and study, are suffered to lie dormant, and the affections are undisciplined, because the outward apparel is considered of more consequence than spiritual loveliness or mental vigor.

The Inward Adorning

Will the followers of Christ seek to obtain the inward adorning, the meek and quiet spirit which God pronounces of great price, or will they squander the few short hours of probation in needless labor for display? The Lord would have woman seek constantly to improve both in mind and heart, gaining intellectual and moral strength that she may lead a useful and happy life—a blessing to the world and an honor to her Creator.

I would ask the youth of today who profess to believe present truth, wherein they deny self for the truth's sake. When they really desire an article of dress, or some ornament or convenience, do they lay the matter before the Lord in prayer to know if His Spirit would sanction this expenditure of means? In the preparation of their clothing, are they careful not to dishonor their profession of faith? Can they seek the Lord's blessing upon the time thus employed? It is one thing to join the church, and quite another thing to be united to Christ. Unconsecrated, world-loving professors of religion are one of the most serious causes of weakness in the church of Christ.

In this age of the world there is an unprecedented rage for pleasure. Dissipation and reckless extravagance everywhere prevail. The multitudes are eager for amusement. The mind becomes trifling and frivolous, because it is not accustomed to meditation, or disciplined to study. Ignorant sentimentalism is current. God requires that every soul shall be cultivated, refined, elevated, and ennobled. But too often every valuable attainment is neglected for fashionable display and superficial pleasure. Women permit their souls to be starved and dwarfed by fashion, and thus they become a curse to society, rather than a blessing. *Review and Herald*, December 6, 1881.

CHAPTER 122

Idolatry of Dress

The idolatry of dress is a moral disease. It must not be taken over into the new life. In most cases, submission to the gospel requirements will demand a decided change in the dress.

There should be no carelessness in dress. For Christ's sake, whose witnesses we are, we should seek to make the best of our appearance. In the tabernacle service, God specified every detail concerning the garments of those who ministered before Him. Thus we are taught that He has a preference in regard to the dress of those who serve Him. Very specific were the directions given in regard to Aaron's robes, for his dress was symbolic. So the dress of Christ's followers should be symbolic. In all things we are to be representatives of Him. Our appearance in every respect should be characterized by neatness, modesty, and purity. But the Word of God gives no sanction to the making of changes in apparel merely for the sake of fashion—that we may appear like the world. Christians are not to decorate the person with costly array or expensive ornaments.

The words of Scripture in regard to dress should be carefully considered. We need to understand that which the Lord of heaven appreciates in even the dressing of the body. All who are in earnest in seeking for the grace of Christ will heed the precious words of instruction inspired by God. Even the style of the apparel will express the truth of the gospel. *Testimonies for the Church*, Vol. 6, p. 96.

CHAPTER 123

True Adornment

Demoralizing extravagance prevails everywhere, and souls are going to ruin because of their love of dress and display. The life of nine tenths of those who are devotees of fashion is a living lie. Deception, fraud, is their daily practice; for they wish to appear that which they are not.

Nobility of soul, gentleness, generosity, are bartered away to gratify the lust after evil things. Thousands sell their virtue that they may have means for following the fashions of the world. Such madness concerning the changing fashions of the world should call forth an army of reformers who would take their position for simple and plain attire. Satan is ever inventing fashions that cannot be followed except through the sacrifice of money, time, and health.

Following the World

Having before us the picture of the world's demoralization upon the point of fashion, how dare professed Christians follow in the path of the worldling? Shall we appear to sanction these demoralizing fashions by adopting them? Many do adopt the fashions of the world, but it is because Christ is not formed within them, the hope of glory. Luxurious living, extravagant dressing, is carried to such an extent as to constitute one of the signs of the last days.

Pride and vanity are manifested everywhere; but those who

are inclined to look into the mirror to admire themselves, have little inclination to look into the law of God, the great moral mirror. This idolatry of dress destroys all that is humble, meek, and lovely in the character. It consumes the precious hours that should be devoted to meditation, to searching the heart, to the prayerful study of God's Word. In the Word of God, Inspiration has recorded lessons especially for our instruction. . . .

Devotion to dress takes from the means intrusted for works of mercy and benevolence, and this extravagant outlay is robbery toward God. Our means have not been given to us for the gratification of pride and love of display. We are to be wise stewards, and clothe the naked, feed the hungry, and give our means to advance the cause of God. If we want adornment, the graces of meekness, humility, modesty, and prudence are suited to every person, in every rank and condition of life.

Shall we not take our stand as faithful sentinels, and by precept and example frown down indulgence in the dissipation and extravagance of this degenerate age? Shall we not set a right example to our youth, and whether we eat or drink, or whatsoever we do, do all to the glory of God? *Review and Herald*, December 12, 1912.

SECTION XIII
Recreation and Amusement

There is a distinction between recreation and amusement. Recreation, when true to its name, re-creation, tends to strengthen and build up. Calling us aside from our ordinary cares and occupations, it affords refreshment for mind and body, and thus enables us to return with new vigor to the earnest work of life. Amusement, on the other hand, is sought for the sake of pleasure, and is often carried to excess; it absorbs the energies that are required for useful work, and thus proves a hindrance to life's true success. Education, *p. 207.*

CHAPTER 124

The Value of Recreation

Christians should be the most cheerful and happy people that live. They may have the consciousness that God is their father and their everlasting friend.

But many professed Christians do not correctly represent the Christian religion. They appear gloomy, as if under a cloud. They often speak of the great sacrifices they have made to become Christians. They appeal to those who have not accepted Christ, representing by their own example and conversation that they must give up everything which would make life pleasant and joyful. They throw a pall of darkness over the blessed Christian hope. The impression is given that God's requirements are a burden even to the willing soul, and that everything that would give pleasure, or that would delight the taste, must be sacrificed.

We do not hesitate to say that this class of professed Christians have not the genuine article. God is love. Whoso dwelleth in God, dwelleth in love. All who have indeed become acquainted, by experimental knowledge, with the love and tender compassion of our Heavenly Father will impart light and joy wherever they may be. Their presence and influence will be to their associates as the fragrance of sweet flowers, because they are linked to God and heaven, and the purity and exalted loveliness of heaven are communicated through them to all that are brought within their influence. This constitutes them the light of the world, the salt of the earth. They are indeed savors of life unto life, but not of death unto death.

Christian Recreation

It is the privilege and duty of Christians to seek to refresh their spirits and invigorate their bodies by innocent recreation, with the purpose of using their physical and mental powers to the glory of God. Our recreations should not be scenes of senseless mirth, taking the form of the nonsensical. We can conduct them in such a manner as will benefit and elevate those with whom we associate, and better qualify us and them to more successfully attend to the duties devolving upon us as Christians.

We cannot be excusable in the sight of God if we engage in amusements which have a tendency to unfit us for the faithful performance of the ordinary duties of life, and thus lessen our relish for the contemplation of God and heavenly things. The religion of Christ is cheering and elevating in its influence. It is above everything like foolish jesting and joking, vain and frivolous chit-chat. In all our seasons of recreation we may gather from the Divine Source of strength fresh courage and power, that we may the more successfully elevate our lives to purity, true goodness, and holiness.

Love of the Beautiful

Even the great God is a lover of the beautiful. He has given us unmistakable evidence of this in the work of His hands. He planted for our first parents a beautiful garden in Eden. Stately trees were caused to grow out of the ground, of every description, for usefulness and ornament. The beautiful flowers were formed, of rare loveliness, of every tint and hue, perfuming the air. The merry songsters, of varied plumage, caroled forth their joyous songs to the praise of their Creator. It was the design of God that man should find happiness in the employment of tending the things He had created, and that his wants should be met with the fruits of the trees of the garden.

God, who made the Eden home of our first parents so surpassingly lovely, has also given the noble trees, the beautiful flowers, and everything lovely in nature, for our happiness. He has given us these tokens of His love that we may have correct views of His character.

He has implanted in the hearts of His children the love of the beautiful. But by many this love has been perverted. The benefits and beauties which God has bestowed upon us have been worshiped, while the glorious Giver has been forgotten. This is stupid ingratitude. We should acknowledge the love of God to us in all His creative works, and our hearts should respond to these evidences of His love by giving Him the heart's best and holiest affections.

The Master Artist

God has surrounded us with nature's beautiful scenery to attract and interest the mind. It is His design that we should associate the glories of nature with His character. If we faithfully study the book of nature, we shall find it a fruitful source for contemplating the infinite love and power of God.

Many extol artistic skill which will produce lovely paintings upon canvas. All the powers of the being are by many devoted to art, yet how far short do these come of the natural. Art can never attain to the perfection seen in nature. Many professed Christians will go into ecstasies over the painting of an evening sunset. They worship the skill of the artist; but they pass by with indifference the actual glorious sunset which it is their privilege to look upon every cloudless evening.

Where does the artist obtain his design? From nature. But the great Master Artist has painted upon heaven's shifting, changing canvas the glories of the setting sun. He has tinted and gilded the heavens with gold, silver, and crimson, as though the portals of high heaven were thrown open, that we might view its gleamings, and our imagination take hold of the glory within. Many turn carelessly from this heavenly wrought picture. They fail to trace the infinite love and power of God in the surpassing beauties seen in the heavens, but are almost entranced as they view and worship the imperfect paintings, in imitation of the Master Artist. *Review and Herald*, July 25, 1871.

Unfitted to Resist Temptation

Do not suppose that you can unite yourself with the amusement-loving, the gay and pleasure-loving, and at the same time resist temptation. *Signs of the Times*, June 20, 1900.

CHAPTER 125

The Love of Worldly Pleasure

It is an alarming fact that the love of the world predominates in the minds of the young as a class. Many conduct themselves as if the precious hours of probation, while mercy lingers, were one grand holiday, and they were placed in the world merely for their own amusement, to be gratified with a continual round of excitement. They find their pleasures in the world, and in the things of the world, and are strangers to the Father and the graces of His Spirit. Many are reckless in their conversation. They choose to forget that by their words they are to be justified or condemned. God is dishonored by the frivolity and the empty, vain talking and laughing that characterize the life of many of our youth. . . .

Satan makes special efforts to lead them to find happiness in worldly amusements, and to justify themselves by endeavoring to show that these amusements are harmless, innocent, and even important for health. He presents the path of holiness as difficult, while the paths of worldly pleasure are strewn with flowers.

In false and flattering colors, he arrays the world with its pleasures before the youth. But the pleasures of earth will soon come to an end, and that which is sown must also be reaped. Are personal attractions, ability, or talents too valuable to devote to God, the author of our being, Him who watches over us every moment? Are our qualifications too precious to devote to God?

The Way of Wisdom

The youth often urge that they need something to enliven and divert the mind. The Christian's hope is just what is needed. Religion will prove to the believer a comforter, a sure guide to the Fountain of true happiness. The young should study the Word of God, giving themselves to meditation and prayer. They will find that their spare moments cannot be better employed. Wisdom's "ways are ways of pleasantness, and all her paths are peace."

Paul, writing to Titus, exhorts the youth to sobriety: "Young men likewise exhort to be sober-minded. In all things showing thyself a pattern of good works: in doctrine showing uncorruptness, gravity, sincerity, sound speech that cannot be condemned; that he that is of the contrary part may be ashamed, having no evil thing to say of you."

I entreat the youth, for their souls' sake, to heed the exhortation of the apostle. All these gracious instructions, warnings, and reproofs will be either a savor of life unto life or of death unto death.

The young are naturally inclined to feel that not much responsibility, caretaking, or burden-bearing is expected of them. But upon every one rests the obligation to reach the Bible standard. The light that shines forth in privileges and opportunities, in the ministry of the Word, in counsels, warnings, and reproofs, will perfect character, or will condemn the careless. This light is to be cherished by the young as well as by those who are older. Who will now take their stand for God, determined to give His service the first place in their lives? Who will be burden-bearers?

"Remember now thy Creator in the days of thy youth." Jesus desires the service of those who have the dew of youth upon them. He wants them to be heirs of immortality. They may grow up into noble manhood and womanhood, notwithstanding the moral pollution that abounds, that corrupts so many of the youth at an early age. They may be free in Christ; the children of light, not of darkness.

God calls upon every young man and young woman to renounce every evil habit, to be diligent in business, fervent in spirit, serving the Lord. They need not remain in indolence, making no effort to overcome wrong habits or to improve the conduct. The sincerity of their prayers will be proved by the vigor of the effort they make to obey God's commands. At every step they may renounce evil habits and associations, believing that the Lord, by the power of His Spirit, will give them strength to overcome.

Faithfulness in Little Things

Individual, constant, united efforts will be rewarded by success. Those who desire to do a great deal of good in our world must be willing to do it in God's way, by doing little things. He who wishes to reach the loftiest heights of achievement by doing something great and wonderful, will fail of doing anything.

Steady progress in a good work, the frequent repetition of one kind of faithful service, is of more value in God's sight than the doing of one great work, and wins for the youth a good report, giving character to their efforts. . . .

The youth can do good in laboring to save souls. God holds them accountable for the use they make of the talents intrusted to them. Let those who claim to be sons and daughters of God aim at a high standard. Let them use every faculty God has given them. *Youth's Instructor*, January 1, 1907.

Unsatisfied Longings

The continual craving for pleasurable amusements reveals the deep longings of the soul. But those who drink at this fountain of worldly pleasure will find their soul-thirst still unsatisfied. They are deceived; they mistake mirth for happiness; and when the excitement ceases many sink down into the depths of despondency and despair. O what madness, what folly, to forsake the "Fountain of living waters" for the "broken cisterns" of worldly pleasure! *Fundamentals of Christian Education*, p. 422.

Opportunities for Witnessing

If you truly belong to Christ, you will have opportunities for witnessing for Him. You will be invited to attend places of amusement, and then it will be that you will have an opportunity to testify to your Lord. If you are true to Christ then, you will not try to form excuses for your non-attendance, but will plainly and modestly declare that you are a child of God, and your principles would not allow you to be in a place, even for one occasion, where you could not invite the presence of your Lord. *Youth's Instructor*, May 4, 1893.

CHAPTER 126

Words of Counsel

It is in the order of God that the physical as well as the mental powers shall be trained; but the character of the physical exercise taken should be in complete harmony with the lessons given by Christ to His disciples. Those lessons should be exemplified in the lives of Christians, so that in all the education and self-training of teachers and students, the heavenly agencies may not record of them that they are "lovers of pleasures." This is the record now being made of a large number, "Lovers of pleasures more than lovers of God." 2 Timothy 3:4.

Thus Satan and his angels are laying their snares for souls. They are working upon the minds of teachers and students to induce them to engage in exercises and amusements which become intensely absorbing, and which are of a character to strengthen the lower passions, and to create appetites and passions that will counteract the operations of the Spirit of God upon human hearts.

All the teachers in a school need exercise, a change of employment. God has pointed out what this should be—useful, practical work. But many have turned away from God's plan to follow human inventions, to the detriment of spiritual life. Amusements are doing more to counteract the working of the Holy Spirit than anything else, and the Lord is grieved. . . .

"Be sober, be vigilant; because your adversary the devil, as a roaring lion, walketh about, seeking whom he may devour," 1

Peter 5:8. He is on the playground, watching your amusements, and catching every soul whom he finds off guard, sowing his seeds in human hearts, and gaining control of human minds. He is present in every exercise in the schoolroom. Those students who allow their minds to be deeply excited over games are not in the best condition to receive the instruction, the counsel, the reproof, most essential for them.

Physical exercise was marked out by the God of wisdom. Some hours each day should be devoted to useful education in lines of work that will help the students in learning the duties of practical life, which are essential for all our youth.

There is need of every one in every school and in every other institution being as was Daniel, in such close connection with the Source of all wisdom that he will be enabled to reach the highest standard in every line. The love and fear of God was before Daniel; and conscious of his amenability to God, he trained all his powers to respond as far as possible to the loving care of the great Teacher. The four Hebrew children would not allow selfish motives and love of amusements to occupy the golden moments of life. They worked with willing heart and ready mind. This is no higher standard than every Christian youth may reach. *Counsels to Teachers, Parents, and Students*, pp. 281-284.

CHAPTER 127

Dangerous Amusements for the Young

The desire for excitement and pleasing entertainment is a temptation and a snare to God's people, and especially to the young. Satan is constantly preparing inducements to attract minds from the solemn work of preparation for scenes just in the future. Through the agency of worldlings he keeps up a continual excitement to induce the unwary to join in worldly pleasures. There are shows, lectures, and an endless variety of entertainments that are calculated to lead to a love of the world; and through this union with the world faith is weakened.

Satan is a persevering workman, an artful, deadly foe. Whenever an incautious word is spoken, whether in flattery or to cause the youth to look upon some sin with less abhorrence, he takes advantage of it, and nourishes the evil seed, that it may take root and yield a bountiful harvest. He is in every sense of the word a deceiver, a skilful charmer. He has many finely woven nets, which appear innocent, but which are skilfully prepared to entangle the young and unwary. The natural mind leans toward pleasure and self-gratification. It is Satan's policy to fill the mind with a desire for worldly amusement, that there may be no time for the question, How is it with my soul?

An Unfortunate Age

We are living in an unfortunate age for the young. The prevailing influence in society is in favor of allowing the youth to follow the natural turn of their own minds. If their children are very wild, parents flatter themselves that when they are older and reason for themselves they will leave off their wrong habits, and become useful men and women. What a mistake! For years they permit an enemy to sow the garden of the heart, and suffer wrong principles to grow and strengthen, seeming not to discern the hidden dangers and the fearful ending of the path that seems to them the way of happiness. In many cases all the labor afterward bestowed upon these youth will avail nothing.

The standard of piety is low among professed Christians generally, and it is hard for the young to resist the worldly influences that are encouraged by many church-members. The majority of nominal Christians, while they profess to be living for Christ, are really living for the world. They do not discern the excellence of heavenly things, and therefore cannot truly love them. Many profess to be Christians because Christianity is considered honorable. They do not discern that genuine Christianity means cross-bearing, and their religion has little influence to restrain them from taking part in worldly pleasures.

Some can enter the ballroom, and unite in all the amusements which it affords. Others cannot go to such lengths as this, yet they can attend parties of pleasure, picnics, shows, and other places or worldly amusement; and the most discerning eye would fail to detect any difference between their appearance and that of unbelievers.

In the present state of society it is no easy task for parents to restrain their children, and instruct them according to the Bible rule of right. Children often become impatient under restraint, and wish to have their own way and to go and come as they please. Especially from the age of ten to eighteen they are inclined to feel that there can be no harm in going to worldly gatherings of young associates. But the experienced Christian parents can see danger. They are acquainted with the peculiar temperaments of their children, and know the influence of these things upon their minds; and from a desire for their salvation, they should keep them back from these exciting amusements.

When the children decide for themselves to leave the pleasures of the world and to become Christ's disciples, what a burden is lifted from the hearts of careful, faithful parents! Yet even then the labors of the parents must not cease. These youth have just commenced in earnest the warfare against sin, and against the evils of the natural heart, and they need in a special sense the counsel and watch-care of their parents.

A Time of Trial Before the Young

Young Sabbath-keepers who have yielded to the influence of the world, will have to be tested and proved. The perils of the last days are upon us, and a trial is before the young which many have not anticipated. They will be brought into distressing perplexity, and the genuineness of their faith will be proved. They profess to be looking for the Son of man; yet some of them have been a miserable example to unbelievers. They have not been willing to give up the world, but have united with the world in attending picnics and other gatherings for pleasure, flattering themselves that they were engaging in innocent amusement. Yet it is just such indulgences that separate them from God, and make them children of the world.

Some are constantly leaning to the world. Their views and feelings harmonize much better with the spirit of the world than with that of Christ's self-denying followers. It is perfectly natural that they should prefer the company of those whose spirit will best agree with their own. And such have quite too much influence among God's people. They take part with them, and have a name among them; but they are a text for unbelievers, and for the weak and unconsecrated ones in the church. In this refining time these professors will either be wholly converted and sanctified by obedience to the truth, or they will be left with the world, to receive their reward with the worldling.

God does not own the pleasure-seeker as His follower. Those only who are self-denying, and who live lives of sobriety, humility, and holiness, are true followers of Jesus. And such cannot enjoy the frivolous, empty conversation of the lover of the world.

Separation From the World

The true followers of Christ will have sacrifices to make. They will shun places of worldly amusement because they find no Jesus there—no influence which will make them heavenly minded and increase their growth in grace. Obedience to the

Word of God will lead them to come out from all these things, and be separate.

"By their fruits ye shall know them" (Matthew 7:20), the Saviour declared. All the true followers of Christ bear fruit to His glory. Their lives testify that a good work has been wrought in them by the Spirit of God, and their fruit is unto holiness. Their lives are elevated and pure. Right actions are the unmistakable fruit of true godliness, and those who bear no fruit of this kind reveal that they have no experience in the things of God. They are not in the Vine. Said Jesus, "Abide in Me, and I in you. As the branch cannot bear fruit of itself, except it abide in the vine; no more can ye, except ye abide in Me. I am the vine, ye are the branches: he that abideth in Me, and I in him, the same bringeth forth much fruit: for without Me ye can do nothing." John 15:4, 5.

Those who would be worshipers of the true God must sacrifice every idol. Jesus said to the lawyer, "Thou shalt love the Lord thy God with all thy heart, and with all thy soul, and with all thy mind. This is the first commandment." Matthew 22:37, 38. The first four precepts of the decalogue allow no separation of the affections from God. Nor must anything share our supreme delight in Him. We cannot advance in Christian experience until we put away everything that separates us from God.

The great Head of the church, who has chosen His people out of the world, requires them to be separate from the world. He designs that the spirit of His commandments, by drawing His followers to Himself, shall separate them from worldly elements.

To love God and keep His commandments is far away from loving the world's pleasures and its friendship. There is no concord between Christ and Belial.

Promises to the Young

The youth who follow Christ have a warfare before them; they have a daily cross to bear in coming out of the world and imitating the life of Christ. But there are many precious promises on record for those who seek the Saviour early. Wisdom calls to the sons of men, "I love them that love me; and those that seek me early shall find me." Proverbs 8:17.

"Wherefore gird up the loins of your mind, be sober, and hope to the end for the grace that is to be brought unto you at the revelation of Jesus Christ; as obedient children, not fashioning yourselves according to the former lusts in your ignorance: but as He which hath called you is holy, so be ye holy in all manner of conversation." 1 Peter 1:13-15. "For the grace of God that bringeth salvation hath appeared to all men, teaching us that, denying ungodliness and worldly lusts, we should live soberly, righteously, and godly, in this present world; looking for that blessed hope, and the glorious appearing of the great God and our Saviour Jesus Christ; who gave Himself for us, that He might redeem us from all iniquity, and purify unto Himself a peculiar people, zealous of good works." Titus 2:11-14. *Counsels to Teachers, Parents, and Students*, pp. 325-330.

CHAPTER 128

Establishing Right Principles in the Youth

The young should be controlled by firm principle, that they may rightly improve the powers which God has given them. But youth follow impulse so much and so blindly, without reference to principle, that they are constantly in danger. Since they cannot always have the guidance and protection of parents and guardians, they need to be trained to self-reliance and self-control. They must be taught to think and act from conscientious principle.

Relaxation and Amusement

Those who are engaged in study should have relaxation. The mind must not be constantly confined to close thought, for the delicate mental machinery becomes worn. The body as well as the mind must have exercise. But there is great need of temperance in amusements, as in every other pursuit. And the character of these amusements should be carefully and thoroughly considered. Every youth should ask himself, What influence will these amusements have on physical, mental, and moral health? Will my mind become so infatuated as to forget God? Shall I cease to have His glory before me?

Card-playing should be prohibited. The associations and tendencies are dangerous. . . . There is nothing in such amusements beneficial to soul or body. There is nothing to strengthen the intellect, nothing to store it with valuable ideas for future use. The conversation is often upon trivial and degrading subjects. . . .

Expertness in handling cards often leads to a desire to put this knowledge and tact to some use for personal benefit. A small sum is staked, and then a larger, until a thirst for gaming is acquired, which leads to certain ruin. How many has this pernicious amusement led to every sinful practice, to poverty, to prison, to murder, and to the gallows! And yet many parents do not see the terrible gulf of ruin that is yawning for our youth.

Among the most dangerous resorts for pleasure is the theater. Instead of being a school for morality and virtue, as is so often claimed, it is the very hotbed of immorality. Vicious habits and sinful propensities are strengthened and confirmed by these entertainments. Low songs, lewd gestures, expressions, and attitudes, deprave the imagination and debase the morals. Every youth who habitually attends such exhibitions will be corrupted in principle. There is no influence in our land more powerful to poison the imagination, to destroy religious impressions, and to blunt the relish for tranquil pleasures and sober realities of life, than theatrical amusements.

The love for these scenes increases with every indulgence, as the desire for intoxicating drink strengthens with its use. The only safe course is to shun the theater, the circus, and every other questionable place of amusement.

There are modes of recreation which are highly beneficial to both body and mind. An enlightened, discriminating mind will find abundant means for entertainment and diversion, from sources not only innocent, but instructive. Recreation in the open air, the contemplation of the works of God in nature, will be of the highest benefit. *Testimonies for the Church*, Vol. 4, pp. 651-653.

Provide Innocent Pleasures

Youth cannot be made as sedate and grave as old age, the child as sober as the sire. While sinful amusements are condemned, as they should be, let parents, teachers, and guardians of youth provide in their stead innocent pleasures, which will not taint or corrupt the morals. Do not bind down the young to rigid rules and restraints that will lead them to feel themselves oppressed, and to break over and rush into paths of folly and destruction. With a firm, kind, considerate hand, hold the lines of government, guiding and controlling their minds and purposes, yet so gently, so wisely, so lovingly, that they will still know that you have their best good in view. *Counsels to Teachers, Parents, and Students*, p. 335.

Recreation in Missionary Work

The hours so often spent in amusement that refreshes neither body nor soul should be spent in visiting the poor, the sick, and the suffering, or in seeking to help some one who is in need. *Testimonies for the Church,* Vol. 6, p. 276.

CHAPTER 129

Unholy Influences at Work

I entreat the students in our schools to be sober-minded. The frivolity of the young is not pleasing to God. Their sports and games open the door to a flood of temptations. They are in possession of God's heavenly endowment in their intellectual faculties, and they should not allow their thoughts to be cheap and low. A character formed in accordance with the precepts of God's Word will reveal steadfast principles, pure, noble aspirations. The Holy Spirit cooperates with the powers of the human mind, and high and holy impulses are the sure result. . . .

The low, common pleasure parties, gatherings for eating and drinking, singing and playing on instruments of music, are inspired by a spirit that is from beneath. They are an oblation unto Satan. . . .

Those who take the lead in these frivolities bring upon the cause a stain not easily effaced. They wound their own souls, and will carry the scars through their lifetime. The evil-doer may see his sins, and repent, and God may pardon the transgressor; but the power of discernment which ought ever to be kept keen and sensitive to distinguish between the sacred and the common, is in a great measure destroyed. *Counsels to Teachers, Parents, and Students*, pp. 366-368.

CHAPTER 130

Joy in Religion

The future abode of the righteous, and their everlasting reward, are high and ennobling themes for the young to contemplate. Dwell upon the marvelous plan of salvation, the great sacrifice made by the King of glory that you might be elevated through the merits of His blood, and by obedience finally be exalted to the throne of Christ. This subject should engage the noblest contemplation of the mind. To be brought into favor with God—what a privilege! . . .

Young friends, I saw that with such employment and diversion as this, you might be happy. But the reason why you are restless is, you do not seek to the only true source for happiness. You are ever trying to find *out* of Christ the enjoyment which is found only *in* Him. In Him are no disappointed hopes. Prayer—oh, how is this precious privilege neglected! The reading of the Word of God prepares the mind for prayer. One of the greatest reasons why you have so little disposition to draw nearer to God by prayer is, you have unfitted yourselves for this sacred work by reading fascinating stories, which have excited the imagination and aroused unholy passions. The Word of God becomes distasteful, the hour of prayer is forgotten. Prayer is the strength of the Christian. When alone, he is not alone; he feels the presence of One who has said, "Lo, I am with you alway."

The young want just what they have not; namely, *religion.* Nothing can take the place of this. Profession alone is nothing.

Names are registered upon the church-books upon earth, but not in the book of life. I saw that there is not one in twenty of the youth who knows what experimental religion is. They serve themselves, and yet profess to be servants of Christ; but unless the spell which is upon them be broken, they will soon realize that the portion of the transgressor is theirs. As for self-denial or sacrifice for the truth's sake, they have found an easier way above it all. As for the earnest pleading with tears and strong cries to God for His pardoning grace, and for strength from Him to resist the temptations of Satan, they have found it unnecessary to be so earnest and zealous; they can get along well without it. Christ, the King of glory, went often alone to the mountains and desert places to pour out His soul's request to His Father; but sinful man, in whom is no strength, thinks he can live without so much prayer. *Testimonies for the Church*, Vol. I, pages 503-505.

The Example of Jesus

Jesus reproved self-indulgence in all its forms, yet He was social in His nature. He accepted the hospitality of all classes, visiting the homes of the rich and the poor, the learned and the ignorant, and seeking to elevate their thoughts from questions of commonplace life to those things that are spiritual and eternal. He gave no license to dissipation, and no shadow of worldly levity marred His conduct; yet he found pleasure in scenes of innocent happiness, and by His presence sanctioned the social gathering. *The Desire of Ages*, pp. 150, 151.

CHAPTER 131

Christian Recreation

While we are seeking to refresh our spirits and invigorate our bodies, we are required of God to use all our powers at all times to the best purpose. We can, and should, conduct our recreations in such a manner that we shall be better fitted for the more successful discharge of the duties devolving upon us, and our influence will be more beneficial upon those with whom we associate. We can return from such occasions to our homes improved in mind and refreshed in body, and prepared to engage in the work anew with better hope and better courage. . .

We are here to benefit humanity and to be a blessing to society; and if we let our minds run in that low channel that many who are seeking only vanity and folly permit their minds to run in, how can we be a benefit to our race and generation? How can we be a blessing to society around us? . . .

Principles Contrasted

Between the associations of the followers of Christ for Christian recreation and worldly gatherings for pleasure and amusement will exist a marked contrast. Instead of prayer and the mentioning of Christ and sacred things, will be heard from the lips of worldlings the silly laugh and the trifling conversation. The idea is to have a general high time. Their amusements commence in folly and end in vanity. Our gatherings should be so conducted, and we should so conduct ourselves, that when we return to our homes we can have a conscience void of offense toward God and man; a consciousness that we have not wounded or injured in any manner those with whom we have been associated, or had an injurious influence over them.

The natural mind leans toward pleasure and self-gratification. It is Satan's policy to manufacture an abundance of this. He seeks to fill the minds of men with a desire for worldly amusement, that they may have no time to ask themselves the question, How is it with my soul? The love of pleasure is infectious. Given up to this, the mind hurries from one point to another, ever seeking for some amusement. Obedience to the law of God counteracts this inclination, and builds barriers against ungodliness. *Counsels to Teachers, Parents, and Students*, pp. 336, 337.

Young men should remember that they are accountable for all the privileges they have enjoyed, for the improvement of their time, and for the right use of their abilities. They may inquire, Shall we have no amusement or recreation? Shall we work, work, work, without variation?

Any amusement in which you can engage asking the blessing of God upon it in faith, will not be dangerous. But any amusement which disqualifies you for secret prayer, for devotion at the altar of prayer, or for taking part in the prayer meeting, is not safe, but dangerous. *Counsels to Teachers, Parents, and Students*, p. 337.

CHAPTER 132

Social Gatherings

Gatherings for social intercourse are made in the highest degree profitable and instructive when those who meet together have the love of God glowing in their hearts; when they meet to exchange thoughts in regard to the Word of God, or to consider methods for advancing His work and doing good to their fellow men. When the Holy Spirit is regarded as a welcome guest at these gatherings, when nothing is said or done to grieve it away, God is honored, and those who meet together are refreshed and strengthened.

But there are social gatherings of a different character, where pride of appearance, hilarity, and trifling are too often seen. In their desire for amusement, those who attend are in danger of forgetting God, and things take place that make the watching angels weep. The scene of pleasure becomes, for the time being, their paradise. All give themselves up to hilarity and mirth. The eyes sparkle, the cheek is flushed; but conscience sleeps.

Lack of Spirituality Revealed

Such enthusiasm and inspiration have not a heavenly origin. They are entirely of this earth. Sadly the angels of heaven look upon the forgetfulness of those for whom Christ has done so much. When sickness and death come to those who have lived merely for self-pleasing, too late they find that they have no oil in their lamps, and that they are utterly unfit to close their life's history.

The tenor of the conversation carried on at many social gatherings reveals what the heart is set upon. The trifling talk, the foolish witticisms, spoken only to create a laugh, do not rightly represent Christ. Those who utter them would not be willing to meet a record of their words. Wrong impressions are made upon the listeners, and reproach is cast upon Christ. O that the youth would guard well their words! for by them they will be justified or by them condemned. Remember that Jesus is beside you wherever you go, noting your actions and listening to your words. Would you be ashamed to hear His voice speaking to you, and to know that He hears your conversation? . . .

The once earnest Christian who takes part in worldly amusements is on dangerous ground. He has left the region pervaded by the vital atmosphere of heaven, and has plunged into an atmosphere of mist and fog; for in many cases pleasure parties and gatherings for amusement are a reproach to the religion of Christ.

He who maintains his connection with God cannot in heart participate in them. The words he hears are not congenial to him; for they are not the language of Canaan. The speakers do not give evidence that they are making melody in their hearts to God.

Subtle Influences

Those who are artificial in character and religious experience too readily gather for pleasure and amusement, and their influence attracts others. Sometimes young men and women who are trying to be Bible Christians are persuaded to join the party. Unwilling to be thought singular, and naturally inclined to follow the example of others, they place themselves under the influence of those who, perhaps, have never felt the divine touch on mind or heart. Had they prayerfully consulted the divine standard, to learn what Christ has said in regard to the fruit to be borne on the Christian tree, they would have discerned that these entertainments were really banquets prepared to keep souls from accepting the invitation to the marriage supper of the Lamb.

It sometimes happens that by frequenting places of amusement, youth who have been carefully instructed in the way of the Lord are carried away by the glamour of human influence, and form attachments for those whose education and training have been of a worldly character. They sell themselves into lifelong bondage by uniting with persons who have not the ornament of a Christlike spirit. Those who truly love and serve God will fear to descend to the world's level by choosing the society of those who have not enthroned Christ in their hearts. They will stand boldly for Christ, even though their course may be one of self-denial and self-sacrifice.

The Antidote for Frivolity

Christ lived a life of toil and sacrifice for us, and can we not deny ourselves for Him? Are not the atonement He has made for us and the righteousness He waits to give us themes worthy of occupying our minds? If the youth will draw from the storehouse of the Bible the treasures it contains, if they will meditate on the pardon, peace, and everlasting righteousness that crown a life of self-denial, they will have no desire for questionable excitement of amusement.

Christ rejoices when the thoughts of the young are occupied by the grand and ennobling themes of salvation. He enters the hearts of all such as an abiding guest, filling them with joy and peace. And the love of Christ in the soul is as "a well of water, springing up into everlasting life." . . . Those who possess this love will delight to talk of the things that God has prepared for them that love Him.

The eternal God has drawn the line of distinction between the saint and the sinner, between converted and unconverted. The two classes do not blend into each other imperceptibly, like the colors of a rainbow, but are as distinct as midday and midnight. God's people cannot with safety enter into intimate associations with those who know the truth, but do not practice it. The patriarch Jacob, when speaking of certain deeds of his sons, which he contemplated with horror, exclaimed, "O my soul, come not thou into their secret; unto their assembly mine honor, be not thou united." He felt that his own honor would be compromised if he associated with sinners in their doings. He lifted the danger signal, warning us to shun wrong associations, lest we become tainted with evil. And the Holy Spirit, through the apostle Paul, utters a similar warning, "Have no fellowship with the unfruitful works of darkness, but rather reprove them." *Youth's Instructor*, February 4, 1897.

Acceptable Social Gatherings

Every talent of influence is to be sacredly cherished and used for the purpose of gathering souls to Christ. Young men and young women should not think that their sports, their evening parties and musical entertainments, as usually conducted, are acceptable to Christ.

Light has been given me, again and again, that all our gatherings should be characterized by a decided religious influence. If our young people would assemble to read and understand the Scriptures, asking, "What shall I do that I may have eternal life?" and then place themselves unitedly upon the side of truth, the Lord Jesus would let His blessing come into their hearts.

O that every church-member, every worker in our institutions, might realize that this life is a school in which to prepare for examination by the God of heaven, with regard to purity, cleanness of thought, unselfishness of action! Every word and act, every thought, is recorded on the record books of heaven. . . .

It is through the power and prevalence of truth that we must be sanctified, and elevated to the true dignity of the standard set forth in the Word. The way of the Lord can be learned only through most careful obedience to His Word. Study the Word. *Youth's Instructor*, August 14, 1906.

CHAPTER 133

How to Spend Holidays

Recreation is needful to those who are engaged in physical labor, and is still more essential for those whose labor is principally mental. It is not essential to our salvation, nor for the glory of God, to keep the mind laboring constantly and excessively, even upon religious themes. There are amusements, such as dancing, card-playing, chess, checkers, etc., which we cannot approve, because Heaven condemns them. These amusements open the door for great evil. They are not beneficial in their tendency, but have an exciting influence, producing in some minds a passion for those plays which lead to gambling and dissipation. All such plays should be condemned by Christians, and something perfectly harmless should be substituted in their place.

I saw that our holidays should not be spent in patterning after the world, yet they should not be passed by unnoticed, for this will bring dissatisfaction to our children. On these days when there is danger that our children will exposed to evil influences, and become corrupted by the pleasures and excitement of the world, let the parents study to get up something to take the place of more dangerous amusements. Give your children to understand that you have their good and happiness in view.

Let several families living in a city or village unite and leave the occupations which have taxed them physically and mentally, and make an excursion into the country, to the side of a fine lake or to a nice grove, where the scenery of nature is beautiful. They should provide themselves with plain, hygienic food, the very best fruits and grains, and spread their table under the shade of some tree, or under the canopy of heaven. The ride, the exercise, and the scenery will quicken the appetite, and they can enjoy a repast which kings might envy.

On such occasions parents and children should feel free from care, labor, and perplexity. Parents should become children with their children, making everything as pleasant for them as possible. Let the whole day be given to recreation.

Exercise in the open air, for those whose employment has been within doors and sedentary, will be beneficial to health. All who can, should feel it a duty to pursue this course. Nothing will be lost, but much gained. They can return to their occupations with new life and new courage to engage in their labor with zeal, and they are better prepared to resist disease. *Testimonies for the Church*, Vol. 1, pp. 514, 515.

Christian Sources of Pleasure

God has provided for every one pleasure that may be enjoyed by rich and poor alike—the pleasure found in cultivating pureness of thought and unselfishness of action, the pleasure that comes from speaking sympathizing words and doing kindly deeds. From those who perform such service, the light of Christ shines to brighten lives darkened by many sorrows. *Testimonies for the Church*, Vol. 9, page 57.

CHAPTER 134

Literary Societies

It is often asked, Are literary societies a benefit to our youth? To answer this question properly, we should consider not only the avowed purpose of such societies, but the influence which they have actually exerted, as proved by experience. The improvement of the mind is a duty which we owe to ourselves, to society, and to God. But we should never devise means for the cultivation of the intellect at the expense of the moral and the spiritual. And it is only by the harmonious development of both the mental and the moral faculties that the highest perfection of either can be attained. Are these results secured by literary societies as they are generally conducted?

Literary societies are almost universally exerting an influence contrary to that which the name indicates. As generally conducted, they are an injury to the youth; for Satan comes in to put his stamp upon the exercises. All that makes men manly or women womanly is reflected from the character of Christ. The less we have of Christ in such societies, the less we have of the elevating, refining, ennobling element which should prevail. When worldlings conduct these meetings to meet their wishes, the spirit of Christ is excluded. The mind is drawn away from serious reflection, away from God, away from the real and substantial, to the imaginary and the superficial. Literary societies—would that the name expressed their true character! What is the chaff to the wheat?

The purposes and objects which lead to the formation of literary societies may be good; but unless wisdom from God shall control these organizations, they will become a positive evil. The irreligious and unconsecrated in heart and life are usually admitted, and are often placed in the most responsible positions. Rules and regulations may be adopted that are thought to be sufficient to hold in check every deleterious influence; but Satan, a shrewd general, is at work to mould the society to suit his plans, and in time he too often succeeds. The great adversary finds ready access to those whom he has controlled in the past, and through them he accomplishes his purpose. Various entertainments are introduced to make the meetings interesting and attractive for worldlings, and thus the exercises of the so-called literary society too often degenerate into demoralizing theatrical performances and cheap nonsense. All these gratify the carnal mind, which is at enmity with God; but they do not strengthen the intellect nor confirm the morals.

The association of the God-fearing with the unbelieving in these societies does not make saints of sinners. When God's people voluntarily unite with the worldly and the unconsecrated, and give them the pre-eminence, they will be led away from Him by the unsanctified influence under which they have placed themselves. For a short time there may be nothing seriously objectionable, but minds that have not been brought under the control of the Spirit of God will not take readily to those things which savor of truth and righteousness. If they had had heretofore any relish for spiritual things, they would have placed themselves in the ranks of Jesus Christ. The two classes are controlled by different masters, and are opposites in their purposes, hopes, tastes, and desires. The followers of Jesus enjoy sober, sensible, ennobling themes, while those who have no love for sacred things cannot take pleasure in these gatherings, unless the superficial and unreal constitutes a prominent feature of the exercises. Little by little the spiritual element is ruled out by the irreligious, and the effort to harmonize principles which are antagonistic in their nature proves a decided failure.

Efforts have been made to devise a plan for the establishment of a literary society which shall prove a benefit to all connected with it—a society in which all the members shall feel a moral responsibility to make it what it should be, and to avoid the evils which often make such associations dangerous to religious principles. Persons of discretion and good judgment, who have a living connection with heaven, who will see the evil tendencies, and, not deceived by Satan, will move straight forward in the path of integrity, continually holding aloft the banner of Christ—such ones are needed to control in these societies. Such an influence will command respect, and make these gatherings a blessing rather than a curse.

If men and women of mature age would unite with the youth to organize and conduct such a literary society, it might become both useful and interesting. But when such gatherings degenerate into occasions for fun and boisterous mirth, they are anything but literary or elevating. They are debasing to both mind and morals.

Bible reading, the critical examination of Bible subjects, essays written upon topics which would improve the mind and impart knowledge, the study of the prophecies or the precious lessons of Christ— these will have an influence to strengthen the mental powers and increase spirituality. A familiar acquaintance with the Scriptures sharpens the discerning powers, and fortifies the soul against the attacks of Satan.

Few realize that it is a duty to exercise control over the thoughts and imaginations. It is difficult to keep the undisciplined mind fixed upon profitable subjects. But if the thoughts are not properly employed, religion cannot flourish in the soul. The mind must be preoccupied with sacred and eternal things, or it will cherish trifling and superficial thoughts. Both the intellectual and the moral powers must be disciplined, and they will strengthen and improve by exercise. . . .

The intellect, as well as the heart, must be consecrated to the service of God. He has claims upon all there is of us. The follower of Christ should not indulge in any gratification, or engage in any enterprise, however innocent or laudable it may appear, which an enlightened conscience tells him would abate his ardor or lessen his spirituality. Every Christian should labor to press back the tide of evil, and save our youth from the influences that would sweep them down to ruin. May God help us to press our way against the current. *Counsels to Teachers, Parents, and Students*, pp. 541-544.

CHAPTER 135

Dancing

The true Christian will not desire to enter any place of amusement or engage in any diversion upon which he cannot ask the blessing of God. He will not be found at the theater, the billiard hall, or the bowling saloon. He will not unite with the gay waltzers, or indulge in any other bewitching pleasure that will banish Christ from the mind.

To those who plead for these diversions, we answer, We cannot indulge in them in the name of Jesus of Nazareth. The blessing of God would not be invoked upon the hour spent at the theater or in the dance. No Christian would wish to meet death in such a place. No one would wish to be found there when Christ shall come.

When we come to the final hour, and stand face to face with the record of our lives, shall we regret that we have attended so few parties of pleasure? that we have participated in so few scenes of thoughtless mirth? Shall we not, rather, bitterly regret that so many precious hours have been wasted in self-gratification—so many opportunities neglected, which, rightly improved, would have secured for us immortal treasures?

It has become customary for professors of religion to excuse almost any pernicious indulgence to which the heart is wedded. By familiarity with sin, they become blinded to its enormity. Many who claim to be children of God gloss over sins which His Word condemns, by linking some purpose of church charity with their godless carousals. Thus they borrow the livery of heaven to serve the devil in. Souls are deceived, led astray, and lost to virtue and integrity by these fashionable dissipations.

In the Path of Dissipation

In many religious families, dancing and card-playing are made a parlor pastime. It is urged that these are quiet, home amusements, which may be safely enjoyed under the parental eye. But a love for these exciting pleasures is thus cultivated, and that which was considered harmless at home will not long be regarded dangerous abroad. It is yet to be ascertained that there is any good to be obtained from these amusements. They do not give vigor to the body nor rest to the mind. They do not implant in the soul one virtuous or holy sentiment. On the contrary, they destroy all relish for serious thought and for religious services. It is true that there is a wide contrast between the better class of select parties and the promiscuous and degraded assemblies of the low dance house. Yet all are steps in the path of dissipation.

The amusement of dancing, as conducted at the present day, is a school of depravity, a fearful curse to society. If all in our great cities who are yearly ruined by this means could be brought together, what histories of wrecked lives would be revealed. How many who now stand ready to apologize for this practice would be filled with anguish and amazement at the result. How can professedly Christian parents consent to place their children in the way of temptation, by attending with them such scenes of festivity? How can young men and young women barter their souls for this infatuating pleasure? *Review and Herald*, February 28, 1882.

The Danger of Amusements

The love of pleasure is one of the most dangerous, because it is one of the most subtle, of the many temptations that assail the children and youth in the cities. Holidays are numerous; games and horse racing draw thousands, and the whirl of excitement and pleasure attracts them away from the sober duties of life. Money that should have been saved for better uses—in many cases the scanty earnings of the poor—is frittered away for amusements. *Fundamentals of Christian Education*, p. 422.

Guided by Principle

Many are so fearful of provoking unfriendly criticism or malicious gossip that they dare not act from principle. They dare not identify themselves with those who follow Christ fully. They desire to conform to worldly customs and secure the approbation of worldlings. Christ gave Himself for us "that He might redeem us from all iniquity, and purify unto Himself a peculiar people, zealous of good works." *Review and Herald*, November 29, 1887.

SECTION XIV
Social Relations

It is through the social relations that Christianity comes in contact with the world. Every man or woman who has received the divine illumination is to shed light on the dark pathway of those who are unacquainted with the better way. Social power, sanctified by the Spirit of Christ, must be improved in bringing souls to the Saviour. The Ministry of Healing, *p. 496.*

CHAPTER 136

Social to Save

The example of Christ in linking Himself with the interests of humanity should be followed by all who preach His Word, and by all who have received the gospel of His grace. We are not to renounce social communion. We should not seclude ourselves from others. In order to reach all classes, we must meet them where they are. They will seldom seek us of their own accord. Not alone from the pulpit are the hearts of men touched by divine truth. There is another field of labor, humbler, it may be, but fully as promising. It is found in the home of the lowly, and in the mansion of the great; at the hospitable board, and in gatherings for innocent social enjoyment.

As disciples of Christ we shall not mingle with the world from a mere love of pleasure, to unite with them in folly. Such associations can result only in harm. We should never give sanction to sin by our words or our deeds, our silence or our presence. Wherever we go, we are to carry Jesus with us, and to reveal to others the preciousness of our Saviour. But those who try to preserve their religion by hiding it within stone walls lose precious opportunities of doing good. Through the social relations, Christianity comes in contact with the world. Every one who has received the divine illumination is to brighten the pathway of those who know not the Light of life.

We should all become witnesses for Jesus. Social power, sanctified by the grace of Christ, must be improved in winning souls to the Saviour. Let the world see that we are not selfishly absorbed in our own interests, but that we desire others to share our blessings and privileges. Let them see that our religion does not make us unsympathetic or exacting. Let all who profess to have found Christ minister as He did for the benefit of men.

We should never give to the world the false impression that Christians are a gloomy, unhappy people. If our eyes are fixed on Jesus, we shall see a compassionate Redeemer, and shall catch light from His countenance. Wherever His spirit reigns, there peace abides. And there will be joy also, for there is a calm, holy trust in God.

Christ is pleased with His followers when they show that, though human, they are partakers of the divine nature. They are not statues, but living men and women. Their hearts, refreshed by the dews of divine grace, open and expand to the Sun of Righteousness. The light that shines upon them they reflect upon others in works that are luminous with the love of Christ. *The Desire of Ages*, pp. 152, 153.

Association Influences Destiny

God's Word places great stress upon the influence of association, even on men and women. How much greater is its power on the developing mind and character of children and youth! The company they keep, the principles they adopt, the habits they form, will decide the question of their usefulness here, and of their future destiny. *Counsels to Teachers, Parents, and Students*, p. 220.

CHAPTER 137

Christian Sociability and Courtesy

Christian sociability is altogether too little cultivated by God's people. This branch of education should not be neglected or lost sight of in our schools.

Students should be taught that they are not independent atoms, but that each one is a thread which is to unite with other threads in composing a fabric. In no department can this instruction be more effectually given than in the school home. Here students are daily surrounded by opportunities which, if improved, will greatly aid in developing the social traits of their characters. It lies in their own power so to improve their time and opportunities as to develop a character that will make them happy and useful. Those who shut themselves up within themselves, who are unwilling to be drawn upon to bless others by friendly associations, lose many blessings; for by mutual contact minds receive polish and refinement; by social intercourse acquaintances are formed and friendships contracted which result in a unity of heart and an atmosphere of love which is pleasing in the sight of heaven.

Especially should those who have tasted the love of Christ develop their social powers, for in this way they may win souls to the Saviour. Christ should not be hid away in their hearts, shut in as a coveted treasure, sacred and sweet, to be enjoyed solely by themselves; nor should the love of Christ be manifested toward those only who please their fancy. Students are to be taught the Christlikeness of exhibiting a kindly interest, a social disposition, toward those who are in the greatest need, even though these may not be their own chosen companions. At all times and in all places Jesus manifested a loving interest in the human family, and shed about Him the light of a cheerful piety. Students should be taught to follow in His steps. They should be taught to manifest Christian interest, sympathy, and love for their youthful companions, and endeavor to draw them to Jesus; Christ should be in their hearts as a well of water springing up into everlasting life, refreshing all with whom they come in contact.

It is this willing, loving ministry for others in times of necessity that is accounted precious with God. Thus even while attending school, students may, if true to their profession, be living missionaries for God. All this will take time; but the time thus employed is profitably spent, for in this way the student is learning how to present Christianity to the world.

Christ did not refuse to mingle with others in friendly intercourse. When invited to a feast by Pharisee or publican, He accepted the invitation. On such occasions every word that He uttered was a savor of life unto life to His hearers; for He made the dinner hour an occasion of imparting many precious lessons adapted to their needs. Christ thus taught His disciples how to conduct themselves when in the company of those who were not religious as well as of those who were. *Testimonies for the Church*, Vol. 6, pp. 172, 173.

CHAPTER 138

Guiding Principles

The heart belongs to Jesus. He has paid an infinite price for the soul; and He intercedes before the Father as our Mediator, pleading not as a petitioner, but as conqueror who would claim that which is His own. He is able to save to the uttermost, for He ever lives to make intercession for us. A young heart is a precious offering, the most valuable gift that can be presented to God. All that you are, all the ability you possess, comes from God a sacred trust, to be rendered back to Him again in a willing, holy offering. You cannot give to God anything that He has not first given you. Therefore when the heart is given to God, it is giving to Him a gift which he has purchased and is His own.

There are many claimants to the time, the affections, and the strength of youth. Satan claims the youth as his property, and a vast number render to him all the ability, all the talent, they possess. The world claims the heart; but that heart belongs to the One who redeemed it. If given to the world, it will be filled with care, sorrow, and disappointed hopes; it will become impure and corrupted. It would be the worst kind of robbery to give to the world your heart's affections and service, for they belong to God. You cannot with profit give your heart to pleasure-seeking.

The enemy of righteousness has every kind of pleasure prepared for youth in all conditions of life; and they are not presented alone in crowded cities, but in every spot inhabited by human beings. Satan loves to secure the youth in his ranks as soldiers. The arch fiend well knows with what material he has to deal; and he has displayed his infernal wisdom in devising customs and pleasures for the youth which will separate their affections from Jesus Christ. . . .

The Prodigal

The lesson of the prodigal is given for the instruction of youth. In his life of pleasure and sinful indulgence, he expends his portion of the inheritance in riotous living. He is friendless, and in a strange country; clad in rags, hungry, longing even for the refuse fed to the swine. His last hope is to return, penitent and humbled, to his father's house, where he is welcomed, forgiven, and taken back to a father's heart. Many youth are doing as he did, living a careless, pleasure-loving, spendthrift life, forsaking the fountain of living waters, the fountain of true pleasure, and hewing out to themselves broken cisterns, which can hold no water.

God's Gracious Invitation

God's invitation comes to each youth, "My son, give Me thine heart; I will keep it pure; I will satisfy its longings with true happiness." God loves to make the youth happy, and that is why He would have them give their hearts into His keeping, that all the God-given faculties of the being may be kept in a vigorous, healthful condition. They are holding God's gift of life. He makes the heart beat; he gives strength to every faculty. Pure enjoyment will not debase one of God's gifts. We sin against our own bodies, and sin against God, when seeking pleasures which separate our affections from God. The youth are to consider that they are placed in the world on trial, to see whether they have characters that will fit them to live with angels.

When your associates urge you into paths of vice and folly, and all around you are tempting you to forget God, to destroy the capabilities God has intrusted to you, and to debase all that is noble in your nature, resist them. Remember that you are the Lord's property, bought with a price, the suffering and agony of the Son of God. . . .

The Lord Jesus claims your service. He loves you. If you doubt His love, look to Calvary. The light reflected from the cross shows you the magnitude of that love which no tongue can tell. "He that keepeth My commandments, he it is that loveth Me." We are to become acquainted by diligent study with the commandments of God; and then show that we are His obedient sons and daughters.

Surrounded by God's Mercies

The mercies of God surround you every moment; and it would be profitable for you to consider how and whence your blessings come every day. Let the precious blessings of God awaken gratitude in you. You cannot number the blessings of God, the constant loving-kindness expressed to you, for they are as numerous as the refreshing drops of rain. Clouds of mercy are hanging over you, and ready to drop upon you. If you will appreciate the valuable gift of salvation, you will be sensible of daily refreshment, of the protection and love of Jesus; you will be guided in the way of peace.

Look upon the glorious things of God in nature, and let your heart go out in gratitude to the Giver. There is in nature's book profitable study for the mind. Be not thankless and reckless. Open the eyes of your understanding; see the beautiful harmony in the laws of God in nature, and be awed, and reverence your Creator, the supreme Ruler of heaven and earth. See him, by the eye of faith, bending over you in love, saying with compassion, "My son, my daughter, give Me thy heart." Make the surrender to Jesus, and then with grateful hearts you can say, "I know that my Redeemer liveth." Your faith in Jesus will give strength to every purpose, consistency to the character.

All your happiness, peace, joy, and success in this life are dependent upon genuine, trusting faith in God. This faith will prompt true obedience to the commandments of God. Your knowledge and faith in God is the strongest restraint from every evil practice, and the motive to all good.

Believe in Jesus as one who pardons your sins, one who wants you to be happy in the mansions He has gone to prepare for you. He wants you to live in His presence; to have eternal life and a crown of glory. *Youth's Instructor*, January 5, 1887.

CHAPTER 139

The Influence of Association

It is inevitable that the youth will have associates, and they will necessarily feel their influence. There are mysterious links that bind souls together, so that the heart of one answers to the heart of another. One catches the ideas, the sentiments, the spirit, of another. This association may be a blessing or a curse. The youth may help and strengthen one another, improving in deportment, in disposition, in knowledge; or, by permitting themselves to become careless and unfaithful, they may exert an influence that is demoralizing.

The matter of choosing associates is one which students should learn to consider seriously. Among the youth who attend our schools there will always be found two classes, those who seek to please God and to obey their teachers, and those who are filled with a spirit of lawlessness. If the youth go with the multitude to do evil, their influence will be cast on the side of the adversary of souls; they will mislead those who have not cherished principles of unswerving fidelity.

It has been truly said, "Show me your company, and I will show you your character." The youth fail to realize how sensibly both their character and their reputation are affected by their choice of associates. One seeks the company of those whose tastes and habits and practices are congenial. He who prefers the society of the ignorant and vicious to that of the wise and good, shows that this own character is defective. His tastes and habits may at first be altogether dissimilar to the tastes and habits of those whose company he seeks; but as he mingles with this class, his thoughts and feelings change; he sacrifices right principles, and insensibly yet unavoidably sinks to the level of his companions. As a stream always partakes of the property of the soil through which it runs, so the principles and habits of youth invariably become tinctured with the character of the company in which they mingle. . . .

The Measure of Strength

Strength of character consists of two things—power of will, and power of self-control. Many youth mistake strong, uncontrolled passion for strength of character; but the truth is that he who is mastered by his passions is a weak man. The real greatness and nobility of the man is measured by his power to subdue his feelings, not by the power of his feelings to subdue him. The strongest man is he, who, while sensitive to abuse, will yet restrain passion and forgive his enemies.

God has given us intellectual and moral power; but to a great extent every one is the architect of his own character. Every day the structure more nearly approaches completion. The Word of God warns us to take heed how we build, to see that our building is founded upon the eternal rock. The time is coming when our work will stand revealed just as it is. Now is the time for all to cultivate the powers that God has given them, that they may form characters for usefulness hereand for a higher life hereafter.

Faith in Christ as a personal Saviour will give strength and solidity to the character. Those who have genuine faith in Christ will be sober-minded, remembering that God's eye is upon them, that the Judge of all men is weighing moral worth, that heavenly intelligences are watching to see what manner of character is being developed.

The reason that so grave mistakes are made by the youth is that they do not learn from the experience of those who have lived longer than they have. Students cannot afford to pass off with jest or ridicule the cautions and instruction of parents and teachers. They should cherish every lesson, realizing at the same time their need of deeper teaching than any human being can give. When Christ abides in the heart by faith, His Spirit becomes a power to purify and vivify the soul. The truth in the heart cannot fail of having a correcting influence upon the life. . . .

Let those students who are away from their homes, no longer under the direct influence of their parents, remember that the eye of their Heavenly Father is upon them. He loves the youth. He knows their necessities, He understands their temptations. He sees in them great possibilities, and is ready to help them to reach the highest standard, if they will realize their need and seek Him for help.

Students, night and day the prayers of your parents are rising to God in your behalf; day by day their loving interest follows you. Listen to their entreaties and warnings, and determine that by every means in your power you will lift yourselves above the evil that surrounds you. You cannot discern how insidiously the enemy will work to corrupt your minds and habits, and develop in you unsound principles.

You may see no real danger in taking the first step in frivolity and pleasure-seeking, and think that when you desire to change your course you will be able to do right as easily as before you yielded yourselves to do wrong. But this is a mistake. By the choice of evil companions many have been led step by step from the path of virtue into depths of disobedience and dissipation to which at one time they would have thought it impossible for them to sink.

The student who yields to temptation weakens his influence for good, and he who by a wrong course of action becomes the agent of the adversary of souls, must render to God an account for the part he has acted in laying stumbling-blocks in the way of others. Why should students link themselves with the great apostate? Why should they become his agents to tempt others? Rather, why should they not study to help and encourage their fellow students and their teachers? It is their privilege to help their teachers bear the burdens and meet the perplexities that Satan would make discouragingly heavy and trying. They may create an atmosphere that will be helpful, exhilarating. Every student may enjoy the consciousness that he has stood on Christ's side, showing respect for order, diligence, and obedience, and refusing to lend one jot of his ability or influence to the great enemy of all that is good and uplifting.

The student who has a conscientious regard for truth and a true conception of duty can do much to influence his fellow students for Christ. The youth who are yoked up with the Saviour will not be unruly; they will not study their own selfish pleasure and gratification. Because they are one with Christ in spirit, they will be one with Christ in action. The older students in our schools should remember that it is in their power to mold the habits and practices of the younger students; and they should seek to make the best of every opportunity. Let these students determine that they will not through their influence betray their companions into the hands of the enemy.

Jesus will be the helper of all who put their trust in Him. Those who are connected with Christ have happiness at their command. They follow the path where their Saviour leads, for His sake crucifying the flesh, with its affections and lusts. They have built their hopes on Christ, and the storms of earth are powerless to sweep them from the sure foundation.

Trustworthy and Faithful

It rests with you, young men and women, to decide whether you will become trustworthy and faithful, ready and resolute to take your stand for the right under all circumstances. Do you desire to form correct habits? Then seek the company of those who are sound in morals, and whose aim tends to that which is good. The precious hours of probation are granted that you may remove every defect from your character, and this you should seek to do, not only that you may obtain the future life, but that you may be useful in this life. A good character is a capital of more value than gold or silver. It is unaffected by panics or failures, and in that day when earthly possessions shall be swept away it will bring rich returns. Integrity, firmness, and perseverance are qualities that all should seek earnestly to cultivate; for they clothe the possessor with a power which is irresistible—a power which makes him strong to do good, strong to resist evil, strong to bear adversity.

The love of truth, and a sense of the responsibility to glorify God, are the most powerful of all incentives to the improvement of the intellect. With this impulse to action the student cannot be a trifler. He will be always in earnest. He will study as under the eye of God, knowing that all heaven is enlisted in the work of his education. He will become noble-minded, generous, kind, courteous, Christlike, efficient. Heart and mind will work in harmony with the will of God. *Counsels to Teachers, Parents, and Students*, pp. 220-226.

CHAPTER 140

Influence

The life of Christ was an ever-widening, shoreless influence, an influence that bound Him to God and to the whole human family. Through Christ, God has invested man with an influence that makes it impossible for him to live to himself. Individually we are connected with our fellow men, a part of God's great whole, and we stand under mutual obligations. No man can be independent of his fellow men; for the well-being of each affects others. It is God's purpose that each shall feel himself necessary to others' welfare, and seek to promote their happiness.

Every soul is surrounded by an atmosphere of its own—an atmosphere, it may be, charged with the lifegiving power of faith, courage, and hope, and sweet with the fragrance of love. Or it may be heavy and chill with the gloom of discontent and selfishness, or poisonous with the deadly taint of cherished sin. By the atmosphere surrounding us, every person with whom we come in contact is consciously or unconsciously affected.

Our Responsibility

This is a responsibility from which we cannot free ourselves. Our words, our acts, our dress, our deportment, even the expression of the countenance, has an influence. Upon the impression thus made there hang results for good or evil which no man can measure. Every impulse thus imparted is seed sown which will produce its harvest. It is a link in the long chain of human events, extending we know not whither. If by our example we aid others in the development of good principles, we give them power to do good. In their turn they exert the same influence upon others, and they upon still others. Thus by our unconscious influence thousands may be blessed.

Throw a pebble into the lake, and a wave is formed; and another and another; and as they increase, the circle widens, until it reaches the very shore. So with our influence. Beyond our knowledge or control it tells upon others in blessing or cursing.

Character is power. The silent witness of a true, unselfish, godly life carries an almost irresistible influence. By revealing in our own life the character of Christ, we cooperate with Him in the work of saving souls. It is only by revealing in our life His character that we can cooperate with Him.

And the wider the sphere of our influence, the more good we may do. When those who profess to serve God follow Christ's example, practicing the principles of the law in their daily life; when every act bears witness that they love God supremely and their neighbor as themselves, then will the church have power to move the world. *Christ's Object Lessons*, pp. 339, 340.

CHAPTER 141

The Choice of Companions

We should choose the society most favorable to our spiritual advancement, and avail ourselves of every help within our reach; for Satan will oppose many hindrances to make our progress toward heaven as difficult as possible. We may be placed in trying positions, for many cannot have their surroundings what they would; but we should not voluntarily expose ourselves to influences that are unfavorable to the formation of Christian character. When duty calls us to do this, we should be doubly watchful and prayerful, that, through the grace of Christ, we may stand uncorrupted.

Lot chose Sodom as a place of residence because he looked more to the temporal advantages he would gain than to the moral influences that would surround himself and his family. What did he gain so far as the things of this world are concerned? His possessions were destroyed, part of his children perished in the destruction of that wicked city, his wife was turned to a pillar of salt by the way, and he himself was saved "so as by fire." Nor did the evil results of his selfish choice end here; but the moral corruption of the place was so interwoven with the character of his children that they could not distinguish between good and evil, sin and righteousness. *Signs of the Times*, May 29, 1884.

CHAPTER 142

The Golden Rule

In your association with others, put yourself in their place. Enter into their feelings, their difficulties, their disappointments, their joys, and their sorrows. Identify yourself with them, and then do to them as, were you to exchange places with them, you would wish them to deal with you. This is the true rule of honesty. It is another expression of the law, "Thou shalt love thy neighbor as thyself." And it is the substance of the teaching of the prophets. It is a principle of heaven, and will be developed in all who are fitted for its holy companionship.

The golden rule is the principle of true courtesy, and its truest illustration is seen in the life and character of Jesus. Oh, what rays of softness and beauty shone forth in the daily life of our Saviour! What sweetness flowed from His very presence! The same spirit will be revealed in His children. Those with whom Christ dwells will be surrounded with a divine atmosphere. Their white robes of purity will be fragrant with perfume from the garden of the Lord. Their faces will reflect light from His, brightening the path for stumbling and weary feet.

No man who has the true ideal of what constitutes a perfect character will fail to manifest the sympathy and tenderness of Christ. The influence of grace is to soften the heart, to refine and purify the feelings, giving a heaven-born delicacy and sense of propriety. *Thoughts from the Mount of Blessing*, pp. 134, 135.

CHAPTER 143

True Refinement

The Lord Jesus demands our acknowledgment of the rights of every man. Men's social rights and their rights as Christians are to be taken into consideration. All are to be treated with refinement and delicacy as the sons and daughters of God.

Christianity will make a man a gentleman. Christ was courteous, even to His persecutors; and His true followers will manifest the same spirit. Look at Paul when brought before rulers. His speech before Agrippa is an illustration of true courtesy as well as persuasive eloquence. The gospel does not encourage the formal politeness current with the world, but the courtesy that springs from real kindness of heart.

The most careful cultivation of the outward proprieties of life is not sufficient to shut out all fretfulness, harsh judgment, and unbecoming speech. True refinement will never be revealed so long as self is considered as the supreme object. Love must dwell in the heart. A thoroughgoing Christian draws his motives of action from his deep heart-love for his Master. Up through the roots of his affection for Christ springs an unselfish interest in his brethren. Love imparts to its possessor grace, propriety, and comeliness of deportment. It illuminates the countenance and subdues the voice; it refines and elevates the whole being. *The Ministry of Healing*, pp. 489, 490.

True Courtesy Needed

There is the greatest necessity that men and women who have a knowledge of the will of God should learn to become successful workers in His cause. They should be persons of polish, of understanding, not having the deceptive outside gloss and simpering affectation of the worldling, but that refinement and true courteousness which savors of heaven, and which every Christian will have if he is a partaker of the divine nature. The lack of true dignity and Christian refinement in the ranks of Sabbath-keepers is against us as a people, and makes the truth which we profess unsavory. The work of educating the mind and manners may be carried forward to perfection. If those who profess the truth do not now improve their privileges and opportunities to grow up to the full stature of men and women in Christ Jesus, they will be no honor to the cause of truth, no honor to Christ. *Testimonies for the Church*, Vol. 4, pp. 358, 359.

Choice of Companions

The youth who are in harmony with Christ will choose companions who will help them in right doing, and will shun society that gives no aid in the development of right principles and noble purposes. In every place are to be found youth whose minds are cast in an inferior mould. When brought into association with this class, those who have placed themselves without reserve on the side of Christ will stand firmly by that which reason and conscience tell them is right. *Counsels to Teachers, Parents, and Students*, p. 226.

CHAPTER 144

Rejecting Worldly Associations

The youth should seriously consider what shall be their purpose and life work, and lay the foundation in such a way that their habits shall be free from taint of corruption. If they would stand in a position where they shall influence others, they must be self-reliant. The lily on the lake strikes its roots down deep beneath the surface of rubbish and slime, and through its porous stem draws those properties that will aid its development, and bring to light its spotless blossom to repose in purity on the bosom of the lake. It refuses all that would tarnish and mar its spotless beauty.

We may learn a lesson from the lily, and although surrounded with influences that would tend to corrupt the morals and bring ruin upon the soul, we may refuse to be corrupted, and place ourselves where evil association shall not corrupt our hearts. Individually the youth should seek for association with those who are toiling upward with unfaltering steps. They should shun the society of those who are absorbing every evil influence, who are inactive and without earnest desire for attainment of a high standard of character, who cannot be relied upon as persons who will be true to principle. Let the youth be found in association with those who fear and love God; for these noble, firm characters are represented by the lily that opens its pure blossom on the bosom of the lake. They refuse to be moulded by the influences that would demoralize, and gather to themselves only that which will aid the development of a pure and noble character. They are seeking to be conformed to the divine model. *Youth's Instructor*, January 5, 1893.

Our Words a Source of Help

There is too little conversation among Christians in regard to the precious chapters in their experience. The work of God is crippled and God is dishonored by the abuse of the talent of speech. Jealousy, evil-surmising, and selfishness are cherished in the heart, and the words show the inward corruption. Evil-thinking and evil-speaking are indulged by many who name the name of Christ. These seldom make mention of the goodness, mercy, and love of God, manifested in giving His Son for the world. This He has done for us, and should not our love and gratitude demand expression? Should we not strive to make our words a source of help and encouragement to one another in our Christian experience? If we truly love Christ, we shall glorify Him by our words. Unbelievers are often convicted as they listen to pure words of praise and gratitude to God. *Review and Herald*, January 25, 1898.

Our Influence

The very example and deportment as well as the words of the Christian should be such as to awaken in the sinner a desire to come to the Fountain of life. *Review and Herald*, November 29, 1887.

CHAPTER 145

Exalted Conversation

The best educated in the sciences are not always the most effective instruments for God's use. There are many who find themselves laid aside, and those who have had fewer advantages of obtaining knowledge of books taking their places, because the latter have a knowledge of practical things that is essential to the uses of everyday life; while those who consider themselves learned often cease to be learners, are self-sufficient, and above being taught, even by Jesus, who was the greatest teacher the world ever knew.

Those who have grown and expanded, whose reasoning faculties have been improved by deep searching of the Scriptures, that they may know the will of God, will come into positions of usefulness; for the Word of God has had an entrance into their life and character. It must do its peculiar work, even to the piercing asunder of the joints and marrow, and discerning the thoughts and intents of the heart. God's Word is to become the nourishment by which the Christian must grow strong, in spirit and in intellect, that he may battle for truth and righteousness.

The Reason for Low Standards

Why is it that our youth, and even those of maturer years, are so easily led into temptation and sin? It is because the Word of God is not studied and meditated upon as it should be. If it were appreciated, there would be an inward rectitude, a strength of spirit, that would resist the temptations of Satan to do evil. A firm, decided will-power is not brought into the life and character, because the sacred instruction of God is not made the study and the subject of meditation. There is not the effort put forth that there should be, to associate the mind with pure, holy thoughts, and to divert it from what is impure and untrue. There is not the choosing of the better part, the sitting at the feet of Jesus, as did Mary, to learn the most sacred lessons of the divine Teacher, that they may be laid up in the heart, and practiced in the daily life. Meditation upon holy things will elevate and refine the mind, and will develop Christian ladies and gentlemen.

God will not accept one of us who is belittling his powers in lustful, earthly debasement, by thought, or word, or action. Heaven is a pure and holy place, where none can enter unless they are refined, spiritualized, cleansed, and purified. There is a work for us to do for ourselves, and we shall be capable of doing it only by drawing strength from Jesus. We should make the Bible our study above every other book; we should love it, and obey it as the voice of God. We are to see and to understand His restrictions and requirements, "thou shalt," and "thou shalt not," and realize the true meaning of the Word of God.

Need of Heavenly-mindedness

When God's Word is made the man of our counsel, and we search the Scriptures for light, angels of heaven come near to impress the mind and enlighten the understanding, so that it can truly be said, "The entrance of Thy words giveth light; it giveth understanding unto the simple." It is no marvel that there is not more heavenly-mindedness shown among the youth who profess Christianity, when there is so little attention given to the Word of God. The divine counsels are not heeded; the admonitions are not obeyed; grace and heavenly wisdom are not sought, that past sins may be avoided and every taint of corruption be cleansed from the character. David's prayer was, "Make me to understand the way of Thy precepts; so shall I talk of Thy wonderful works."

If the minds of our youth, as well as those of more mature age, were directed aright when associated together, their conversation would be upon exalted themes. When the mind is pure, and the thoughts elevated by the truth of God, the words will be of the same character, "like apples of gold in pictures of silver." But with the present understanding, with the present practices, with the low standard which even professed Christians are content to reach, the conversation is cheap and profitless. It is "of the earth, earthy," and savors not of the truth, or of heaven, and does not come up even to the standard of the more cultured class of worldlings.

A Vigorous Process of Sanctification

When Christ and heaven are the themes of contemplation, the conversation will give evidence of the fact. The speech will be seasoned with grace, and the speaker will show that he has been obtaining an education in the school of the divine Teacher. Says the psalmist, "I have chosen the way of truth: Thy judgments have I laid before me," He treasured the Word of God. It found an entrance to his understanding, not to be disregarded, but to be practiced in his life. . . .

Day by day, and hour by hour, there must be a vigorous process of self-denial and of sanctification going on within; and then the outward works will testify that Jesus is abiding in the heart by faith. Sanctification does not close the avenues of the soul to knowledge, but it comes to expand the mind, and to inspire it to search for truth, as for hidden treasure; and the knowledge of God's will advances the work of sanctification. There is a heaven, and O, how earnestly we should strive to reach it.

I appeal to the students of our schools and colleges, to believe in Jesus as your Saviour. Believe that He is ready to help you by His grace, when you come to Him in sincerity. You must fight the good fight of faith. You must be wrestlers for the crown of life. Strive, for the grasp of Satan is upon you; and if you do not wrench yourselves from Him, you will be palsied and ruined. The foe is on the right hand and on the left, before you and behind you; and you must trample him under your feet. Strive, for there is a crown to be won. Strive, for if you win not the crown, you lose everything in this life and in the future life. Strive, but let it be in the strength of your risen Saviour. *Review and Herald*, August 21, 1888. (See also *Fundamentals of Christian Education*, pp. 129-137.)

CHAPTER 146

Sowing Wild Oats

A little time spent in sowing your wild oats, dear young friends, will produce a crop that will embitter your whole life; an hour of thoughtlessness—once yielding to temptation—may turn the whole current of your life in the wrong direction. You can have but one youth; make that useful. When once you have passed over the ground, you can never return to rectify your mistakes. He who refuses to connect with God, and puts himself in the way of temptation, will surely fall.

God is testing every youth. Many have excused their carelessness and irreverence, because of the wrong example given them by more experienced professors. But this should not deter any from right-doing. In the day of final accounts you will plead no such excuses as you plead now. You will be justly condemned, because you knew the way, but did not choose to walk in it.

Temptation

Satan, that arch-deceiver, transforms himself into an angel of light, and comes to the youth with his specious temptations, and succeeds in winning them, step by step, from the path of duty. He is described as an accuser, a deceiver, a liar, a tormentor, and a murderer. "He that committeth sin is of the devil." Every transgression brings the soul into condemnation, and provokes the divine displeasure. The thoughts of the heart are discerned of God.

When impure thoughts are cherished, they need not be expressed by word or act to consummate the sin and bring the soul into condemnation. Its purity is defiled, and the tempter has triumphed.

Every man is tempted when he is drawn away of his own lusts and enticed. He is turned away from the course of virtue and real good by following his own inclinations. If the youth possessed moral integrity, the strongest temptations might be presented in vain. It is Satan's act to tempt you, but your own act to yield. It is not in the power of all the host of Satan to force the tempted to transgress. There is no excuse for sin.

While some of the youth are wasting their powers in vanity and folly, others are disciplining their minds, storing up knowledge, girding on the armor to engage in life's warfare, determined to make it a success. But they cannot make life a success, however high they may attempt to climb, unless they center their affections upon God. If they will turn to the Lord with all the heart, rejecting the flatteries of those who would in the slightest degree weaken their purpose to do right, they will have strength and confidence in God.

Vain Amusement Not True Happiness

Those who love society frequently indulge this trait until it becomes an overruling passion. To dress, to visit places of amusement, to laugh and chat upon subjects altogether lighter than vanity—this is the object of their lives. They cannot endure to read the Bible and contemplate heavenly things. They are miserable unless there is something to excite. They have not within them the power to be happy; but they depend for happiness upon the company of other youth as thoughtless and reckless as themselves. The powers which might be turned to noble purposes, they give to folly. . . .

The youth who finds joy and happiness in reading the Word of God and in the hour of prayer is constantly refreshed by draughts from the Fountain of life. He will attain a height of moral excellence and a breadth of thought of which others cannot conceive. Communion with God encourages good thoughts, noble aspirations, clear perceptions of truth, and lofty purposes of action. Those who thus connect their souls with God are acknowledged by Him as His sons and daughters. They are constantly reaching higher and still higher, obtaining clearer views of God and of eternity, until the Lord makes them channels of light and wisdom to the world. . . .

Those who abide in Jesus will be happy, cheerful, and joyful in God. A subdued gentleness will mark the voice, reverence for spiritual and eternal things will be expressed in the actions, and music, joyful music, will echo from the lips; for it is wafted from the throne of God. This is the mystery of godliness, not easily explained, but none the less felt and enjoyed. A stubborn and rebellious heart can close its doors to all the sweet influences of the grace of God, and all the joy in the Holy Ghost; but the ways of wisdom are ways of pleasantness, and all her paths are peace. The more closely we are connected with Christ, the more will our words and actions show the subduing, transforming power of His grace. *Testimonies for the Church*, Vol. 4, pp. 622-626.

CHAPTER 147

Irreligious Visitors

It is not safe for Christians to choose the society of those who have no connection with God, and whose course is displeasing to Him. Yet how many professed Christians venture upon the forbidden ground. Many invite to their homes relatives who are vain, trifling, and ungodly; and often the example and influence of these irreligious visitors produce lasting impressions upon the minds of the children in the household. The influence thus exerted is similar to that which resulted from the association of the Hebrews with the godless Canaanites. . . .

Many feel that they must make some concessions to please their irreligious relatives and friends. As it is not always easy to draw the line, one concession prepares the way for another, until those who were once true followers of Christ are in life and character conformed to the customs of the world. The connection with God is broken. They are Christians in name only. When the test hour comes, then their hope is seen to be without foundation. They have sold themselves and their children to the enemy. They have dishonored God, and in the revelation of His righteous judgments, they will reap what they have sown. Christ will say to them, as He said to ancient Israel, "Ye have not obeyed My voice. Why have ye done this?" *Signs of the Times*, June 2, 1881.

SECTION XV
Courtship and Marriage

The family tie is the closest, the most tender and sacred, of any on earth. It was designed to be a blessing to mankind. And it is a blessing wherever the marriage covenant is entered into intelligently, in the fear of God, and with due consideration for its responsibilities. The Ministry of Healing, *pp. 356, 357.*

CHAPTER 148

True Love

Love is a precious gift, which we receive from Jesus. Pure and holy affection is not a feeling, but a principle. Those who are actuated by true love are neither unreasonable nor blind. Taught by the Holy Spirit, they love God supremely, and their neighbor as themselves.

Let those who are contemplating marriage weigh every sentiment and watch every development of character in the one with whom they think to unite their life destiny. Let every step toward a marriage alliance be characterized by modesty, simplicity, sincerity, and an earnest purpose to please and honor God. Marriage affects the after life both in this world and in the world to come. A sincere Christian will make no plans that God cannot approve.

Seeking Counsel

If you are blessed with God-fearing parents, seek counsel of them. Open to them your hopes and plans, learn the lessons which their life experiences have taught, and you will be saved many a heartache. Above all, make Christ your counselor. Study His Word with prayer.

Under such guidance let a young woman accept as a life companion only one who possesses pure, manly traits of character, one who is diligent, aspiring, and honest, one who loves and fears God. Let a young man seek one to stand by his side who is fitted to bear her share of life's burdens, one whose influence will ennoble and refine him, and who will make him happy in her love.

"A prudent wife is from the Lord." "The heart of her husband doth safely trust in her. . . . She will do him good and not evil all the days of her life." "She openeth her mouth with wisdom; and in her tongue is the law of kindness. She looketh well to the ways of her household, and eateth not the bread of idleness. Her children arise up, and call her blessed; her husband also, and he praiseth her," saying, "Many daughters have done virtuously, but thou excellest them all." He who gains such a wife, "findeth a good thing, and obtaineth favor of the Lord." *The Ministry of Healing*, pp. 358, 359.

Choice of Companions

Great care should be taken by Christian youth in the formation of friendships and in the choice of companions. Take heed, lest what you now think to be pure gold turns out to be base metal. Worldly associations tend to place obstructions in the way of your service to God, and many souls are ruined by unhappy unions, either business or matrimonial, with those who can never elevate or ennoble. Never should God's people venture upon forbidden ground. Marriage between believers and unbelievers is forbidden by God. But too often the unconverted heart follows its own desires, and marriages unsanctioned by God are formed. *Fundamentals of Christian Education*, p. 500.

CHAPTER 149

Wrong Forms of Courtship*

The lack of firmness and self-denial in your character is a serious drawback in obtaining a genuine religious experience that will not be sliding sand. Firmness and integrity of purpose should be cultivated. These qualities are positively necessary to a successful Christian life. If you have integrity of soul you will not be swayed from the right. No motive will be sufficient to move you from the straight line of duty; you will be loyal and true to God. The pleadings of affection and love, the yearnings of friendship, will not move you to turn aside from truth and duty; you will not sacrifice duty to inclination.

If you, my brother, are allured to unite your life-interest with a young, inexperienced girl, who is really deficient in education in the common, practical, daily duties of life, you make a mistake; but this deficiency is small compared with her ignorance in regard to her duty to God. She has not been destitute of light; she has had religious privileges, and yet she has not felt her wretched sinfulness without Christ.

Influence on Religious Experience

If, in your infatuation, you can repeatedly turn from the prayer-meeting, where God meets with His people, in order to enjoy the society of one who has no love for God, and who sees no attrac-

*From a personal testimony.

tions in the religious life, how can you expect God to prosper such a union?

Be not in haste. Early marriages should not be encouraged. If either young women or young men have no respect for the claims of God, if they fail to heed the claims which bind them to religion, there will be danger that they will not properly regard the claims of the husband or of the wife. The habit of frequently being in the society of the one of your choice, and that, too, at the sacrifice of religious privileges and of your hours of prayer, is dangerous; you sustain a loss that you cannot afford.

The habit of sitting up late at night is customary, but it is not pleasing to God, even if you are both Christians. These untimely hours injure health, unfit the mind for the next day's duties, and have an appearance of evil. My brother, I hope you will have self-respect enough to shun this form of courtship. If you have an eye single to the glory of God, you will move with deliberate caution. You will not suffer lovesick sentimentalism to so blind your vision that you cannot discern the high claims that God has upon you as a Christian. *Testimonies for the Church*, Vol. 3, pp. 44, 45.

Early Marriages

Early marriages are not to be encouraged. A relation so important as marriage and so far-reaching in its results should not be entered upon hastily, without sufficient preparation, and before the mental and physical powers are well developed. *The Ministry of Healing*, p. 358.

CHAPTER 150

Engagement With Unbelievers

Dear Sister: I have learned of your contemplated marriage with one who is not united with you in religious faith, and I fear that you have not carefully weighed this important matter. Before taking a step which is to exert an influence upon all your future life, I urge you to give the subject careful and prayerful deliberation. Will this new relationship prove a source of true happiness? Will it be a help to you in the Christian life? Will it be pleasing to God? Will your example be a safe one for others to follow?

Tests of Love

Before giving her hand in marriage, every woman should inquire whether he with whom she is about to unite her destiny is worthy. What has been his past record? Is his life pure? Is the love which he expresses of a noble, elevated character, or is it a mere emotional fondness? Has he the traits of character that will make her happy? Can she find true peace and joy in his affection? Will she be allowed to preserve her individuality, or must her judgment and conscience be surrendered to the control of her husband? As a disciple of Christ, she is not her own; she has been bought with a price. Can she honor the Saviour's claims as supreme? Will body and soul, thoughts and purposes, be preserved pure and holy? These questions have a vital bearing upon the well-being of every woman who enters the marriage relation.

Religion is needed in the home. Only this can prevent the grievous wrongs which so often embitter married life. Only where Christ reigns, can there be deep, true, unselfish love. Then soul will be knit with soul, and the two lives will blend in harmony. Angels of God will be guests in the home, and their holy vigils will hallow the marriage chamber. Debasing sensuality will be banished. Upward to God will the thoughts be directed; to Him will the heart's devotion ascend.

Results of Disobedience

The heart yearns for human love, but this love is not strong enough, or pure enough, or precious enough, to supply the place of the love of Jesus. Only in her Saviour can the wife find wisdom, strength, and grace to meet the cares, responsibilities, and sorrows of life. She should make Him her strength and her guide. Let woman give herself to Christ before giving herself to any earthly friend, and enter into no relation which shall conflict with this. Those who find true happiness must have the blessing of Heaven upon all that they possess and all that they do. It is disobedience to God that fills so many hearts and homes with misery. My sister, unless you would have a home where the shadows are never lifted, do not unite yourself with one who is an enemy of God.

As one who expects to meet these words in the judgment, I entreat you to ponder the step you contemplate taking. Ask yourself, "Will not an unbelieving husband lead my thoughts away from Jesus? He is a lover of pleasure more than a lover of God; will he not lead me to enjoy the things that he enjoys?"

The path to eternal life is steep and rugged. Take no additional weights to retard your progress. . . .

I would warn you of your danger before it shall be too late. You listen to smooth, pleasant words, and are led to believe that all will be well; but you do not read the motives that prompt these fair speeches. You cannot see the depths of wickedness hidden in the heart. You cannot look behind the scenes, and discern the snares that Satan is laying for your soul. He would lead you to pursue such a course that he can obtain easy access, to aim his shafts of temptation against you. Do not give him the least advantage. While God moves upon the minds of his servants, Satan works through the children of disobedience. There is no concord between Christ and Belial. The two cannot harmonize. To connect with an unbeliever is to place yourself on Satan's ground. You grieve the Spirit of God and forfeit His protection. Can you afford to have such terrible odds against you in fighting the battle for everlasting life?

A Broken Engagement

You may say, "But I have given my promise, and shall I now retract it?" I answer, If you have made a promise contrary to the Scriptures, by all means retract it without delay, and in humility before God repent of the infatuation that led you to make so rash a pledge. Far better take back such a promise, in the fear of God, than keep it, and thereby dishonor your Maker.

Remember, you have a heaven to gain, an open path to perdition to shun. God means what He says. When He prohibited our first parents from eating the fruit of the tree of knowledge, their disobedience opened the floodgates of woe to the whole world. If we walk contrary to God, He will walk contrary to us. Our only safe course is to render obedience to all His requirements, at whatever cost. All are founded in infinite love and wisdom. *Testimonies for the Church*, Vol. 5, pp. 361-365.

Mature Judgment Essential

The good of society, as well as the highest interest of the students, demands that they shall not attempt to select a life partner while their own character is yet undeveloped, their judgment immature, and while they are at the same time deprived of parental care and guidance. . . .

Those who are seeking to shield the youth from temptation and to prepare them for a life of usefulness are engaged in a good work. We are glad to see in any institution of learning a recognition of the importance of proper restraint and discipline for the young. May the efforts of all such instructors be crowned with success. *Fundamentals of Christian Education*, pp. 62, 63.

CHAPTER 151

Need of Counsel and Guidance

In these days of peril and corruption, the young are exposed to many trials and temptations. Many are sailing in a dangerous harbor. They need a pilot; but they scorn to accept the much-needed help, feeling that they are competent to guide their own bark, and not realizing that it is about to strike a hidden rock that may cause them to make shipwreck of faith and happiness. They are infatuated with the subject of courtship and marriage, and their principal burden is to have their own way. In this, the most important period of their lives, they need an unerring counselor, an infallible guide. This they will find in the Word of God. Unless they are diligent students of that Word, they will make grave mistakes, which will mar their happiness and that of others, both for the present and the future life.

There is a disposition with many to be impetuous and headstrong. They have not heeded the wise counsel of the Word of God; they have not battled with self, and obtained precious victories; and their proud, unbending will has driven them from the path of duty and obedience. Look back over your past life, young friends, and faithfully consider your course in the light of God's Word. Have you cherished that conscientious regard for your obligations to your parents that the Bible enjoins? Have you treated with kindness and love the mother who has cared for you from infancy? Have you regarded her wishes, or have you brought pain and sadness to her heart by carrying out your own desires and plans? Has the truth you profess sanctified your heart, and softened and subdued your will? If not, you have close work to do to make past wrongs right.

A Perfect Guide

The Bible presents a perfect standard of character. This sacred book, inspired by God, and written by holy men, is a perfect guide under all circumstances of life. It sets forth distinctly the duties of both young and old. If made the guide of life, its teachings will lead the soul upward. It will elevate the mind, improve the character, and give peace and joy to the heart. But many of the young have chosen to be their own counselor and guide, and have taken their cases in their own hands. Such need to study more closely the teachings of the Bible. In its pages they will find revealed their duty to their parents and to their brethren in the faith. The fifth commandment reads, "Honor thy father and thy mother, that thy days may be long upon the land which the Lord thy God giveth thee." Again we read, "Children, obey your parents in the Lord; for this is right."

One of the signs that we are living in the last days is that children are disobedient to parents, unthankful, unholy. The Word of God abounds in precepts and counsels enjoining respect for parents. It impresses upon the young the sacred duty of loving and cherishing those who have guided them through infancy, childhood, and youth, up to manhood and womanhood, and who are now in a great degree dependent upon them for peace and happiness. The Bible gives no uncertain sound on this subject; nevertheless, its teachings have been greatly disregarded.

The young have many lessons to learn, and the most important one is to learn to know themselves. They should have correct ideas of their obligations and duties to their parents, and should be constantly learning in the school of Christ to be meek and lowly of heart. While they are to love and honor their parents, they are also to respect the judgment of men of experience with whom they are connected in the church.

Honorable Conduct

A young man who enjoys the society and wins the friendship of a young lady unknown to her parents does not act a noble Christian part toward her or toward her parents. Through secret communications and meetings he may gain an influence over her mind; but in so doing he fails to manifest that nobility and integrity of soul which every child of God will possess. In order to accomplish their ends, they act a part that is not frank and open and according to the Bible standard, and prove themselves untrue to those who love them and try to be faithful guardians over them. Marriages contracted under such influences are not according to the Word of God. He who would lead a daughter away from duty, who would confuse her ideas of God's plain and positive commands to obey and honor her parents, is not one who would be true to the marriage obligations.

The question is asked, "Wherewithal shall a young man cleanse his way?" and the answer is given, "By taking heed thereto according to Thy word." The young man who makes the Bible his guide need not mistake the path of duty and of safety. That blessed book will teach him to preserve his integrity of character, to be truthful, to practice no deception. "Thou shalt not steal," was written by the finger of God upon the tables of stone; yet how much underhand stealing of affections is practiced and excused.

A deceptive courtship is maintained, private communications are kept up, until the affections of one who is inexperienced, and knows not whereunto these things may grow, are in a measure withdrawn from her parents and placed upon him who shows by the very course he pursues that he is unworthy of her love. The Bible condemns every species of dishonesty, and demands right-doing under all circumstances. He who makes the Bible the guide of his youth, the light of his path, will obey its teachings in all things. He will not transgress one jot or tittle of the law in order to accomplish any object, even if he has to make great sacrifices in consequence. If he believes the Bible, he knows that the blessing of God will not rest upon him if he departs from the strict path of rectitude. Although he may appear for a time to prosper, he will surely reap the fruit of his doings.

The curse of God rests upon many of the ill-timed, inappropriate connections that are formed in this age of the world. If the Bible left these questions in a vague uncertain light, then the course that many youth of today are pursuing in their attactments for one another would be more excusable. But the requirements of the Bible are not half-way injunctions; they demand perfect purity of thought, of word, and of deed. We are grateful to God that His Word is a light to the feet, and that none need mistake the path of duty. The young should make it a business to consult its pages and heed its counsels; for sad mistakes are always made in departing from its precepts.

Need of Sound Judgment

If there is any subject that should be considered with calm reason and unimpassioned judgment, it is the subject of marriage. If ever the Bible is needed as a counselor, it is before taking a step that binds persons together for life. But the prevailing sentiment is that in this matter the feelings are to be the guide; and in too many cases love-sick sentimentalism takes the helm and guides to certain ruin. It is here that the youth show less intelligence than on any other subject; it is here that they refuse to be reasoned with. The question of marriage seems to have a bewitching power over them. They do not submit themselves to God. Their senses are enchained, and they move forward in secretiveness, as if fearful that their plans would be interfered with by some one.

The underhand way in which courtships and marriages are carried on is the cause of a great amount of misery, the full extent of which is known only to God. On this rock thousands have made shipwreck of their souls. Professed Christians, whose lives are marked with integrity, and who seem sensible upon every other subject, make fearful mistakes here. They manifest a set, determined will that reason cannot change. They become so fascinated with human feelings and impulses that they have no desire to search the Bible and come into close relationship with God.

Satan knows just what elements he has to deal with, and he displays his infernal wisdom in various devices to entrap souls to their ruin. He watches every step that is taken, and makes many suggestions, and often these suggestions are followed rather than the counsel of God's Word. This finely woven, dangerous net is skillfully prepared to entangle the young and unwary. It may often be disguised under a covering of light; but those who become its victims pierce themselves through with many sorrows. As the result, we see wrecks of humanity everywhere.

Parents to Be Consulted

When will our youth be wise? How long will this kind of work go on? Shall children consult only their own desires and inclinations, irrespective of the advice and judgment of their parents? Some seem never to bestow a thought upon their parents' wishes or preferences, nor to regard their matured judgment. Selfishness has closed the door of their hearts to filial affection. The minds of the young need to be aroused in regard to this matter. The fifth commandment is the only commandment to which is annexed a promise; but it is held lightly, and is even positively ignored by the lover's claim. Slighting a mother's love, dishonoring a father's care, are sins that stand registered against many youth.

One of the greatest errors connected with this subject is that the young and inexperienced must not have their affections disturbed, that there must be no interference in their love experience. If there ever was a subject that needed to be viewed from every standpoint, it is this. The aid of the experience of others, and a calm, careful weighing of the matter on both sides, is positively essential. It is a subject that is treated altogether too lightly by the great majority of people.

Take God and your God-fearing parents into your counsel, young friends. Pray over the matter. Weigh every sentiment, and watch every development of character in the one with whom you think to link your life destiny. The step you are about to take is one of the most important in your life, and should not be taken hastily. While you may love, do not love blindly.

Examine carefully to see if your married life would be happy, or inharmonious and wretched. Let the questions be raised, Will this union help me heavenward? will it increase my love for God? and will it enlarge my sphere of usefulness in this life? If these reflections present no drawback, then in the fear of God move forward.

But even if an engagement has been entered into without a full understanding of the character of the one with whom you intend to unite, do not think that the engagement makes it a positive necessity for you to take upon yourself the marriage vow, and link yourself for life to one whom you cannot love and respect. Be very careful how you enter into conditional engagements; but better, far better, break the engagement before marriage than separate afterward, as many do.

Treatment of Mother an Index

True love is a plant that needs culture. Let the woman who desires a peaceful, happy union, who would escape future misery and sorrow, inquire before she yields her affections, Has my lover a mother? What is the stamp of her character? Does he recognize his obligations to her? Is he mindful of her wishes and happiness? If he does not respect and honor his mother, will he manifest respect and love, kindness and attention, toward his wife? When the novelty of marriage is over, will he love me still? Will he be patient with my mistakes, or will he be critical, overbearing, and dictatorial? True affection will overlook many mistakes; love will not discern them.

Impulse Not Reliable

The youth trust altogether too much to impulse. They should not give themselves away too easily, nor be captivated too readily by the winning exterior of the lover. Courtship, as carried on in this age, is a scheme of deception and hypocrisy, with which the enemy of souls has far more to do than the Lord. Good common sense is needed here if anywhere; but the fact is, it has little to do in the matter.

If children would be more familiar with their parents, if they would confide in them, and unburden to them their joys and sorrows, they would save themselves many a future heartache. When perplexed to know what course is right, let them lay the matter just as they view it before their parents, and ask advice of them. Who are so well calculated to point out their dangers as godly parents? Who can understand their peculiar temperaments so well as they?

Children who are Christians will esteem above every earthly blessing the love and approbation of their God-fearing parents. The parents can sympathize with the children, and pray for and with them that God will shield and guide them. Above everything else they will point them to their never-failing Friend and Counselor, who will be touched with the feeling of their infirmities. He who was tempted in all points like as we are, yet without sin, knows how to succor those who are tempted. *Review and Herald*, January 26, 1886.

Divine Love

In your life union your affections are to be tributary to each other's happiness. Each is to minister to the happiness of the other. This is the will of God concerning you. But while you are to blend as one, neither of you is to lose his or her individuality in the other. God is the owner of your individuality. . . .

Living for God, the soul sends forth to Him its best and highest affections. Is the greatest outflow of your love toward Him who died for you? If it is, your love for each other will be after heaven's order. *Testimonies for the Church*, Vol. 7, pp. 45, 46.

CHAPTER 152

Premature Marriage

Boys and girls enter upon the marriage relation with unripe love, immature judgment, without noble, elevated feelings, and take upon themselves the marriage vows, wholly led by their boyish, girlish passions. . . .

The Danger of Early Attachments

Attachments formed in childhood have often resulted in very wretched unions, or in disgraceful separations. Early connections, if formed without the consent of parents, have seldom proved happy. The young affections should be restrained until the period arrives when sufficient age and experience will make it honorable and safe to unfetter them. Those who will not be restrained will be in danger of dragging out an unhappy existence. A youth not out of his teens is a poor judge of the fitness of a person as young as himself to be his companion for life. After their judgment has become more matured, they view themselves bound for life to each other, and perhaps not at all calculated to make each other happy. Then, instead of making the best of their lot, recriminations take place, the breach widens, until there is settled indifference and neglect of each other. To them there is nothing sacred in the word home. The very atmosphere is poisoned by unloving words and bitter reproaches. *A Solemn Appeal*, pp. 11, 12 (Edition: Signs Publishing Company Limited).

CHAPTER 153

Marriages, Wise and Unwise

Immature marriages are productive of a vast amount of the evils that exist today. Neither physical health nor mental vigor is promoted by a marriage that is entered on too early in life. Upon this subject altogether too little reason is exercised. Many youth act from impulse. This step, which affects them seriously for good or ill, to be a lifelong blessing or curse, is too often taken hastily, under the impulse of sentiment. Many will not listen to reason or instruction from a Christian point of view. . . .

The world is full of misery and sin today in consequence of ill-assorted marriages. In many cases it takes only a few months for husband and wife to realize that their dispositions can never blend; and the result is that discord prevails in the home where only the love and harmony of heaven should exist.

By contention over trivial matters, a bitter spirit is cultivated. Open disagreements and bickering bring inexpressible misery into the home, and drive asunder those who should be united in the bonds of love. Thus thousands have sacrificed themselves, soul and body, by unwise marriages, and have gone down in the path of perdition.

Unequally Yoked

It is a dangerous thing to form a worldly alliance. Satan well knows that the hour which witnesses the marriages of many young men and women closes the history of their religious experience and usefulness. For a time they may make an effort to live a Christian life, but all their strivings are made against a steady influence in the opposite direction. Once they felt it a privilege to speak of their joy and hope; but soon they become unwilling to make this a subject of conversation, knowing that the one with whom they have linked their destiny takes no interest in these things. Thus Satan insidiously weaves about them a web of skepticism, and faith in the precious truth dies out of the heart.

It is Satan's studied effort to secure the youth in sin; for then he is sure of the man. The enemy of souls is filled with intense hatred against every endeavor to influence the youth in the right direction. He hates everything that will give correct views of God and of Christ. His efforts are especially directed against those who are placed in a position favorable for receiving light from heaven; for he knows that any movement on their part to come into connection with God will give them power to resist his temptations. As an angel of light he comes to the youth with his specious devices, and too often succeeds in winning them, step by step, from the path of duty.

Proper Association

Young persons who are thrown into one another's society may make their association a blessing or a curse. They may edify, strengthen, and bless one another, improving in deportment, in disposition, in knowledge; or, by permitting themselves to become careless and unfaithful, they may exert only a demoralizing influence. *Youth's Instructor*, August 10, 1899.

Hasty Marriages

Satan is constantly busy to hurry inexperienced youth into a marriage alliance. But the less we glory in the marriages which are now taking place, the better. When the sacred nature and the claims of marriage are understood, it will even now be approved of Heaven, and the result will be happiness to both parties, and God will be glorified. . . .

True religion ennobles the mind, refines the taste, sanctifies the judgment, and makes its possessor partaker of the purity and influences of Heaven; it brings angels near, and separates more and more from the spirit and influence of the world. *Testimonies for the Church*, Vol. 2, pp. 252, 253.

Influenced to Marriage by Satan

Satan is busily engaged in influencing those who are wholly unsuited to each other to unite their interests. He exults in this work, for by it he can produce more misery and hopeless woe to the human family than by exercising his skill in any other direction. *Testimonies for the Church*, Vol. 2, p. 248.

CHAPTER 154

Marrying and Giving in Marriage

God has placed men in the world, and it is their privilege to eat, to drink, to trade, to marry, and to be given in marriage; but it is safe to do these things only in the fear of God. We should live in this world with reference to the eternal world. The great crime in the marriages of the days of Noah was that the sons of God formed alliances with the daughters of men. Those who professed to acknowledge and revere God associated with those who were corrupt of heart; and without discrimination they married whom they would. There are many in this day who have no depth of religious experience, who will do exactly the same things as were done in the days of Noah. They will enter into marriage without careful and prayerful consideration. Many take upon themselves the sacred vows as thoughtlessly as they would enter into a business transaction; true love is not the motive for the alliance.

Unholy Infatuation

The thought of marriage seems to have a bewitching power upon the minds of many of the youth. Two persons become acquainted; they are infatuated with each other, and their whole attention is absorbed. Reason is blinded, and judgment is overthrown. They will not submit to any advice or control, but insist on having their own way, regardless of consequence.

Like some epidemic, or contagion, that must run its course, is the infatuation that possesses them; and there seems to be no such thing as putting a stop to it. Perhaps there are those around them who realize that, should the parties interested be united in marriage, it could only result in life-long unhappiness. But entreaties and exhortations are given in vain. Perhaps, by such a union, the usefulness of one whom God would bless in His service will be crippled and destroyed; but reasoning and persuasion are alike unheeded.

All that can be said by men and women of experience proves ineffectual; it is powerless to change the decision to which their desires have led them. They lose interest in the prayer meeting, and in everything that pertains to religion. They are wholly infatuated with each other, and the duties of life are neglected, as if they were matters of little concern. Night after night, these young people burn the midnight oil to talk with each other—in reference to subjects of serious and solemn interest?—O no. Rather of frivolous things that are of no importance.

Violating the Laws of Health and Modesty

Satan's angels are keeping watch with those who devote a large share of the night to courting. Could they have their eyes opened, they would see an angel making a record of their words and acts. The laws of health and modesty are violated. It would be more appropriate to let some of the hours of courtship before marriage run through the married life. But as a general thing, marriage ends all the devotion manifested during the days of courtship!

These hours of midnight dissipation, in this age of depravity, frequently lead to the ruin of both parties thus engaged. Satan exults, and God is dishonored when men and women dishonor themselves. The good name of honor is sacrificed under the spell of this infatuation, and the marriage of such persons cannot be solemnized under the approval of God. They are married because passion moved them, and when the novelty of the affair is over, they will begin to realize what they have done. In six months after the vows are spoken, their sentiments toward each other have undergone a change. Each has learned in married life more of the character of the companion chosen. Each discovers imperfections that, during the blindness and folly of their former association, were not apparent. The promises at the altar do not bind them together. In consequence of hasty marriages, even among the professed people of God, there are separations, divorces, and great confusion in the church.

Disregard for Counsel

This kind of marrying and giving in marriage is one of Satan's special devices, and he succeeds in his plans almost every time. I have the most painful sense of helplessness when parties come to me for counsel upon this subject. I may speak to them the words that God would have me; but they frequently question every point, and plead the wisdom of carrying out their own purposes; and eventually they do so.

They seem to have no power to overcome their own wishes and inclinations, and will marry at all hazards. They do not consider the matter carefully and prayerfully, leaving themselves in the hands of God, to be guided and controlled by His Spirit. The fear of God does not seem to be before their eyes. They think they understand the matter fully, without wisdom from God or counsel from man.

When it is too late, they find that they have made a mistake, and have imperiled their happiness in this life and the salvation of their souls. They would not admit that any one knew anything about the matter but themselves, when if counsel had been received, they might have saved themselves years of anxiety and sorrow. But advice is only thrown away on those who are determined to have their own way. Passion carries such individuals over every barrier that reason and judgment can interpose.

Characteristics of True Love

Love is a plant of heavenly origin. It is not unreasonable; it is not blind. It is pure and holy. But the passion of the natural heart is another thing altogether. While pure love will take God into all its plans, and will be in perfect harmony with the Spirit of God, passion will be headstrong, rash, unreasonable, defiant of all restraint, and will make the object of its choice an idol.

In all the deportment of one who possesses true love, the grace of God will be shown. Modesty, simplicity, sincerity, morality, and religion will characterize every step toward an alliance in marriage. Those who are thus controlled will not be absorbed in each other's society, at a loss of interest in the prayer meeting and the religious service. . . .

Seeking Divine Guidance

If men and women are in the habit of praying twice a day before they contemplate marriage, they should pray four times a day when such a step is anticipated. Marriage is something that will influence and affect your life, both in this world and in the world to come. A sincere Christian will not advance his plans in this direction without the knowledge that God approves his course. He will not want to choose for himself, but will feel that God must choose for him. We are not to please ourselves, for Christ pleased not Himself. I would not be understood to mean that anyone is to marry one whom he does not love. This would be sin. But fancy and the emotional nature must not be allowed to lead on to ruin. God requires the whole heart, the supreme affections.

The majority of the marriages of our time, and the way in which they are conducted, make them one of the signs of the last days. Men and women are so persistent, so headstrong, that God is left out of the question. Religion is laid aside, as if it had no part to act in this solemn and important matter. But unless those who profess to believe the truth are sanctified through it, and exalted in thought and character, they are not in as favorable a position before God as the sinner who has never been enlightened in regard to its claims. *Review and Herald*, September 25, 1888.

CHAPTER 155

Responsibilities of Marriage

Many have entered the marriage relation who have not acquired property, and who have had no inheritance. They did not possess physical strength or mental energy to acquire property. It has been just such ones who have been in haste to marry, and who have taken upon themselves responsibilities of which they had no just sense. They did not possess noble, elevated feelings, and had no just idea of the duty of a husband and father, and what it would cost them to provide for the wants of a family. And they manifested no more propriety in the increase of their families than that shown in their business transactions. . . .

The marriage institution was designed of Heaven to be a blessing to man; but, in a general sense, it has been abused in such a manner as to make it a dreadful curse. Most men and women have acted in entering the marriage relation as though the only question for them to settle was whether they loved each other. But they should realize that a responsibility rests upon them in the marriage relation farther than this. They should consider whether their offspring will possess physical health, and mental and moral strength. But few have moved with high motives, and with elevated considerations which they could not lightly throw off—that society had claims upon them, that the weight of their family's influence would tell in the upward or downward scale. *A Solemn Appeal*, pp. 63, 64 (Edition: Signs Publishing Company Limited).

CHAPTER 156

Good Judgment and Self-control in Marriage

Those professing to be Christians should not enter the marriage relation until the matter has been carefully and prayerfully considered from an elevated standpoint, to see if God can be glorified by the union. Then they should duly consider the result of every privilege of the marriage relation, and sanctified principle should be the basis of every action.

Looking Ahead

Before increasing their family, they should take into consideration whether God would be glorified or dishonored by their bringing children into the world. They should seek to glorify God by their union from the first, and during every year of their married life. They should calmly consider what provision can be made for their children. They have no right to bring children into the world to be a burden to others. Have they a business that they can rely upon to sustain a family, so that they need not become a burden to others? If they have not, they commit a crime in bringing children into the world to suffer for want of proper care, food, and clothing.

The Domination of Passion

In this fast, corrupt age these things are not considered. Lustful passion bears away, and will not submit to control, although feebleness, misery, and death are the result of its reign. Women are forced to a life of hardship, pain, and suffering, because of the uncontrollable passions of men who bear the name of husband—more rightly could they be called brutes. Mothers drag out a miserable existence, with children in their arms nearly all the time, managing every way to put bread into their mouths and clothes upon their backs. Such accumulated misery fills the world.

There is but little real, genuine, devoted pure love. This precious article is very rare. Passion is termed love. Many a woman has had her fine and tender sensibilities outraged, because the marriage relation allowed him whom she called husband to be brutal in his treatment of her. His love she found to be of so base a quality that she became disgusted.

Necessity of Self-control

Very many families are living in a most unhappy state, because the husband and father allows the animal in his nature to predominate over the intellectual and moral. The result is that a sense of languor and depression is frequently felt, but the cause is seldom divined as being the result of their own improper course of action. We are under solemn obligations to God to keep the spirit pure and the body healthy, that we may be a benefit to humanity, and render to God perfect service. *Testimonies for the Church*, Vol. 2, pp. 380, 381.

CHAPTER 157

The Example of Isaac

No one who fears God can without danger connect himself with one who fears Him not. “Can two walk together, except they be agreed?” The happiness and prosperity of the marriage relation depends upon the unity of the parties; but between the believer and the unbeliever there is a radical difference of tastes, inclinations, and purposes. They are serving two masters, between whom there can be no concord. However pure and correct one’s principles may be, the influence of an unbelieving companion will have a tendency to lead away from God.

He who has entered the marriage relation while unconverted is by his conversion placed under stronger obligation to be faithful to his companion, however widely they may differ in regard to religious faith; yet the claims of God should be placed above every earthly relationship, even though trials and persecution may be the result. With the spirit of love and meekness, this fidelity may have an influence to win the unbelieving one. But the marriage of Christians with the ungodly is forbidden in the Bible. The Lord’s direction is “Be ye not unequally yoked together with unbelievers.

Isaac was highly honored by God, in being made inheritor of the promises through which the world was to be blessed; yet when he was forty years of age he submitted to his father’s judgment in appointing his experienced, God-fearing servant to choose a wife for him. And the result of that marriage, as presented in the Scriptures, is a tender and beautiful picture of domestic happiness: "Isaac brought her unto his mother Sarah's tent, and took Rebekah, and she became his wife; and he loved her: and Isaac was comforted after his mother's death."

What a contrast between the course of Isaac and that pursued by the youth of our time, even among professed Christians! Young people too often feel that the bestowal of their affections is a matter in which self alone should be consulted—a matter that neither God nor their parents should in any wise control. Long before they have reached manhood or womanhood, they think themselves competent to make their own choice, without the aid of their parents. A few years of married life are usually sufficient to show them their error, but often too late to prevent its baleful results. For the same lack of wisdom and self-control that dictated the hasty choice is permitted to aggravate the evil, until the marriage relation becomes a galling yoke. Many have thus wrecked their happiness in this life, and their hope of the life to come.

If there is any subject which should be carefully considered, and in which the counsel of older and more experienced persons should be sought, it is the subject of marriage; if ever the Bible was needed as a counselor, if ever divine guidance should be sought in prayer, it is before taking a step that binds persons together for life.

Parents should never lose sight of their own responsibility for the future happiness of their children. Isaac's deference of his father's judgment was the result of the training that had taught him to love a life of obedience. While Abraham required his children to respect parental authority, his daily life testified that that authority was not a selfish or arbitrary control, but was founded in love, and had their welfare and happiness in view.

Fathers and mothers should feel that a duty devolves upon them to guide the affections of the youth, that they may be placed upon those who will be suitable companions. They should feel it a duty, by their own teaching and example, with the assisting grace of God, to so mold the character of the children from their earliest years that they will be pure and noble, and will be attracted to the good and true. Like attracts like; like appreciates like. Let the love for truth and purity and goodness be early implanted in the soul, and the youth will seek the society of those who possess these characteristics. . . .

True love is a high and holy principle, altogether different in character from that love which is awakened by impulse, and which suddenly dies when severely tested. It is by faithfulness to duty in the parental home that the youth are to prepare themselves for homes of their own. Let them here practice self-denial, and manifest kindness, courtesy, and Christian sympathy. Thus love will be kept warm in the heart, and he who goes out from such a household to stand at the head of a family of his own will know how to promote the happiness of her whom he has chosen as a companion for life. Marriage, instead of being the end of love, will be only its beginning. *Patriarchs and Prophets*, pp. 174-176.

Index of Scriptural References

General Index

F

N

Reference Index

The Desire of Ages

Testimonies on S. S. Work

Christian Temperance and Bible Hygiene

Testimonies to Ministers

Counsels to Teachers, Parents, and Students

A Solemn Appeal

Ministry of Healing

Fundamentals of Christian Education

Counsels on Health

Education

Christ's Object Lessons

Patriarchs and Prophets

Gospel Workers

Thoughts From the Mount of Blessing